# Productive and Efficient Data Science with Python

## With Modularizing, Memory Profiles, and Parallel/GPU Processing

Dr. Tirthajyoti Sarkar

Apress®

*Productive and Efficient Data Science with Python: With Modularizing, Memory Profiles, and Parallel/GPU Processing*

Dr. Tirthajyoti Sarkar
Fremont, CA, USA

ISBN-13 (pbk): 978-1-4842-8120-8
https://doi.org/10.1007/978-1-4842-8121-5

ISBN-13 (electronic): 978-1-4842-8121-5

Managing Director, Apress Media LLC: Welmoed Spahr
Acquisitions Editor: Celestin Suresh John
Development Editor: James Markham
Coordinating Editor: Aditee Mirashi
Copy Editor: Mary Behr

Cover designed by eStudioCalamar

Cover image designed by Freepik (www.freepik.com)

Distributed to the book trade worldwide by Springer Science+Business Media New York, 1 New York Plaza, Suite 4600, New York, NY 10004-1562, USA. Phone 1-800-SPRINGER, fax (201) 348-4505, e-mail orders-ny@springer-sbm.com, or visit www.springeronline.com. Apress Media, LLC is a California LLC and the sole member (owner) is Springer Science + Business Media Finance Inc (SSBM Finance Inc). SSBM Finance Inc is a **Delaware** corporation.

For information on translations, please e-mail booktranslations@springernature.com; for reprint, paperback, or audio rights, please e-mail bookpermissions@springernature.com.

Apress titles may be purchased in bulk for academic, corporate, or promotional use. eBook versions and licenses are also available for most titles. For more information, reference our Print and eBook Bulk Sales web page at www.apress.com/bulk-sales.

Any source code or other supplementary material referenced by the author in this book is available to readers on GitHub (https://github.com/Apress/Sarkar_Productive-and-Efficient-Data-Science-with-Python). For more detailed information, please visit www.apress.com/source-code.

Printed on acid-free paper

*Dedicated to the memory of my loving parents, Jyotirindra Nath Sarkar and Sarmistha Sarkar, who instilled in me the quest for knowledge and taught me the most valuable lessons of life*

# Table of Contents

# About the Author

**Dr. Tirthajyoti Sarkar** lives and works in the San Francisco Bay area, California. He currently serves as the Senior Director, AI/ML Platform at Rhombus Power Inc. where he builds solutions for problems of vital national and global importance using AI, data, and mathematics.

Most recently, he worked as a Data Science Manager at a startup developing an edge-computing platform for the semiconductor manufacturing industry. Before that, he spent more than a decade in the semiconductor and electronics industries where he developed power semiconductor technology and applied artificial intelligence and machine learning techniques for design automation and product innovation. Dr. Sarkar regularly publishes AI and data science articles on top online platforms and teaches machine learning in various workshops and forums. He has published 30+ papers in IEEE and holds multiple US patents. He has authored two data science books. Dr. Sarkar is a Senior Member of IEEE, a former Chair of the Semiconductor Committee of the PSMA (the world's largest power supply organization consortium), and an Industry Advisory Member for ValleyML, a non-profit AI/ML organization. He holds a Ph.D. in Electrical Engineering from the University of Illinois at Chicago and an MS in Data Analytics from Georgia Tech.

# About the Technical Reviewer

**Joos Korstanje** is a data scientist with over five years of industry experience in developing machine learning tools, a large part of which are forecasting models. He currently works at Disneyland Paris where he develops machine learning for a variety of tools.

# Acknowledgments

This book has been a great journey for me, and it will not be complete without acknowledging some of the people who helped me in this quest.

First, I would like to thank my editor, Aditee Mirashi, who guided me patiently on the authoring process and its specifics as this is my first collaboration with Apress. She has been unfailingly helpful and understanding while I navigated through the chapters and technical reviews.

I would like to acknowledge some of the open-source developers and data science communicators whose work I have cited or used in various chapters, with their kind permissions. Khyuen Tran has contributed greatly to the community by publishing efficient data science tricks (with Python) and I have had the pleasure of discussing these ideas with her. Her work is cited in Chapter 13. Moez Ali, the creator of the low-code AutoML library PyCaret, has graciously allowed me to use some portions of his documentation when I cite low-code libraries in Chapter 12. I have also interacted with Helin Cao, the maintainer and chief evangelist for the wonderful PyWebIO library that I demonstrate in Chapter 7, for many illuminating discussions. The folks at Saturn Cloud kindly offered me quick help and support when I used their amazing service in a RAPIDS-based demonstration in Chapter 11.

My wife, Chitrita Chakravarti, an accomplished DataOps Solutions Architect herself, has provided support both professionally and personally while I was working on this book. She deserves my sincere gratitude.

Lastly, I am eternally grateful to all my friends and professional connections, especially on LinkedIn, who always had kind and encouraging words for me when I described the painstaking process of working through this project. Their support and words have been a primary source of motivation.

# Introduction

Data science and machine learning can be practiced with various degrees of efficiency and productivity. This book focuses specifically on Python-based tools and techniques to help data scientists, beginners and seasoned professionals alike, become highly productive at all aspects of typical data science tasks.

This book is specifically intended for those who wish to leapfrog beyond the standard way of performing data science and machine learning tasks, and utilize the full spectrum of the Python data science ecosystem for a much higher level of productivity. You will be taught how to look out for inefficiencies and bottlenecks in the standard process and how to think beyond the box. Automation of repetitive data science tasks is a key mindset that you will develop from reading this book. In many cases, you will also learn how to extend existing coding practices to handle larger datasets, with high efficiency, with the help of advanced software tools that already exist in the Python ecosystem but are not taught in any standard data science book.

This is not a regular Python cookbook that teaches standard libraries like NumPy or Pandas. Rather, it focuses on useful techniques such as how to measure the memory footprint and execution speed of ML models, modularize a data science or deep learning task, write object-oriented code for a data science library or web app development, and so on. It also covers Python libraries, which come in handy for automating and speeding up the day-to-day tasks of any data scientist. Furthermore, it touches upon tools and packages that help a data scientist tackle large and complex datasets in a far more optimal way than what would have been possible by following standard Python data science technology wisdom.

If you take away a mentality of probing and measuring inefficiency in your data science code, and you learn tricks to discover effective solutions for those productivity issues, I will consider this book to be successful. This will be an immense reward for me.

## Source Code

All source code used in this book's examples can be downloaded from
https://github.com/Apress/Sarkar_Productive-and-Efficient-Data-Science-with-Python

# CHAPTER 1

# What Is Productive and Efficient Data Science?

The goal of this chapter is to introduce you to the benefits of performing data science tasks efficiently and productively. I also illustrate some potential pitfalls in the everyday work of a regular data scientist to drive home the point of *efficient data science*.

Like any other computing (and non-computing) task in life, data science (DS) and machine learning (ML) can be practiced with varying degrees of efficiency and productivity. This book focuses specifically on **Python-based tools and techniques** to help a data scientist, beginner and seasoned professional alike, become **highly productive at all aspects of typical DS stacks** (e.g., statistical analysis, visualization, model selection, feature engineering, code quality testing, modularization, parallel processing, and even easy web app deployment).

But why strive to achieve efficiency in data science? What could go wrong in a regular data science pipeline if these aspects of efficiency and productivity are not kept in mind and practiced with diligence?

To understand these issues, you need to examine a typical data science pipeline first. Let me take you through that journey.

## A Typical Data Science Pipeline

Data science is a vast and dynamic field. In the modern business and technology space, the discipline of data science has assumed the role of a truly transformative force. Every kind of industry and socio-economic field from healthcare to transportation and from online retail to on-demand music uses DS tools and techniques in myriad ways.

© Dr. Tirthajyoti Sarkar 2022
T. Sarkar, *Productive and Efficient Data Science with Python*, https://doi.org/10.1007/978-1-4842-8121-5_1

Every day exabytes of business and personal data flow through increasingly complex *dataflow pipelines* architected by sophisticated *DataOps architectures* to be ingested, processed, and analyzed by database engines or machine learning algorithms, leading to insightful business decisions or technological breakthroughs.

However, to illustrate the point of efficient data science practices, let's take the generic example of a typical data science task flow shown in Figure 1-1. You may have encountered this in your introductory data science course or practiced it in your everyday work.

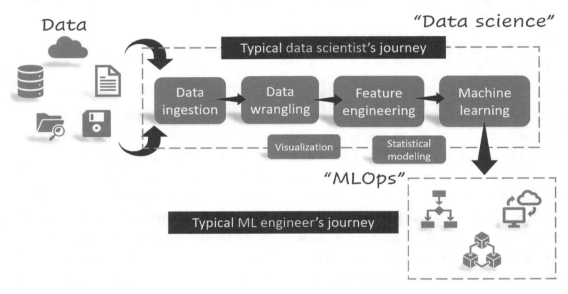

***Figure 1-1.*** *A typical data science pipeline showing various stages of ingestion, wrangling, visualization, modeling, and even MLOps*

You are probably suspecting that **there could be a high chance of writing inefficient code in the data wrangling or ingesting phase**. However, you may wonder what could go wrong in the machine learning/statistical modeling phase as you may be using the out-of-the-box methods and routines from highly optimized Python libraries like `Scikit-learn`, `Scipy`, or `TensorFlow`. Furthermore, you may wonder why tasks like quality testing and app deployments should be included in a productive data science pipeline anyway.

In the next section, I will answer these questions through simple examples.

# Typical Examples of Inefficient Practices in Data Science

Some modules of the DS pipeline in Figure 1-1, such as data wrangling, visualization, statistical modeling, ML training, and testing, are more directly impacted by inefficient programming styles and practices than others.

Let me show some simple examples and take you through some data science stories.

## Iterating Over a pandas DataFrame

As data scientists, all of us have been there.

We are given a large pandas DataFrame and asked to check some relationships between various fields in the columns, in a row-by-row fashion. It could be a logical operation or a sophisticated mathematical transformation on the raw data.

Essentially, it is a simple case of **iterating over the rows of the DataFrame** and doing some processing at each iteration. However, it may not be that simple in terms of choosing the most efficient method of executing this apparently simple task. For example, you can choose from the following approaches.

## Brute-Force for Loop

The code for this naïve approach will go something like this:

```
for i in range(len(df)):
    if (some condition is satisfied):
        <do some calculation with> df.iloc[i]
```

Essentially, you are iterating over each row (df.iloc[i]) using a generic for loop and processing it one at a time. There's nothing wrong with the logic and you will get the correct result in the end.

But this is guaranteed to be inefficient. If you try this approach with a DataFrame with a large number of rows, say ~1,000,000 (1 million) and 10 columns, the total iteration may run for tens of seconds or more (even on a fast machine).

Now, you may think that being able to process a million records in tens of seconds is still acceptable. But, as you increase the number of columns or the complexity of the calculation (or of the condition checking done at each iteration), you will see that they quickly add up and *this approach should be avoided as much as possible when*

3

*building scalable DS pipelines*. On top of that, if you have to repeat such iteration tasks for hundreds of datasets on a regular basis (in a standard business/production environment), the inefficiencies will stack up over time.

## Better Approaches: df.iterrows and df.values

Depending on the situations at hand, you may have choices of two better approaches for this iteration task.

- The pandas library has a dedicated method for iterating over rows named `iterrows()`, which might be handy to use in this particular situation. Depending on the DataFrame size and the complexity of the row operations, this may reduce the total execution time by ~10X over the `for` loop approach.

- pandas offers a method for returning a NumPy representation of the DataFrame named `df.values()`. This can significantly speed things up (even better than `iterrows`). However, this method removes the axis labels (column names) and therefore you must use the generic NumPy array indexing like 0, 1, to process the data.

# Scatterplot Everything in a Large Dataset

Often, at the beginning of a data analysis task, we are tempted to visualize the pairwise interrelationships between all kinds of numeric features that are present in the given dataset. This is often a necessary step for exploratory data analysis (EDA; see `https://en.wikipedia.org/wiki/Exploratory_data_analysis`) and can reveal significant insights about the general pattern of the dataset. However, for large datasets with hundreds of features (columns), this may put extreme pressure on the visualization routine, leading to poor plots and a slow response.

## Combinatorial Explosion

It is easy to explain why this apparently simple (pairwise) scatter plot task can become quickly intractable. The reason is combinatorial explosion (`https://en.wikipedia.org/wiki/Combinatorial_explosion`). Essentially, you are trying to plot all combinations of two-way relationships and therefore you have $^nC_2$ possible combinations to plot where **_n_** is the number of numeric features and $C$ denotes the combinatorial sign. Some concrete examples will help.

- $^{4}C_2 = \mathbf{6}$ so you have 6 plots for pairwise plotting 4 features in a dataset

- $^{6}C_2 = \mathbf{15}$ so you have 15 plots for pairwise plotting 6 features in a dataset

- $^{10}C_2 = \mathbf{45}$ so you have 45 plots for pairwise plotting 10 features in a dataset

- $^{20}C_2 = \mathbf{190}$ so you have 190 plots for pairwise plotting 20 features in a dataset

As you can see in Figure 1-2, the number of plots increases rather quickly! On top of that, if you have a large dataset (with millions of samples), then each plot needs to have millions of data points rendered on the screen. It is computationally prohibitive to render millions of points on a web browser for hundreds of plots.

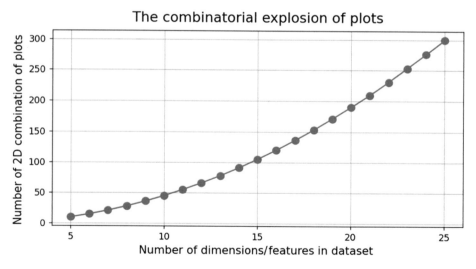

**Figure 1-2.** *How the combinatorial explosion leads to a large number of possible two-dimensional plots for even a modest dataset*

| WHY DID I MENTION A WEB BROWSER? |
| --- |

Jupyter notebook is the most popular choice for data scientists to do these exploratory data analyses (and advanced machine learning in many cases). At its core, the Jupyter notebook system runs a web server which lets you write code, markdown text, and render plots in a browser window (using JavaScript code in many cases). Therefore, if you try to render hundreds of plots with millions of points, your browser memory may be taxed and it can crash!

# Writing Similar Plotting Code Multiple Times

This is a very common practice by data scientists: to copy-paste the same plotting code (using, for example, the `Matplotlib` or `Seaborn` library) repeatedly in an analysis Jupyter notebook. While, inherently, this may not increase the total running time of the code, this is a bad software engineering practice that violates the principle of DRY (don't repeat yourself; https://en.wikipedia.org/wiki/Don%27t_repeat_yourself).

Essentially, you are giving up the opportunity of code refactoring (https://en.wikipedia.org/wiki/Code_refactoring) when you copy-paste the same plotting code in multiple places, thereby increasing the chance of introducing bugs and making the code difficult to read and maintain in the long term.

## Write a Generic Function Instead

Instead, you should try to write a generic function that can produce the desired plot with the right styling that you need and then just pass variables to this function for plotting. A pseudo-code example would be something like this:

```
def plot_linechart(x):
    """
    Plots line chart of given 'x' variable from dataframe df
    """
    # Extracts the values from the dataframe as Numpy array
    x_array = df[x].values
    # Mean and upper and lower limits calculations
    x_mean = x_array.mean()
```

```
x_upper = x_mean+2*x_array.std()
x_lower = x_mean-2*x_array.std()
# Data length
data_len = len(x_array)
# Size and title
plt.figure(figsize=(15,3))
plt.title(x,fontsize=15)
# Main plot
plt.plot(x_array,color='blue',alpha=0.6)
# Mean, upper limit, lower limit horizontal lines
plt.hlines(y=x_mean,xmin=0,xmax=data_len,
           linestyle='--',color='k',linewidth=4)
plt.hlines(y=x_upper,xmin=0,xmax=data_len,
           linestyle='--',color='red',linewidth=2.5)
plt.hlines(y=x_lower,xmin=0,xmax=data_len,
           linestyle='--',color='red',linewidth=2.5)
# Show
plt.show()
```

Here, there is already a pandas DataFrame df in the workspace. This function just plots various columns from that DataFrame as a line chart along with showing the mean, upper limit, and lower limit lines. The column name is passed as the only argument of the function.

## IS THIS A COMMON SCENARIO?

This is a typical data analytics scenario with, perhaps, some manufacturing process or quality testing data where you may have a tabular dataset of a large number of parameters (i.e., a dataframe with a number of columns) and you want to plot multiple line charts side by side or on top of each other to compare the performance or investigate some pattern. You avoid inefficient and error-prone code by writing a well-planned function first and then refactoring that again and again.

## Not Writing A Test Module

Testing improves the delivery, performance, and long-term profitability of any software product/service for all kinds of businesses and industries. It should be, therefore, a no-brainer that **data science and machine learning should also embrace this habit of testing every important piece of code**.

We are increasingly expecting a high-quality and robust software framework behind various ML services that predict favorite restaurants or guide us when we are lost in a new city. Trust in these services, which often seem magical, can only come if we know that the software behind the scenes was tested using a proven and robust methodology.

In many cases, the pace of the development of these new types of services is even higher than that of traditional software products. Hastening the development of a product often comes at the price of compromising its quality. A good software testing strategy can help offset this trade-off.

Put another way, **a sound testing strategy can save a lot of development time in the long term for a data science task flow** while guaranteeing a high quality of the finished product. Saving time in the coding and software engineering stages is an inherently productive and efficient endeavor.

# Some Pitfalls to Avoid

It is clear from the previous sections that a data scientist can fall into the trap of inefficient data science practices in myriad ways. It is almost impossible to capture all of these ways, but here I list some common pitfalls to avoid while working on a data science task for your business or scientific exploration.

## Don't Live in Ignorance. Measure Efficiency.

*How fast or efficient is your code*? Don't leave it to guesswork. Without a solid metric, you cannot compare multiple coding styles or options and choose the best one. In short, **without some sort of measurement of efficiency, you can never even start to improve**.

Therefore, always try to include some sort of timing/speed measurement code in your analysis or test module so that you can test and measure various DS tasks or function blocks on how efficient they really are. We will revisit this topic in more detail in Chapter 2.

# Don't Leave Your Code as Orphans. Modularize Them.

If you focus on building a modularized and expressive data science pipeline, it will pay you back in terms of improved productivity. But what can prevent you from doing so? Surprisingly, it may be the very programming language that we all have come to adopt and appreciate for its power and simplicity: Python.

## The Python-Powered Data Science Legacy May Have a Problem

We use Python a lot for our data science work. Why? Because it's awesome for ML and the data science community. It is on its way to becoming the fastest-growing major language for modern data-driven analytics and artificial intelligence (AI) apps. It is also used for simple scripting purposes, to automate stuff, to test a hypothesis, to create interactive plots for brainstorming, to control lab instruments, and so on.

However, Python for software development and Python for scripting are not the same beast, at least in the domain of data science. **Scripting is (mostly) the code you write for yourself. Software is the assemblage of code you (and other teammates) write for others.**

It's wise to admit that when (a majority of) data scientists, who do not come from a software engineering background, write Python programs for AI/ML models and statistical analysis, *they tend to write such code for themselves*. They just want to get to the heart of the pattern hidden in the data. Fast. Without thinking deeply about normal mortals (users). They write a block of code to produce a rich and beautiful plot. But they don't create a function out of it to use later. They import lots of methods and classes from standard libraries. But they don't create a subclass of their own by inheritance and add methods to it for extending the functionality.

## Embrace OOP Principles As Much As You Can

Functions, inheritance, methods, classes: they are at the heart of robust object-oriented programming (OOP; `www.educative.io/blog/object-oriented-programming`) but they are somewhat avoidable if all you want to do is create a Jupyter notebook with your data analysis and plots.

You can avoid the initial pain of using OOP principles but this almost always renders your Notebook code non-reusable and non-extensible. In short, that piece of code serves only you (until you forget what logic exactly you coded) and no one else.

But readability (and thereby reusability) is critically important. That is the true test of the merit of what you produced. Not for yourself. But for others.

Therefore, don't fall into this trap of writing disjoint code pieces with the aim of doing a quick and dirty analysis. Try to put your code into well-planned functions and modules (class and subclass) as much as possible. We will revisit this topic in much more detail and with actual code examples in Chapters 5 and 6.

# Don't Be Limited by Hardware or Traditional Tools

Many data scientists feel somewhat helpless in the face of large-scale data, say on the order of hundreds of gigabytes (GB) or multiple terabytes (TB). While enterprise-grade software solutions routinely handle this kind of data volume every day, individual data science practitioners may still run into scalability and execution issues with this kind of dataset. This, of course, impacts their overall productivity.

## Local Hardware Memory Limitation Is a Real Issue

Most data science tasks, especially the initial data ingestion, wrangling, exploratory analysis, statistical modeling, and feature engineering, happen on the local hardware of a single data scientist (or a team). This is a fact of the way this enterprise works. With the advent of AutoML tools and the emphasis on the "citizen data scientist," individuals are more and more encouraged to take up data science tasks and start the ball rolling on the analytics workload that is in high demand for every conceivable business today.

This has great potential to revolutionize the whole field and to propel it to greater heights. However, it also comes with the caveat that, in many cases, an individual data scientist may run into the back wall of local hardware memory or compute limit when dealing with a terabyte (or even multi-gigabyte) scale dataset.

Individual laptop memory (RAM) runs up to 16 GB or 32 GB at best, thereby limiting the size of a dataset that can be loaded into the working memory in its entirety. Even for a dataset of a modest 10 GB size, traditional analytics tools like pandas can become excruciatingly slow when you load the entire data into a single DataFrame object. Many of these widely used Python data science packages do not support parallel computing at all.

**Note**    A gigabyte (GB) is ~$10^9$ bytes or 1,000 MB. A terabyte (TB) is 1,000GB or ~$10^{12}$ bytes. A petabyte (PB) is 1,000TB or ~$10^{15}$ bytes. It is estimated that the entire collection of the Library of Congress including photos, sound recordings, and movies might take ~3,000TB of storage.

## GPU-Accelerated Computing Has Not Focused on Data Science as a Whole

From a compute perspective, GPUs have been a blessing for advanced machine learning with big datasets. However, they are much more discussed and practiced for deep learning tasks than anything else. As great a success story as deep learning may be for the rise of AI and ML, a majority of data science and analytics workflows still have little use for GPUs.

Therefore, it is a common scenario that a data scientist has access to a GPU-powered workstation or a multi-GPU cloud computing instance but cannot utilize those hardware resources effectively for the analytics tasks that they want to accomplish (Figure 1-3).

*Figure 1-3.* *GPU-based accelerated computing needs to become an essential component of mainstream data analytics (even without any deep learning component)*

## Always Explore Alternative Libraries/Frameworks

It is, therefore, clear from the discussion above that to practice productive and efficient data science, practitioners must learn

> How to handle large and complex datasets efficiently (which would have been difficult with traditional DS tools) with libraries that support parallel computing and multi-tasking out of the box

> How to fully utilize GPU and multi-core processors for all kinds of data science and analytics tasks, and not just for specialized deep learning modeling

We will discuss many of these issues at length and show some emerging (and exciting) alternatives to the traditional tools and frameworks in Chapters 10–12.

# Efficiency and Productivity Go Hand in Hand

This is one of the poorly understood and less appreciated facts about data science, or about any technical enterprise for that matter: **being efficient and tidy and avoiding bugs and errors directly leads to productivity** in all aspects of professional life. While some of the connections are easy to spot, others are less obvious. Therefore, in this section, I provide key examples of techniques for high efficiency with regard to the practice of data science.

## Measuring Efficiency Goes a Long Way

As discussed in the preceding section, if you develop a habit of measuring the efficiency of your code or function, you will automatically create an environment where you are keeping track of those metrics and how you are improving over time. In this way, you can become much more productive in your daily tasks as they can be probed and improved upon with clear targets when they start showing any sign of lag. Measuring the memory and compute footprint is one prominent example; I talk about this in detail in Chapter 9.

This habit helps to increase productivity at a large enterprise scale, too. For example, you may feel confident before committing a large piece of ML prediction code that was written by you or your team **only when you know that your team has measured the code execution efficiency thoroughly** and ensured that the code won't blow up the API endpoint in the face of gigabytes of real-time streaming data.

# Testing Reduces the Chance of Rework

The more unit or functional testing modules are planned and written at the development stage of a data science pipeline or ML predictive framework, the fewer chances of discovering critical bugs at the deployment stage. While for pure exploratory analysis, testing has less impact on the overall speed of the development cycle, the productivity of any real-life deployment will depend on building this habit.

However, **traditional software testing best practices may not be 100% applicable to data science and ML code testing since they involve a lot of probabilistic features or randomized input/output patterns**. Therefore, careful planning and a deep familiarity with the stochastic nature of these systems are essential ingredients for building a high-performance testing framework. This necessitates some sort of data science expertise on the part of the test engineering team as well.

# Planning ML Model Development

ML model development and tuning is often done in an ad-hoc manner, with the sole focus of obtaining the highest accuracy or some similar model performance metric. Long-term productivity improvement is not considered a major goal of such experimentation and model iteration.

However, making small changes to the process like logging hyperparameters and metrics properly, or creating a model iteration routine that systematically stores and visualizes the tuning process, can go a long way to reducing waste in repeatable work. I talk about some of these best practices in Chapter 4.

It is important, however, to identify the productivity of a complete ML platform in a holistic manner **which places greater emphasis on the overall system productivity rather than on the speed of developing individual models**. Incorporating model tracking, logging, and visualization code certainly places some overhead on the individual modeling components, but the benefit is realized in the longer run in a system-wide manner. This must be realized and supported by the higher management for the data science team to execute with confidence.

# Knowledge of GUI Programming/Web App Development Is Quite Helpful

This may sound counterintuitive but learning a bit of GUI/API programming can often lead to overall productivity improvement for your data science pipeline. This happens, of course, when you use that knowledge to wrap the GUI around a piece of ML model or data analytics code to make it presentable to a wide user base.

Let me illustrate with a concrete example. Often, the essential first step in getting approval for a large-scale ML platform development is to produce a working prototype for the internal users or stakeholders such as higher management or the Sales and Marketing departments. This audience will understand the purpose and utility of the prototype much better if they see it in a visual manner and, even better, if they can play around with the platform (Figure 1-4).

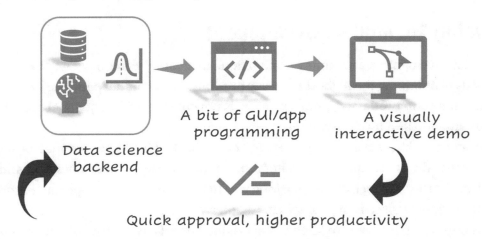

***Figure 1-4.*** *A quick demo of working data science prototypes to higher management often increases the overall productivity of the team*

This requires not only the back-end development of the ML models and data analytics pipeline but a front-end app demonstrating the inner workings in as visually intuitive and interactive manner as possible. A data science team may not write the exact code for creating this demo app, but a deep knowledge of how those front-end elements and components should be designed and integrated into the back-end ML platform will go a long way towards faster development of the prototype. Reducing the time gap in this phase automatically means a quicker decision timeline and overall improvement in the time-to-market and productivity of the whole team. Web/browser-based apps are a natural choice for this type of task, and I discuss some of these tools (that can quickly create a web app to showcase your data science work) in Chapter 12.

# Skills and Attitude for Practicing Productive Data Science

It goes without saying that you must work consciously towards developing the specific set of skills and aptitude to move into the realm of productive and efficient data science. By its very nature, data science welcomes and embraces professionals from all kinds of technical backgrounds and professional training. While this is a wonderful thing for the field in general, it also means that anybody who wants to break the cycle of inefficiency must make a focused effort to develop these skills.

No book or course can cover the entire spectrum of possible skills and topics that need to be taught to propel a data scientist towards the path of productive and efficient data science. However, if I had to imagine some specific components for such an ideal book, I would expect it to

> Teach how to look out for inefficiencies and bottlenecks in the standard data science code and how to think beyond the box to solve those problems.

> Teach how to write modularized, efficient data analysis and machine learning code to improve productivity in a variety of situations such as exploratory data analysis, visualization, deep learning, and more.

> Cover a wide range of side topics such as software testing, module development, GUI programming, and ML model deployment as a web app, which are invaluable skillsets for budding data scientists to possess.

> Teach how to whip up quick GUI apps for the demo of a data science/ML idea or model tuning, or how to easily (and quickly) deploy ML models and data analysis code at a web app endpoint.

> Cover parallel computing, out-of-core (larger than the system memory) scalability, and GPU-powered data science stack with hands-on examples.

Expose and guide the readers to a larger and ever-expanding Python ecosystem of data science tools that are connected to the broader aspects of software engineering and production-level deployment.

And, above all, **instill and reinforce the sense of inquisitiveness about the efficiency** of one's data science pipeline so that the practitioner can continuously research and develop their own methods and best practices for probing the code and systems they are working with.

# Summary

In this introductory chapter, I covered a lot of ground to give you a fairly detailed idea about the emerging concepts of productive and efficient data science. I talked about what it means from a technical point of view and how it helps the organization as a whole. I pointed out that inefficiencies can seep into any stage of a typical data science pipeline: ingestion, wrangling, visualization, EDA, ML modeling, or even the demo stage.

I delved deeply into some concrete examples that appear frequently in a typical data science task such as iteration over a large dataset or visualization practices with a complex dataset. In particular, I talked about embracing good OOP principles and developing the mentality of a test engineer while working on DS tasks.

I described common pitfalls to avoid in these aspects. I placed special emphasis on not limiting yourself with local hardware or traditional tools while dealing with large terabyte-scale datasets. GPU-accelerated computing, which has not received much attention beyond deep learning, was discussed. I also touched upon parallel computing ideas that will be explored in more detail later in this book.

Next, I showed, with concrete examples, how productivity and efficiency go hand in hand in typical data science tasks or platforms. The use of GUI/app development as a tool to accelerate the decision-making process was discussed in this regard.

Finally, I talked about the ideal skills and aptitudes to develop in order to embrace the habit of productive data science. You will explore these ideas with hands-on examples in the following chapters.

# CHAPTER 2

# Better Programming Principles for Efficient Data Science

The goal of this chapter is to introduce you to the concepts of certain programming styles and habits that play an essential part in developing efficient data science (DS) and machine learning (ML) systems and pipelines. I will illustrate the concepts through brief examples (or pseudo-codes wherever applicable) and talk about how to measure or track inefficiency.

I will start by introducing the concepts of time and space complexities (https://levelup.gitconnected.com/time-and-space-complexity-725dcba31902) in programming and algorithms. You will also get to see Big-O notation (https://en.wikipedia.org/wiki/Big_O_notation) used in this context. These are foundational concepts for analyzing the runtime or efficiency of any algorithm and can be used to measure and describe the efficiency of standard ML algorithms, as an example. I will also talk briefly about why complexity measures matter for data science tasks in particular.

Then I will demonstrate practical examples of common, inefficient data science and ML coding practices. This is by no means meant to be an exhaustive illustration of every kind of inefficient data science programming. However, I will try to give you a glimpse of typical inefficient code snippets that do not scale well or make some aspects of the overall system design inefficient. Hopefully, you can internalize these examples and apply the same thought process to your own analytics work to become more productive.

In most of these cases, I will also show some more examples of what can be done instead, such as how you can improve the efficiency of the same task using a better programming style or choice of a different tool or function (within the Python ecosystem).

© Dr. Tirthajyoti Sarkar 2022
T. Sarkar, *Productive and Efficient Data Science with Python*, https://doi.org/10.1007/978-1-4842-8121-5_2

Finally, I will introduce tools and techniques to measure the execution time of your code or function blocks. I will cover both generic Python modules and Jupyter magic commands in this regard.

# The Concept of Time and Space Complexities plus Big-O Notation

The time and space complexities of an algorithm are related to the worst-case (generally) execution time and the memory/storage space it takes to run that algorithm for a given input. Because the time and space almost always depend on the size of the input (for example, number of elements in an array), these complexity measures are expressed as functions of the input size, thus $f(n)$ or $g(n)$ for the **n**-element array where **f** or **g** denote the time and space complexities, respectively.

## A Simple Example: Searching for an Element

Let's demonstrate this using a simple example. Consider the following Python program for searching for a given element inside a list. Note that you could have written the code in more *Pythonic* way with `if ele in lst`, but for demonstration purpose, let's write it using naïve list traversing code:

```python
def ele_in_lst(ele,lst):
    len_lst = len(lst)
    for i in range(len_lst):
        if lst[i] == ele:
            return True
    return False
```

If you test this function with the following input, you get `True`:

```python
ele_in_lst(ele=2,lst=[3,4,5,2,9])
>> True
```

But if you test with the following input, you get `False`:

```python
ele_in_lst(ele=2,lst=[3,4,5,5,9,11,3,4,-1,3,5,7,12,15])
>> False
```

In the second example above, the loop is traversed entirely, so the equality check operation of if lst[i] == ele is done 14 times (the length of the list). This is the core operation of the program, which is performed by the CPU and factors into the time complexity of the code.

So, what is the time complexity of this search method? It is clear that **in the worst case**, where the ele is not in the given lst, **the time taken will always be proportional to the length of the** lst (if we assume that each equality operation takes a constant time to perform). This is denoted by the function $O(n)$ where $n$ denotes the number of elements in the input array.

# The Big-O Notation

This notation of **O** in the function $O(n)$ is called the Big-*O* notation. As per Wikipedia, "*it describes the limiting behavior of a function when the argument tends towards a particular value or infinity*" (https://en.wikipedia.org/wiki/Big_O_notation). In particular, this is an example of the worst-case time complexity for this situation (because the element is not present in the given list), but in the limiting case, this is what every computer programmer should be concerned about.

One may wonder why we are not calculating the *average case* time complexity. As it turns out, in most cases, it is quite difficult to calculate or even estimate what that average case looks like, whereas the worst case is generally defined and understood in a much simpler manner. Furthermore, the notation of $O(n)$ is understood in an asymptotic sense, thus the worst-case time taken will not deviate from this linear trend when $n$ becomes large.

Why *linear* trend? Because $O(n)$ denotes the first power of $n$. Similarly, we have algorithms of $O(n^2)$ or $O(n^3)$ complexities that show quadratic or cubic trends. In other words, the time taken will grow looking like a quadratic or cubic function of the problem size $n$.

The origin of this Big-O notation is deeply rooted in the more advanced mathematics of analytic number theory (https://en.wikipedia.org/wiki/Analytic_number_theory), and it shows up in discussions of many mathematical theorems as well. But, in the context of computer science and programming, this is the standard notation to denote the time/space complexity of a given algorithm.

# Complexities: Linear, Logarithmic, Quadratic, and More

So, if this is **O(*n*)**, can the search be made better? Yes, as it turns out, the search can be made to run as fast as **O(log$_2$(*n*))** **if the list is presorted**. The specific algorithm to be used in that case is called the *binary search*. And, as you can guess, the naïve algorithm that we wrote above is called the *linear search*.

## How Much Faster?

And just how much faster is **O(log$_2$(n))** than **O(*n*)**, anyway? We can find that out by simply plotting the two functions **f(*n*) = *n*** and **g(*n*) = log$_2$(*n*)** as the number *n* grows. For a better illustration, see Figure 2-1. It contains two plots: one with the direct comparison between these two functions and another where the logarithmic function is multiplied by a large constant number like 25.

What does the second case in Figure 2-1 represent? It is for a situation where we are using a **O(log$_2$(*n*))** algorithm but we also have a large overhead for the unit computation, so where the fundamental unit of computing is much slower than the corresponding unit operation with the **O(*n*)** linear algorithm.

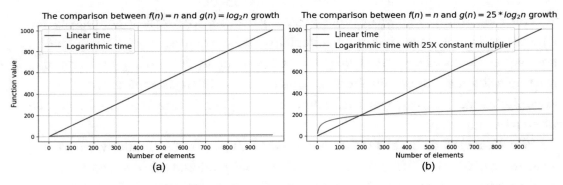

***Figure 2-1.*** *Function value growth comparison between logarithmic and linear-time complexity algorithms. In (a), both have the constant multiplier 1. In (b), the log algorithm has a multiplier of 25*

What is abundantly clear from Figure 2-1 is that no matter the constant multiplier (1 or 25), the **O(log$_2$(*n*))** algorithm becomes much faster than the **O(*n*)** algorithm as *n* grows, so the function value, which represents the time taken by the algorithm, grows much slower with *n*. Therefore, we should **always use a logarithmic complexity algorithm in place of a linear complexity algorithm for the same task (if we can get our hands on such an algorithm)**.

For the search example, this needs presorting of the list, which has its own algorithmic complexity (see sorting algorithms complexity at `www.geeksforgeeks.org/time-complexities-of-all-sorting-algorithms`). But this is often done given that, in a typical application scenario, *you might have to sort the list much less frequently than you have to search through it.*

## What's Beyond Linear?

Although the linear-time complexity looked worse compared to the logarithmic-time one, it is, in fact, a remarkably efficient algorithm in the context of common computing algorithms that we generally encounter (both in data science and non-data-science work). As you can guess, complexities with higher powers of $n$ are pretty common and are denoted accordingly:

> **O($n^2$)** for quadratic-time complexity
>
> **O($n^3$)** for cubic-time complexity
>
> **O($2^n$)** for exponential-time complexity (yes, those hellish things exist!)

Let me show you quick (and naïve) examples of **O($n^2$)** and **O($n^3$)** algorithms. Here is a simple algorithm iterating over the dimensions of a given NumPy array and counting the elements that are greater than zero (you surely know about the NumPy library and arrays at `https://numpy.org/doc/stable/user/whatisnumpy.html` if you are interested in data science, don't you?):

```python
import numpy as np
array_2D = np.random.normal(size=(5,5))

def count_positives(array):
    """
    Counts positives in a random 2-D array
    """
    m,n = array.shape
    count = 0
    for i in range(m):
```

```
        for j in range(n):
            if array[i][j] > 0.0:
                count+=1

    return count
```

How many times is the core unit of computation (if `array[i][j] > 0.0`) performed? Clearly, it is done 5 x 5 = 25 times here for this 2D array of dimension (5, 5). If we change the code for the dimension to be (100, 100) then the computation will be performed 100 x 100 = 10,000 times!

Therefore, the time-complexity here is $O(m \times n)$ where $(m, n)$ are the dimensions of the 2D array. For square arrays, it is roughly equivalent to our familiar $O(n^2)$.

# Why Complexity Matters for Data Science

All these discussions about algorithmic complexity may make you wonder how you might utilize this knowledge in your data science work, especially for productive data science. To answer that, first you need to see some common examples of data science tasks that may have high algorithmic complexity. I covered the linear, logarithmic, and quadratic ones in the last section. Let me show you two more (worse) complexity examples in the context of data science tasks.

## Image Data: Cubic-Complexity Algorithms

As a natural progression to the code example from the $O(n^2)$ case, if we increase the number of loops to 3, as in a 3D array, then the time complexity becomes $O(n^3)$. A prominent example of a 3D array, specifically in the context of data science, is image data where a 2D array represents the coordinates of the pixel, and in each pixel, there is another number representing the color depth (https://en.wikipedia.org/wiki/Color_depth) or the grayscale value (examples shown in Figure 2-2).

Since you may have to work frequently with image data as a data scientist, you have a high chance of running into $O(n^3)$ algorithms. In fact, you may be facing a more complex computing task at each pixel, as it can be a vector of multiple color values (e.g., RGB) instead of a single floating-point number.

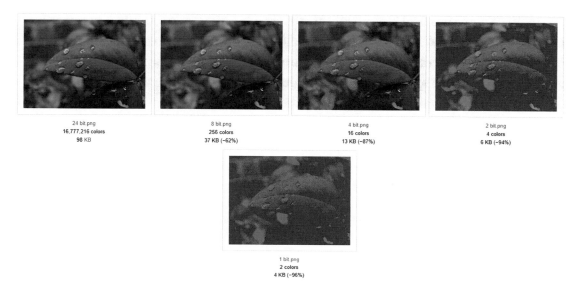

*Figure 2-2.*  *Color-depth and grayscale images example (Source: Wikimedia, GNU Free Documentation License)*

# Best Regression Model: Exponential Complexity

What about the dreaded $O(2^n)$ complexity? Do you really encounter them in everyday data science work? Yes, it turns out that there is a simple data science example for that too.

Consider the exercise of **determining the best linear regression model for a large dataset with many features**. All of the features may not be impactful or equally important. Only a specific subset of features is optimum for most practical cases. Determining that optimum set sounds like a common data science task.

As we know, adding more features to the model will increase the simple $R^2$ coefficient but when we take into consideration advanced metrics such as adjusted-R2 (www.statisticshowto.com/probability-and-statistics/statistics-definitions/adjusted-r2/) or AIC criterion (https://en.wikipedia.org/wiki/Akaike_information_criterion), then we need to experiment with multiple combinations of features to find out the best combination. In short, we need to **search through the space of all possible combinations of features**, build a regression model for each combination, calculate the desired performance metric, and pick the best one at the end (e.g., for which the performance metric is highest).

In more mathematical terms, this translates to **finding the best subset among all subsets of a given set.** This is an exponentially hard problem to compute. This means that the algorithmic complexity is **$O(2^n)$**. Moreover, this is just for building the set of all subsets of the feature space, not even considering the computational cost of building the actual regression model for each combination.

Why? Because of this simple equation that we may remember from high school math. Basically, the sum total of all combinations taken 1, 2, 3, ..., $n$ from $n$ possible items is $2^n$. In the context of our regression problem, we are choosing 1, 2, 3, or more features at a time and building the models.

$$\Sigma\left(C^n_1 + C^n_2 + \dots + C^n_n\right) = 2^n$$

This is the reason **exhaustive search is almost never encouraged for a regression model optimization**. Instead, we have greedy search (`https://en.wikipedia.org/wiki/Greedy_algorithm`) methods such as forward- and backward-selection algorithms (`https://quantifyinghealth.com/stepwise-selection/`), which cut down the search time drastically and yet find a reasonably good solution for almost all practical cases.

# Relative Growth Comparison

To illustrate the benefit (or disadvantage) of having algorithms with various complexity orders, we can draw the kind of simple chart shown in Figure 2-3. It is clear that the logarithm-time algorithm grows slowest, followed by the linear-time one. Algorithms with higher powers grow quickly and the exponential type just takes off like a ballistic missile!

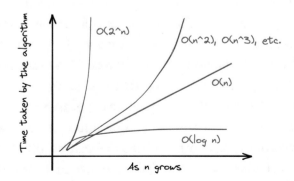

***Figure 2-3.***  *Relative growth of various time-complexity algorithms (not to scale)*

It is also noteworthy to state that, because these complexity measures and the Big-$O$ notation are really defined in an asymptotic sense, as in the limit of large values of $n$, they really need to be treated as belonging to entirely separate classes of computing difficulty. This means no matter what actual complexity function a particular algorithm may be reduced to, if it is cubic, then it is always worse than a linear or quadratic algorithm in the long run.

The quickest way to judge is to **look at the highest degree of the algorithm** and determine the rank. Exponentials are always worse than polynomials, and polynomials are always worse than linear. Some quick examples are as follows:

An algorithm of **$O(200*n+3)$** complexity is better than one with **$O(0.1*n^2+12)$**.

An algorithm of **$O(3*n^3+2^n+5)$** complexity is worse than one with **$O(100*n^2+12)$**.

An algorithm of **$O(4^{0.1n})$** complexity is worse than one with **$O(100*n^{100})$**.

---

The last one in the above list must have surprised you! You are encouraged to calculate these two functions starting from small to large values of $n$ and overlay them to get an understanding of how the first function overtakes the second one at large values of $n$. Therefore, judging from an asymptotic sense, you should still prefer the polynomial-degree algorithm (even with a term like $n^{100}$) over the exponential one ($4^{0.1n}$).

---

# AI Is Intractable, but It Works

*Deep learning networks have been trained to recognize speech, caption photographs, and translate text between languages at high levels of performance. Although applications of deep learning networks to real-world problems have become ubiquitous, our understanding of why they are so effective is lacking. **These empirical results should not be possible according to sample complexity** in statistics and nonconvex optimization theory.*

*Terrence J. Sejnowski (www.salk.edu/scientist/terrence-sejnowski/), "The unreasonable effectiveness of deep learning in artificial intelligence" (www.pnas.org/doi/10.1073/pnas.1907373117), PNAS, December 2020*

It is a big jump, going from simple searching and sorting algorithms to the world of gradient descent and backpropagation (https://blog.paperspace.com/intro-to-optimization-in-deep-learning-gradient-descent/) used in deep learning, but it's necessary to make the point of AI algorithms being intractable yet manageable.

So, what is **intractability?** It is a whole new subject in itself, beyond the scope of this book, albeit closely related to the topic of algorithmic complexity discussed in the previous subsections. Simply put, **intractable problems are computational problems for which no efficient algorithm (that solves them) can be found**. Here, the term *efficient* means, under most circumstances, polynomial-time algorithms, so algorithms with complexities at most $O(n^k)$ but not the ones with $O(2^n)$ or $O(n!)$.

Unfortunately, in the field of AI, most of the common problems can be shown to be intractable in theory. In particular, for AI problems, their most optimum solution needs some kind of algorithm that searches through a space that is exponential in nature, such as the number of all possible trees (and branches) in a decision tree or the number of all possible models in a simple multivariate regression. As these traditional ML tasks fall into the realm of intractability, it is no surprise that deep learning networks will also be plagued by the same computational difficulty.

However, despite the theoretical impossibility (of finding the best possible solution), common ML algorithms and solutions work for almost all practical situations by employing clever techniques such as greedy search (www.programiz.com/dsa/greedy-algorithm), heuristics (https://en.wikipedia.org/wiki/Heuristic_(computer_science)), dynamic programming (www.programiz.com/dsa/dynamic-programming), randomized algorithms (https://en.wikipedia.org/wiki/Randomized_algorithm), and more. Concretely, the **practical techniques do not seek to find the absolute best solution but a "good enough" solution that can be found efficiently and with reasonable computing resources**. They also utilize domain knowledge and inductive bias heavily to trim the search space of potential solutions.

Heuristic search techniques are often called *informed search* as they tend to use additional information about the problem and the environment (that an AI agent may be in). Imagine you are in a foreign country and don't have access to Google Maps! You have a choice of driving to a few cities from the place you are currently in, as the first step of the journey to reach your ultimate destination. You may not know the exact driving distance of these cities, but you may have heard from your friend that it took her less time for a train journey to city *A* than it took to travel to city *B*. This is *additional information* about the environment and, although it does not guarantee that the actual driving distance to City *A* is less than that to City *B*, there is a good chance of it being true. It's called a *heuristic* and you can use it to determine the optimal path to take on your journey. A great many AI algorithms use this technique for efficient search.

Therefore, to summarize, the intent of the preceding sections on computational complexity and Big-*O* notation was to introduce the idea of efficiency of common algorithms and to illustrate that there are, indeed, separate classes of algorithms that perform quite differently when the input size grows. This was done to instill a sense of probing in your mind, to check your code and implementation for weakness, even if you are not required to rigorously analyze and mathematically derive the exact Big-*O* function for a particular solution. Moreover, this is also to assure you that **clever solution techniques exist to handle even seemingly intractable problems** with big data, and you should explore them at every chance.

# Inefficient Programming in Data Science

Data science code can be plagued by inefficient practices and design patterns in countless ways. One of the major reasons for this happening is that data scientists often come from diverse backgrounds (e.g., physics, biology, economics, statistics, electrical engineering, etc.) and they don't follow the well-established software engineering design patterns (https://en.wikipedia.org/wiki/Software_design_pattern) all the time. Data science boot camps, workshops, and online courses, which are often the places where a lot of budding data scientists get their training from, teach a plethora of topics covering Python coding, statistics, and machine learning but not necessarily these high-efficiency programming techniques.

However, it is to be noted at the outset that this book is not a primer on software engineering for data science. In particular, the goal of this chapter is to showcase some of the most obvious and widely repeated inefficient programming patterns that are found in data science tasks so that you can recognize and learn from these examples. This is precisely what I set forth to do in the next sections. Also, for good measure, I show workarounds and alternatives that are supposed to be more efficient.

# Canonical Examples

In this section, I show some examples of *inefficient programming patterns* that occur frequently in regular data science workflow. I follow an approach that is practical and hands-on rather than pedagogical. That means I am not taking a rigorous mathematical approach to calculate and prove the algorithmic complexities of various functions and code snippets. Instead, you are encouraged to measure the execution times of code snippets using various tools and explore possible improvement strategies on your own. There is no one right answer on how to improve upon these snippets.

It is to be noted that **I am not talking about specific libraries like NumPy or pandas in this section**. In fact, I will discuss efficient best practices with these libraries in the next chapter. Here, I am showing examples of basic Python coding patterns that you can utilize for many situations (data science and beyond).

---

A note to the reader: I intend to keep the code snippets compact and therefore I am not making them self-contained and exhaustive. This means code snippets are not meant to be run on their own. Accompanying notebooks will have the full runnable code.

---

## Use a Filter Instead of a for Loop

There are countless articles written about avoiding a for loop for simple repetitive tasks that can be cast with some other form of mathematical logic. Now, for many complicated logic and iteration situations, you cannot avoid for loops. However, in many situations you can use alternate methods and you should be on the lookout for them. Python provides some built-in methods to be used in specific situations like data filtering.

Consider the following code block with three function definitions:

```
ONE_MILLION = list(range(int(1e6)))

def for_loop():
    result = []
    for ele in ONE_MILLION:
        if not ele % 3:
            result.append(ele)
    return result

def list_comprehension():
    return [num for num in ONE_MILLION if not num % 3]

def filter_fn():
    return filter(lambda x: not x % 3, ONE_MILLION)
```

The first function contains a plain vanilla for loop and list appending. The second one is much cleaner and uses Python's list comprehension (https://realpython.com/list-comprehension-python/). Finally, the third function uses the built-in `filter` function and the lambda expression (https://realpython.com/python-lambda/) to achieve the same goal.

Let's use Jupyter Notebook's built-in magic command (https://stackoverflow.com/questions/29280470/what-is-timeit-in-python) `%%timeit` to measure the execution speed.

For the `for_loop` function,

```
%%timeit -r20 -n5
for_loop()
>> 56.6 ms ± 3.03 ms per loop (mean ± std. dev. of 20 runs, 5 loops each)
```

For the `list_comprehension` function,

```
%%timeit -r20 -n5
list_comprehension()
>> 44.2 ms ± 2.21 ms per loop (mean ± std. dev. of 20 runs, 5 loops each)
```

For the `filter_fn` function,

```
%%timeit -r20 -n5
filter_fn()
>> 440 ns ± 93.6 ns per loop (mean ± std. dev. of 20 runs, 5 loops each)
```

The list comprehension is slightly faster than the plain `for` loop whereas the filter-based method is much faster. Clearly, for this kind of situation, where you are essentially doing data filtering (by iterating over a list and creating a new list based on whether each element meets a specific criterion), you should try the `filter` function whenever possible.

---

One thing to remember about these examples, strewn throughout this book, is that the exact numerical result of a timing measurement will vary wildly from machine to machine, or even from one execution to the next. The timing profile is a tricky subject and difficult to standardize. You may get a totally different result depending on the hardware you are using and local software settings. Nonetheless, (in most cases) the overall trend will be apparent from the examples.

---

## Use Sets to Find Unique Elements

Sets are a powerful data structure (https://realpython.com/python-sets/) in Python, and they can be used creatively for situations where you want to find the unique elements from a long list or array. Consider the following code with two function definitions:

```
import random
random_lst = [random.randint(1,100) for _ in range(100000)]

def unique_for_loop():
    unique_elements = []
    for ele in random_lst:
        if ele not in random_lst:
            unique_elements.append(ele)
    return unique_elements

def unique_set():
    return list(set(random_lst))
```

As usual, you run tests using the Jupyter `%%timeit` command and get the following with the `for` loop function:

```
%%timeit -r20 -n5
unique_for_loop()
>> 109 ms ± 4 ms per loop (mean ± std. dev. of 20 runs, 5 loops each)
```

You get the following result using `set`:

```
%%timeit -r20 -n5
unique_set()
>> 788 µs ± 181 µs per loop (mean ± std. dev. of 20 runs, 5 loops each)
```

The method with `set` is much faster! Therefore, it makes sense to use it any time you have a situation involving finding unique elements in a long array.

Furthermore, the `in` operator is designed to be very fast when working on sets. Therefore, if you want to check the membership of an element in a long list (i.e., check if that element exists in the list), and you have reason to believe that the list contains many duplicate entries, then you can reduce the search time significantly by first removing all the duplicates and creating a set out of that list. A pseudo-code will look something like

```
a_long_list = ...
duplicates_removed = set(a_long_list)
ele = ...
if ele in duplicates_removed:
    print(f"The element {ele} exists in the list")
```

---

The method shown above is not a fundamental principle of changing the algorithmic complexity of the search operation (as discussed in the previous section). It is a **trick to take advantage of in specific situations using the built-in data structures** of Python and their optimized methods and operators. In data science tasks (or, in general, with programming), you should keep your eyes open for these sorts of tricks as they can be found everywhere and in every programming language.

---

# Use a Specialized Data Structure for Counting

In many situations, you may need to count the frequency of variables or elements from a large corpus of text or blob of data. One natural instinct is to construct a dictionary where the variables are stored as keys and their corresponding count as the integer values. A simple way to do this is to write a function like this:

```
def word_counts(text):
    dict_words = {}
    for w in text.split(' '):
        if w in dict_words.keys():
            dict_words[w]+=1
        else:
            dict_words[w] = 1
    return dict_words
```

Run it on a text sample (from the familiar *A Tale of Two Cities*):

```
text = """It was the best of times, it was the worst of times,
it was the age of wisdom, it was the age of foolishness,
it was the epoch of belief, it was the epoch of incredulity,
it was the season of Light, it was the season of Darkness,
it was the spring of hope, it was the winter of despair,
we had everything before us, we had nothing before us,
we were all going direct to Heaven, we were all going direct the other
way - in short, the period was so far like the present period, that some of
its noisiest authorities insisted on its being received, for good or for
evil, in the superlative degree of comparison only
"""
```

You get the following result:

```
%%timeit -r1000 -n10
word_counts(text)
>> 28.6 µs ± 13.9 µs per loop (mean ± std. dev. of 1000 runs, 10
loops each)
```

For this kind of situation involving counting, you can use a specialized data structure called Counter from the collections module (https://docs.python.org/3/library/collections.html#collections.Counter) of Python. You will see that by using this built-in data structure, you can make the code compact, organized, and faster.

Here is the single-line code to create a Counter object from the given text:

```
counter_words = Counter(text.split(' '))
```

This counter_words object has a dictionary-like API just like the dict_words object returned by the word_counts function. For example, you can easily print the counts (of each unique word) using the .items() method:

```
counter_words.items()
>> dict_items([('It', 1), ('was', 11), ('the', 14), ('best', 1), ('of', 12),
('times,', 2), ('it', 5), ('worst', 1), ('\nit', 4), ('age', 2),
('wisdom,', 1), ('foolishness,', 1), ('epoch', 2), ...
```

```
Truncated output to save space
```

Observe that counter_words has more useful built-in methods than the regular dictionary dict_words. For example, one of the most common data science tasks (used repeatedly in Natural Language Processing or NLP pipelines) is to list the top 5 (or 10) most common words. If you were to use the native Python dictionary approach, then you would have to write a small additional code to get that list:

```
dict_words = word_counts(text)
top_5 = sorted([(v,i) for i,v in dict_words.items()], reverse=True)[:5]
```

This would get you the list of tuples with the five most frequently appearing words:

```
[(14, 'the'), (12, 'of'), (11, 'was'), (5, 'it'), (4, '\nit')]
```

But you can get the same result using the built-in most_common() method, which takes a single argument of the number of top words you want to extract:

```
counter_words.most_common(5)
>> [('the', 14), ('of', 12), ('was', 11), ('it', 5), ('\nit', 4)]
```

Not only is this approach faster (you are encouraged to measure the execution speed using the Jupyter magic command) but also it is cleaner and less error-prone because you don't have to write your own code with a separate list variable like top_5. You just pass on the number as an argument to the built-in method and get back a list.

# Use the itertools Library for Combinatorial Structures

Suppose you are working on a machine learning model with a dataset that has four numerical and four categorical features. You want to build all combinations of two feature models combining one numerical and one categorical feature and compare the performance of all such models.

A naïve way to build a list combining numerical and categorical features would be using nested for loops, like so:

```
lst_features = []
for i in num_features:
    for j in cat_features:
        lst_features.append((i,j))
```

The resulting list may look like this:

```
[('num_feature-1', 'cat_feature-1'),
 ('num_feature-1', 'cat_feature-2'),
 ('num_feature-1', 'cat_feature-3'),
 ('num_feature-1', 'cat_feature-4'),
 ('num_feature-2', 'cat_feature-1'),
 ('num_feature-2', 'cat_feature-2'),
 ('num_feature-2', 'cat_feature-3'),
 ('num_feature-2', 'cat_feature-4'),
 ('num_feature-3', 'cat_feature-1'),
 ('num_feature-3', 'cat_feature-2'),
 ('num_feature-3', 'cat_feature-3'),
 ('num_feature-3', 'cat_feature-4'),
 ('num_feature-4', 'cat_feature-1'),
 ('num_feature-4', 'cat_feature-2'),
 ('num_feature-4', 'cat_feature-3'),
 ('num_feature-4', 'cat_feature-4')]
```

For such combinatorial data structures, you can use the itertools module (built-in Python). You can get the same result as above by using the product function from the library. Here is the single-line code:

```
lst_features = list(product(num_features, cat_features, repeat=1))
```

You are encouraged to measure the timing on these two approaches. It is highly likely that the itertools function will run faster.

Furthermore, you may want to build all combinations of five-feature models by mixing the numerical and categorical features together. Again, one line of code is sufficient to build the whole combination using the combinations function from the library. Note the argument r=5 in the function denoting that you want a five-feature combination:

```
comb_features = list(combinations(num_features+cat_features, r=5))
```

It looks like following (truncated output):

```
Model 0: num_feature-1, num_feature-2, num_feature-3, num_feature-4,
cat_feature-1,
Model 1: num_feature-1, num_feature-2, num_feature-3, num_feature-4,
cat_feature-2,
Model 2: num_feature-1, num_feature-2, num_feature-3, num_feature-4,
cat_feature-3,
Model 3: num_feature-1, num_feature-2, num_feature-3, num_feature-4,
cat_feature-4,
Model 4: num_feature-1, num_feature-2, num_feature-3, cat_feature-1,
cat_feature-2,
Model 5: num_feature-1, num_feature-2, num_feature-3, cat_feature-1,
cat_feature-3,
```

# Lessons Learned from the Examples

In the examples above, you covered important computing tasks such as

- Filtering

- Finding unique elements

- Counting the frequency of occurrence and most common elements

- Building combinatorial data structures

In all of these cases, I first showed a somewhat naïve way of accomplishing the task using Python code and then demonstrated a faster and cleaner way to accomplish the same task using specialized data structures or built-in functions in Python. Although these examples cover a lot of common tasks in any data science workflow, there are so many more situations where you can apply the lessons learned here.

So, what are the core lessons learned? Here is a short list.

> Always look for an **optimum data structure** to use to store and manipulate your data. For different situations, different data structures can be optimal.

> **No need to restrict yourself to just the default containers** like lists, sets, tuples, and dictionaries. Python has other modules with specialized containers and data structures which can come in handy in many situations and deliver faster performance.

> **Cleaner code is efficient and productive code**. A clean and compact single-line code may not be faster than the five lines of code it replaces, but it enhances the maintainability and readability of the overall codebase. This leads to increased productivity and higher efficiency in the long run.

> Always take care to **measure the execution time** and experiment with various options (as listed above) to determine the best one for your particular situation. Without measuring, you cannot say anything for certain.

# Measuring Code Execution Timing

You saw in the examples in the preceding section the importance of measuring the execution time and speed of your code and functions. But what are some of the standard methods to accomplish this? In this section, I will cover a few approaches (Figure 2-4).

***Figure 2-4.*** *Measuring the execution speed is the first essential step towards making your data science code more efficient and productive*

# Python's time Module Is Your Friend

For almost any timing measurement situation, you can use functions from the time module of Python. It has a few different functions to offer, and you should utilize them in a certain way to get accurate results.

## Basic Usage Example

One of the fundamental functions in the time module is also named time() and it gives back the current system time. Here is a simple code example to illustrate its usage:

```
from time import time, sleep

# Function which just sleeps for 2 seconds
def sleep_fn():
    sleep(2)

# The main timing block
t1 = time()
sleep_fn()
t2 = time()

print("Elapsed time: ", t2-t1)
```

You may get the following:

```
Elapsed time:  2.0102791786193848
```

You could have any piece of code (however long and complex) in place of `sleep_fn` in the code above and the timing block would have measured `t1` and `t2` before and after the code executes. From those measurements, you would get the difference or the runtime of the code. Therefore, this is the basic usage pattern:

```
t1 = time()
<data science code or function>
t2 = time()
time_delta = t2-t1
```

It looks simple, doesn't it? However, there are a few caveats which I discuss next.

## Many Loops Needed for a Fast Code Block

The returned value in the function time is in seconds, so it may return zero if you are trying to measure a fast code block. For example,

```
t1 = time()
s = sum([i for i in range(10)])
t2 = time()
print("Sum: ", s)
print("Elapsed time: ", t2-t1)
```

You will get the correct sum, but the elapsed time will show up as zero. It is that fast.

```
Sum:  45
Elapsed time:  0.0
```

So, what can you do? Just run the same code many times so that the total time is in the range of at least milliseconds. Then, calculate the average.

```
NUM_LOOPS = 10000
t1 = time()
for _ in range(NUM_LOOPS):
    s=sum([i for i in range(10)])
t2 = time()
print("Sum: ", s)
print("Elapsed time: ", t2-t1)
print("Average time: ", (t2-t1)/NUM_LOOPS)
```

You may get something like:

```
Sum:   45
Elapsed time:  0.006996631622314453
Average time:  6.996631622314453e-07
```

So, you ran the summation code 10,000 times and found out that it takes approximately 0.7 microseconds or 699 nanoseconds to sum numbers 1 through 10. As you can surely appreciate, **averaging the measurements for 10,000 runs also eliminated any kind of variance** and provided a stable measurement.

## A Timing Decorator

Writing the timing code as above is fine but in the spirit of refactoring and the DRY principle of software engineering (https://thevaluable.dev/dry-principle-cost-benefit-example/) it would be great to avoid writing the same code again and again. Instead, it's better to have **a mechanism at which you can throw any data science function and it will tell you the execution time**. Needless to say, this mechanism should be able to accept functions with arbitrary arguments and keywords (Figure 2-5).

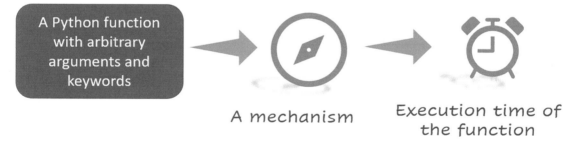

***Figure 2-5.*** *A mechanism to measure the execution time of any arbitrary Python function*

Fortunately, Python provides a couple of clever constructs to accomplish just that. You can use Python decorators and wrapping constructs from the `functools` module to get what you want.

Here is the boilerplate code for your reference:

```
from functools import wraps
from time import time
```

```
def timing(func):
    @wraps(func)
    def wrap(*args, **kw):
        ts = time()
        result = func(*args, **kw)
        te = time()
        print (f"Function '{func.__name__}' with arguments {args},
        keywords {kw} took {te-ts} seconds to run")
        return result
    return wrap
```

This code basically allows you to define any function func with arbitrary arguments and keywords and to measure its execution time. Here is a simple example where you use the @timing as the decorator to the function std_dev, which takes a large integer n as input, generates that many random numbers using the NumPy library, and calculates their standard deviation:

```
import numpy as np
@timing
def std_dev(n=10000):
    a = np.random.randint(1,1000,size=n)
    s = a.std()
    return s
```

Once decorated by @timing, whenever you run the function, you may get output like the following:

```
std_dev(n=1000000)
>> Function 'std_dev' with arguments (), keywords {'n': 1000000} took
0.012999773025512695 seconds to run
```

If you rerun the function with 10 million as argument (n=10000000), you get

```
std_dev(n=10000000)
>> Function 'std_dev' with arguments (), keywords {'n': 10000000} took
0.1154332160949707 seconds to run
```

It took almost 10X time for an input 10X larger. So, the timing calculation is automatic and updated with every instance of the function execution.

The topic of Python decorators is a vast one and merits its own mini-book or course. You can utilize them in various ways for productive data science work. Go to `https://realpython.com/primer-on-python-decorators/` for a quick introduction. You should also look at the `functools` module and to explore what it can do.

## Using the Decorator to Measure Complexity

Let me show a quick example of how to use the timing decorator to measure the time complexity of a particular piece of code. Suppose you want to measure the complexity of the matrix multiplication method of your favorite NumPy package. This is, of course, because you use that algorithm or function (`numpy.matmul`) in many places of your machine learning code. You may just wonder *how much time it takes for the function to execute as the size of matrices go up.*

The following code wraps a test function with the timing decorator:

```python
def gettime(func):
    @wraps(func)
    def wrap(*args, **kw):
        ts = time()
        result = func(*args, **kw)
        te = time()
        tdelta= round(1000*(te-ts),3)
        return tdelta
    return wrap
@gettime
def matrix_mult(n=100):
    matrix_1 = np.random.normal(size=(n,n))
    matrix_2 = np.random.normal(size=(n,n))
    result = np.matmul(matrix_1,matrix_2)
    return result
```

Note that you are returning the time difference (`tdelta`) after multiplying it by 1,000 to turn the result in milliseconds and rounding it off to three decimal places (`round(1000*(te-ts),3)`) for better readability. Your test function generates two 2D

41

matrices (size=(n,n)) with random Gaussian numbers (np.random.normal) to perform the matrix multiplication. Now you can just invoke matrix_mult() with a size parameter n to get the time (in milliseconds) it takes for the multiplication operation.

Refer to the accompanying Jupyter notebook with this book for the details of the plotting code. When you calculate the execution times for a range of matrix size from 1,000 to 10,000, you get the result shown in Figure 2-6. The curve does look like a polynomial function of $n$, doesn't it? Is it following $O(n^2)$ complexity? You are also encouraged to experiment with 3D matrices and see what happens to the computational complexity. Will it become $O(n^3)$ as we talked about in the previous chapter for image processing tasks?

---

Matrix multiplications are so fundamental and ubiquitous for machine learning tasks that their execution time and performance often determine the computational efficiency of the overall machine learning pipeline. Even the simple-looking linear regression uses matrix multiplication (and inverse) to obtain the best coefficients when using an ordinary-least-square solution technique. For a simple article explaining this method, go to www.kdnuggets.com/2016/11/linear-regression-least-squares-matrix-multiplication-concise-technical-overview.html. When you move into the realm of deep learning, matrix multiplications are pervasive and everywhere. In fact, it is hard to improve the algorithmic complexity beyond what has already been done, thus current emphasis is on designing hardware architectures that are optimized for matrix multiplication (go to https://maitrix.com/dsr-modular-computation/hardware-matrix-multiplication/). These novel hardware solutions are finding increasing use in AI/ML applications in the form of AI-optimized ICs or processors.

---

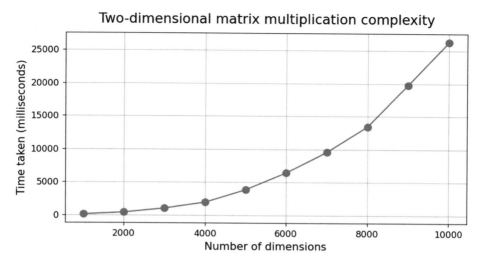

*Figure 2-6.* *Two-dimensional matrix multiplication time with a NumPy function*

# Jupyter/IPython Magic Command

The Jupyter notebook came out of the IPython (or Interactive-Python) project (`https://ipython.org/`), which also provides the core kernel behind the Jupyter front end. With its language-agnostic notebook format and seamless support for code, graphics rendering, and markdown texts, Jupyter Notebook (and, more recently, Jupyter Lab) quickly became the de-facto standard and prototyping tool for data scientists.

Among its powerful features, a set of magic commands (`www.tutorialspoint.com/jupyter/ipython_magic_commands.htm`) is worth mentioning. They can do many useful things like

- Execute system commands (change directory, show present directory, etc.)

- Open a default text editor from a Jupyter cell

- List environmental variables

The particular set of magic commands (`%timeit` and `%%timeit`) can also help measure the code execution time. You have already seen these commands in this book for measuring the efficiency of various pieces of code within the Jupyter notebook environment.

## %timeit: Execution Time for Single-Line Code

This magic command is also called a "line command" as it is used in single-line command situations. For example,

```
%timeit sum(range(100000))
>> 2.25 ms ± 199 µs per loop (mean ± std. dev. of 7 runs, 100 loops each)
```

It measures the time taken to sum numbers 0 through 99999. Because the core operation is quite fast, it runs 100 loops of 7 runs and calculates the average and variance as well.

This kind of magic command is particularly useful to showcase the distinct improvement you can get by using specialized numeric computing packages like NumPy over native Python functions. For the same task as above, you can use %timeit with NumPy code to get the following result:

```
%timeit np.sum(np.arange(100000))
>> 91.6 µs ± 3.47 µs per loop (mean ± std. dev. of 7 runs, 10000
loops each)
```

Note how %timeit automatically increased the number of loops to calculate the individual code runtime accurately as the np.sum runs much faster than the built-in Python sum function.

## %%timeit: Measuring Execution Time for a Block of Code in a Cell

These magic commands are also called "cell magic" because they apply to the contents of a complete Jupyter notebook cell (which is usually a multi-line code block, rather than a single line of code). You used one earlier in this book. In fact, they are the preferred tool to measure the performance of a function or logic conditional loop.

Following the same summation example as above, this would look like

```
%%timeit
s = 0
for i in range(100000):
    s+=i

>> 5.08 ms ± 724 µs per loop (mean ± std. dev. of 7 runs, 100 loops each)
```

Note, however, that there are no print statements in this piece of code. This is because including one will alter the total time slightly because of the additional function call.

This is important to remember and practice: **when you are measuring the performance of a piece of code, focus on measuring the time taken for that exact code, no more and no less.** This means you should only be interested in the timing measurement and not the actual computation result.

While the `%%timeit` command automatically adjusts the number of loops intelligently, you may want to control that for comparison among different functions that may vary in speed. All you have to do is insert a couple of extra runtime arguments in the command. For example, the following code will time the same summation code with 50 loops and 10 runs each. Note the command line arguments -n50 and -r10, denoting the number of loops and runs, respectively:

```
%%timeit -n50 -r10
s = 0
for i in range(100000):
    s+=i
```

# Summary

In this chapter, I started with a discussion of the concepts of algorithmic complexity and the asymptotic behavior of common algorithms (for example, searching or sorting) in terms of the size of the input. In that regard, I introduced the concept of the Big-$O$ notation and what it means for comparing and analyzing the relative performance of algorithms and computing tasks in general.

Thereafter, I talked about why this concept is important for common data science tasks as I drew on examples of polynomial-degree and exponential complexities from regular data science jobs like image data analysis and evaluating the best regression model for a feature-rich dataset. I gave a sneak peek of how quickly exponential growth occurs as compared to polynomial-time growth and why an exhaustive search for the best model is almost never done. In this context, I further discussed the intractability of AI algorithms in general, and why their practical applications are hugely successful these days.

Next, I illustrated the idea of inefficient programming patterns in data science with Python code snippets in the context of common tasks like filtering, searching, and counting. I showed more efficient alternatives, which I hope will generate new ideas in your mind.

Finally, I dealt with the matter of measuring inefficiency itself with the help of timing tools and commands. I explored in detail the various usages of the `time` module that comes built-in with Python. In particular, I showed how to create a timing decorator to measure the execution time of any generic function. Jupyter magic commands constitute a second set of tools in this regard, and they were also discussed with simple examples. I will revisit the topic of time profiling with the help of dedicated tools in Chapter 8.

This chapter had the central objective of instilling a sense of probing into your mind, which you can use anywhere and everywhere in their codebase, *to dig deep and probe the efficiency of your implementations and compare among alternative solutions*. I hope that such efforts were successful in that regard.

# CHAPTER 3

# How to Use Python Data Science Packages More Productively

Python is, without any doubt, the most used and fastest growing programming language of choice for data scientists (and other related professionals such as machine learning engineers or artificial intelligence researchers) all over the world. There are many reasons for this explosive growth of Python as the *lingua franca* of data science (mostly in the last decade or so). It has an easy learning curve, it supports dynamic typing, it can be written both script-type and in object-oriented fashion, and more.

However, probably the most important reason for its growth is the amazing open-source community activity and the resulting ecosystem of powerful and rich libraries and frameworks focused on data science work. The default, barebone installation of Python cannot be used to do any meaningful data science task. However, with minimal extra work, any data scientist can install and use a handful of feature-rich, well-tested, production-grade libraries that can jumpstart their work immediately.

Some of the most popular and widely used among these jump-starter packages are the following:

- **NumPy** for numerical computing (used as the foundation of almost all data science Python libraries)

- **pandas** for data analytics with tabular, structured data

- **Matplotlib/Seaborn** for powerful graphics and statistical visualization

© Dr. Tirthajyoti Sarkar 2022
T. Sarkar, *Productive and Efficient Data Science with Python*, https://doi.org/10.1007/978-1-4842-8121-5_3

However, just because these libraries provide easy APIs and smooth learning curves does not mean that everybody uses them in a highly productive and efficient manner. One must explore these libraries and understand both their powers and limitations to exploit them fully for productive data science work.

This is the goal of this chapter: to show how and why these libraries should be used in various typical data science tasks for achieving high efficiency. You'll start with the NumPy library as it is also the foundation of pandas and SciPy. Then you'll explore the pandas library, followed by a tour of the Matplotlib and Seaborn packages.

It is to be noted, however, that my goal is not to introduce you to typical features and functions of these libraries. There are plenty of excellent courses and books for that purpose. You are expected to have basic knowledge of and experience with using some, if not all, of these libraries. I will show you **canonical examples of how to use these packages to do your data science work in a productive manner**.

You may also wonder where another widely used Python ML package named scikit-learn fits in this scheme. I cover that in Chapter 4. Additionally, in Chapter 7, I cover how to use some lesser-known Python packages to aid NumPy and pandas to use them more efficiently and productively.

# Why NumPy Is Faster Than Regular Python Code and By How Much

NumPy (or Numpy), short for **Num**erical **Py**thon, is the fundamental package used for high-performance scientific computing and data analysis in the Python ecosystem. It is the foundation on which nearly all of the higher-level data science tools and frameworks such as pandas and Scikit-learn are built.

Deep learning libraries such as TensorFlow and PyTroch use, as their fundamental building block, NumPy arrays, on top of which they build their specialized Tensor objects and graph flow routines for deep learning tasks. Most of the machine learning algorithms make heavy use of linear algebra operations on a long list/vector/matrix of numbers for which NumPy code and methods have been optimized.

# NumPy Arrays are Different

The fundamental data structure introduced by NumPy is the ndarray or **N-dimensional numerical arrays**. For beginners in Python, sometimes these arrays look similar to a Python list. But they are anything but similar. Let's demonstrate this using a simple example.

Consider the following code which creates two Python lists. When you use the + operator on them, the second list gets appended to the first one.

```
lst1 = [i for i in range(1,11)]
lst2 = [i*10 for i in range(1,11)]
print(lst1+lst2)
>> [1, 2, 3, 4, 5, 6, 7, 8, 9, 10, 10, 20, 30, 40, 50, 60, 70, 80, 90, 100]
```

The treatment of the elements in the lists feel object-like, not very numerical, doesn't it? If these were numerical vectors instead of a simple list of numbers, you would expect the + operator to act slightly different and add the numbers from the first list to the corresponding numbers in the second list *element-wise.*

That's precisely what the NumPy array version of these lists does:

```
import numpy as np
arr1 = np.array(lst1)
arr2 = np.array(lst2)
arr1+arr2
>> array([ 11,  22,  33,  44,  55,  66,  77,  88,  99, 110])
```

What is np.array? It is nothing but the array method called from the NumPy module (the first line of the code did that with import numpy as np).

Perhaps the easiest way to see the richness of this array representation is to check the list of all methods associated with the data structure. You can do that using the dir function like this:

```
for p in dir(lst1):
    if '__' not in p:
        print(p, end=', ')
>> append, clear, copy, count, extend, index, insert, pop, remove,
reverse, sort,
```

If you run similar code for the `arr1` object, you will see the following output:

```
>> T, all, any, argmax, argmin, argpartition, argsort, astype, base,
byteswap, choose, clip, compress, conj, conjugate, copy, ctypes, cumprod,
cumsum, data, diagonal, dot, dtype, dump, dumps, fill, flags, flat,
flatten, getfield, imag, item, itemset, itemsize, max, mean, min, nbytes,
ndim, newbyteorder, nonzero, partition, prod, ptp, put, ravel, real,
repeat, reshape, resize, round, searchsorted, setfield, setflags, shape,
size, sort, squeeze, std, strides, sum, swapaxes, take, tobytes, tofile,
tolist, tostring, trace, transpose, var, view,
```

There are so many more (and different looking) functions and attributes available with the NumPy array object. In particular, take note of methods such as `mean`, `std`, and `sum`, as they clearly indicate a **focus on numerical/statistical computing** with this kind of array objects. And these operations are fast too. How fast? You will see that now.

# NumPy Array vs. Native Python Computation

NumPy is much faster due to its **vectorized implementation** and the fact that many of its core routines were originally written in the C language (based on the CPython framework). NumPy arrays are densely packed arrays of homogeneous types. Python lists, by contrast, are arrays of pointers to objects, even when all of them are of the same type. So, we get the benefits of the locality of reference.

Many NumPy operations are implemented in the C language, **avoiding the general cost of loops in Python, pointer indirection, and elementwise dynamic type checking**. In particular, the boost in speed depends on what operation you are performing. For data science and ML tasks, this is an invaluable advantage because it avoids looping in long and multi-dimensional arrays.

---

Locality of reference (`www.geeksforgeeks.org/locality-of-reference-and-cache-operation-in-cache-memory/`) is one of the main reasons behind NumPy arrays being much faster and more efficient than Python list objects. Spatial locality in memory access patterns results in performance gains notably due to the CPU cache operations. The cache loads bytes in chunks from RAM to the CPU registers (the fastest memory in a computer system, located next to the processor). Adjacent items in memory are then loaded very efficiently.

---

# NumPy and Native Python Implementation

Let's illustrate this using the familiar @timing decorator from the last chapter. Here is a code wrapping the decorator around two functions, std_dev and std_dev_python, implementing the calculation of standard deviation of a list/array with NumPy and native Python code, respectively.

```
@timing
def std_dev(a):
    if isinstance(a,list):
        a = np.array(a)
    s = a.std()
    return s

from math import sqrt
@timing
def std_dev_python(lst):
    s = sum(lst)
    av = s/len(lst)
    sumsq = 0
    for i in lst:
        sumsq+=(i-av)**2
    sumsq_av = sumsq/len(lst)
    result = sqrt(sumsq_av)
    return result
```

Next, you define two objects, a NumPy array and a Python list, of the same length (1,000,000) and calculate the time it takes for the standard deviation computation:

```
a = np.arange(1000000)
lst = [i for i in range(1000000)]
```

For the NumPy function,

```
std_dev(a)
>> Function 'std_dev' took 8.996 milliseconds to run
>> 288675.1345946685
```

For the Python function,

```
std_dev_python(lst)
>> Function 'std_dev_python' took 212.995 milliseconds to run
>> 288675.1345958226
```

So, the NumPy implementation is much faster and should be used for data science tasks by default.

## Conversion Adds Overhead

If you look at the code for the NumPy function, you will notice a small but significant code for type checking and coercion at the beginning. This to handle the situation of a NumPy function receiving a list object instead of the NumPy array it was expecting.

```
if isinstance(a,list):
        a = np.array(a)
```

If you pass the lst object to std_dev function, you may see something like this:

```
std_dev(lst)
>> Function 'std_dev' took 84.004 milliseconds to run
>> 288675.1345946685
```

This is interesting. The operation is still quite a bit faster than the native Python implementation, but definitely much slower than the case where a NumPy array was passed into the function. The result is also slightly different (only after five decimal places though). This is because of the conversion of the lst object to the NumPy array type inside the function that takes the extra time. The conversion also impacts the numerical precision leading to the slightly different result.

Therefore, although type-checking and conversion should be part of your code, you should focus on **converting numerical lists or tables to NumPy arrays as soon as possible at the beginning of a data science pipeline** and work on them afterwards, so that you do not lose any extra time at the computation stage.

# Using NumPy Efficiently

NumPy offers a dizzying array of functions and methods to use on numerical arrays and matrices for advanced data science and ML engineering. You can find a plethora of resources going deep into those aspects and features of NumPy.

Since this book is about productive data science, I am focusing more on the fundamental aspect of *how to use NumPy for building efficient programming pattern* in data science work. I prefer to illustrate that by showing typical examples of inefficient coding style and how to use the NumPy-based code correctly to increase your productivity. Let's start on that path.

## Conversion First, Operation Later

Although not a guaranteed outcome, it is almost always better to **vectorize your data first** (Figure 3-1). In other words, convert it to NumPy arrays as early as possible and run the mathematical operations on those array objects rather than running native Python functions and then converting them to an array.

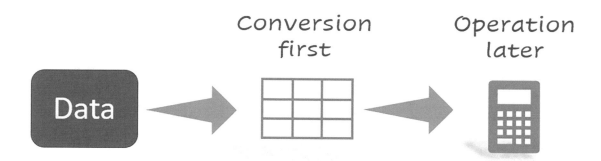

***Figure 3-1.*** *NumPy is best taken advantage of when you vectorize your data first and then do the necessary operations*

Here's a list of numbers and a mathematical operation function:

```
lst_of_nums = [i for i in range(100000)]

def calc_nums(x):
    return (x+1)/(x+1000)
```

It is a bad practice to do the following, yet this kind of code pattern is ubiquitous in the data science world:

```
result_lst = []
for i in lst_of_nums:
    result_lst.append(calc_nums(i))
result_array = np.array(result_lst)
```

Instead, first convert to the array format and then apply the mathematical operations directly on the array. You don't even need to write a separate Python function.

```
array_of_nums = np.array(lst_of_nums)
result_array = (array_of_nums+1)/(array_of_nums+1000)
```

If you test the execution time, you will see the second option is 2X to 3X faster for this data. For a bigger data size, this much improvement may prove significant.

---

Data in real-life situations comes from business operations and databases. Data comes either in streaming or batch mode. Data can also come in web APIs in the format of JSON or XML. It almost will never come in a nicely NumPy-formatted manner. This is why it is so important to understand the pros and cons of array conversion, operations like appending to and updating an array, back conversion to a Python list in case you must stream the data back to another API through a JSON interface, and so on.

---

## Vectorize Logical Operations

You can also vectorize a list where you need to check for logical condition before doing the mathematical operation directly with NumPy. Suppose from the previous example you want to apply the function only to the numbers that are integral multiples of 7. You may be tempted to write this code:

```
result_lst = []
for i in lst_of_nums:
    if i%7==0:
        result_lst.append(calc_nums(i))
result_array = np.array(result_lst)
```

Instead, you should use the NumPy operations directly in this manner:

```
array_of_nums = np.array(lst_of_nums)
array_div7 =  array_of_nums[array_of_nums%7==0]
result_array = (array_div7+1)/(array_div7+1000)
```

The second line of this code uses the **Boolean indexing with NumPy** where you create a Boolean NumPy array with `array_of_nums%7==0` and then use this array as an index of the main array. This effectively creates an array with only the elements that are divisible by 7. Finally, you run your operation on this shorter `array_div7`. In a way, this is a filtering operation too where you filter the main array into a shorter array based on a logical check.

# Use the Built-In Vectorize Function

NumPy provides a built-in vectorizing function to help many user-defined functions to be vectorized as easily as possible. The exact improvement in speed and efficiency depends on the type and complexity of the specific function in question. Here is an example of a function that works on two floating point numbers and performs certain math operation based on their mutual relationship:

```
from math import sin
def myfunc(x,y):
    if (x>0.5*y and y<0.3):
        return (sin(x-y))
    elif (x<0.5*y):
        return 0
    elif (x>0.2*y):
        return (2*sin(x+2*y))
    else:
        return (sin(y+x))
```

In such situations, you can almost mechanically apply the `numpy.vectorize` method in the following way:

```
vectfunc = np.vectorize(myfunc,
                        otypes=[np.float64],
                        cache=False)
result_array=vectfunc(lst_x,lst_y)
```

Here you pass on the custom function object `myfunc` as the first argument in the `np.vectorize` and define the object types it should expect by the `otypes` parameter. The great thing is that although the main `myfunc` works on individual floating point numbers `x` and `y`, the resulting `vectfunc` can accept any array (or even a Python list) with the `np.float64` data type (or even native Python floating point data, which will be coerced into the `np.float64` type automatically).

# Avoid Using the .append Method

Appending new or incoming data to an array is a common data science operation. Often the situation is that the data is generated by a stochastic or random process (e.g., a financial transaction or a sensor measurement) and it has to be recorded in a NumPy array (for later use in an ML algorithm, for example).

**NumPy has an append method but it is quite inefficient** because of its behavior of copying the entire data array into memory every time the update happens. You have two choices for appending this kind of random data to an NumPy array:

- If you know the final length of the array, then initialize an empty NumPy array (with the `numpy.empty` method) or an array of zeroes/ones and just put the new piece of data in the present index while iterating over the range.

- Alternatively, you can use a Python list, append to it, and then convert to a NumPy array at the end. You can use this with a `while` loop until the random process terminates, so you don't need to know the length beforehand.

You can see this is directly contrary to what we discussed in the subsection "Conversion First, Operation Later." However, the situation is subtly different here because, in this case, you are updating the array with incoming data that results from an unknown process, so you don't know what precise mathematical operation to perform on the array.

As an example, the following code initializes an empty NumPy array with a known shape (equal to the known data length of 1,000), records a Gaussian random number 1,000 times, and puts the square of that number in the array:

```
desired_length = 1000
results = np.empty(desired_length)
```

```
for i in range(desired_length):
    sample = np.random.normal()
    results[i] = sample**2
```

The following code **emulates a situation when the length of the data is itself uncertain**. The process terminates when the variable TERMINATE itself goes over 2.0.

```
TERMINATE = np.random.normal()
result_lst = []
while TERMINATE < 2.0:
    sample = np.random.normal()
    result_lst.append(sample**2)
    TERMINATE = np.random.normal()
result_array = np.array(result_lst)
```

As discussed, because of the uncertainty in the length of the data or the process that generates it, it is advisable to use a Python list to append the data as it comes in. When the data collection is finished, go back to the "conversion first, operation later" principle and convert the Python list to a NumPy array before doing any sophisticated mathematical operation over it.

---

**When does** TERMINATE **become greater than 2.0?** In the code above, since the variable TERMINATE is generated from a normal distribution with a zero mean and a unity standard deviation, any value greater than 2.0 will be located more than two standard deviations from the mean. That means it will have ~5% chance of producing a value greater than 2.0 at each iteration. If you run this code repeatedly, you will have a new NumPy array of a different length each time you rerun the code.

---

# Utilizing NumPy Reading Utilities

How would you read a text file where numerical data is stored in a CSV format into a NumPy array? This situation is extremely common in a regular data science pipeline as CSV (comma-separated value) remains one of the most popular file formats in use across all platforms (Windows, Linux, Mac OS, etc.).

Of course, you can use the csv module that comes with Python and read line by line. But, conveniently enough, NumPy provides many utility functions to read from file or string objects. Using them makes the code cleaner and thereby more productive. These routines are well-optimized for speed too, so your code remains efficient.

## Reading from a Flat Text File

The method numpy.fromfile can be used for this purpose. It is a highly efficient way of reading binary data with a known datatype, as well as parsing simply formatted text files. For example, you may be reading a bunch of numeric data written on a text file with a comma separator:

```
with open('fdata.txt') as f:
    data = f.readline()
data = data.split(',')
fr = np.array(data[:-1],dtype=float)
```

Note that when you use the native Python readline with an opened file, you get a string object. So, you need to split the string with the comma separator and then read the resulting list as a NumPy array with the dtype set to float. You can do the same reading with just one line of code:

```
fr = np.fromfile('fdata.txt',sep=',')
```

It is clear that there is less chance of bugs and errors in this approach than the native Python file-reading code.

## Utility for Tabular Data in a Text File

Numpy offers another similar text-reading utility called loadtxt, which is even more powerful and feature-rich. It **works with text file where data is written in tabular format** (i.e., in rows and columns) and loads data directly into a multi-dimensional array as long as the number of entries in each row remains same. Figure 3-2 illustrates this.

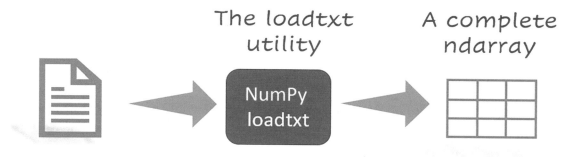

**Figure 3-2.** *Showing how the loadtxt utility works in NumPy*

For example, suppose you have a CSV text file with three rows and three columns of data, as shown in Figure 3-3.

**Figure 3-3.** *A simple text file with tabulated comma-separated data to be read*

One line of code can read the contents of this file into a 3x3 NumPy array/matrix:

```
np.loadtxt('npread.txt',delimiter=',')
>> array([[  9.2,   22.1,  -33.6],
       [   6.4,    2.3,   -5.4],
       [  12.2,    4.5,    7.2]])
```

You can even **read selective columns** from the file. This is particularly useful if you always get a massive data file from a customer, but you know that only certain specific columns are useful for your data science work. Then, you can load only selective data into memory and make your pipeline fast and efficient.

```
np.loadtxt('npread.txt',delimiter=',',usecols=(0,2))
>> array([[  9.2, -33.6],
       [  6.4,  -5.4],
       [ 12.2,   7.2]])
```

Imagine the amount of custom text-reading code you would have to write if you did not have this utility function from NumPy. In the spirit of productive data science and keeping your code clean and readable, use these utilities whenever possible.

# Using pandas Productively

After covering some of the best practices and productive utilities of the NumPy library, let's now look at the most widely used data analytics package in the Python ecosystem: pandas. This package is used by almost every data scientist and analyst that you may come across.

pandas uses NumPy at its foundation and interfaces with other highly popular Python libraries like Scikit-learn so that you can do data analytics and wrangling work in pandas and transport the processed data seamlessly to an ML algorithm. It also provides a rich set of data-reading options from various kinds of common data sources (e.g., a web page, HTML, CSV, Microsoft Excel, JSON formatted object, and even zip files) which makes it invaluable for data wrangling tasks.

However, it is a large library with many methods and utilities that can be used in myriad ways to accomplish the same end goal. This makes it highly likely that different data scientists (even within the same team) are using different programming styles and patterns with pandas to get the same job done. Some of these patterns yield faster and cleaner execution than others and should be preferred. In this subsection, I cover a few of these areas with simple examples.

## Setting Values in a New DataFrame

pandas provides a variety of options to index, select particular data, and set it to a given value. In many situations, you will find yourself with a Python list or NumPy array that you want to set at a particular position (row) in your DataFrame.

For demonstration, let's define a simple list with six values:

- First name (a Python string object)

- Last name (a Python string object)

- Age (a Python integer object)

- Address (a Python string object)

- Price (a Python float object)

- Date (a Python datetime object)

```
profile_data = ['First name', 'Last name', 30, 'An address', 25.2, today]
```

You have a few options to insert this data to the rows of a DataFrame. Note that in reality you will have a dictionary or a few thousand such lists (all different). Just for the speed demonstration, I show inserting the same list data in the DataFrame.

You can create an empty DataFrame like this, defining the column names explicitly:

```
df = pd.DataFrame(columns = ['FirstName', 'LastName', 'Age', 'Address', 'Price', 'Date'])
```

Now comes the part where you iterate and insert the data into one row after another.

## The .at or .iloc Methods Are Slow

A lot of data scientists use the .at or .iloc methods for indexing and slicing data once they start working with a DataFrame. They are very useful methods to have at your disposal, and they are fine to use for indexing purpose. However, try to avoid them for inserting/setting data when you are building a DataFrame from scratch.

Set N = 2000 for the speed test and run the following code to measure the speed of setting data with these methods:

```
%%timeit -n5 -r10
for i in range(N):
    df.at[i] = profile_data
>> 207 ms ± 58.6 ms per loop (mean ± std. dev. of 10 runs, 5 loops each)
```

and

```
%%timeit -n5 -r10
for i in range(N):
    df.iloc[i] = profile_data
>> 116 ms ± 5.63 ms per loop (mean ± std. dev. of 10 runs, 5 loops each)
```

In this instance, the .iloc method is slightly faster, but this depends on the type of the data and other aspects. In general, inserting data this way should be avoided as much as possible.

## Use .values to Speed Things Up Significantly

The method pandas.DataFrame.values returns a NumPy representation of the DataFrame and therefore is optimized for speed in the best possible manner. So, if you run the following code, you get much faster execution time:

```
%%timeit -n5 -r10
for i in range(N):
    df.values[i] = profile_data
>> 12 ms ± 2.63 ms per loop (mean ± std. dev. of 10 runs, 5 loops each)
```

Note that for this to work, you must have a pre-existing DataFrame with 2,000 rows. Now, with this code you can set new values much faster than using .at or .iloc methods. This won't work on a newly created, empty DataFrame.

## Specify Data Types Whenever Possible

Making pandas guess data types is one of the most frequent inefficient code patterns and it happens with almost all data scientists. It is inefficient because when you import data into a DataFrame without specifically telling pandas the datatypes of the columns, it will read the entire dataset into memory just to figure out the data types. Quite naturally, it hogs the system memory and results in a highly wasteful process that can be avoided with more explicit code.

So, how do you do it as a standard practice? Reading data from the disk is often done with some sort of plain text file like a CSV. You can read just the first few lines of the CSV file, determine the data types, create a dictionary, and pass it on for the full file read, or use it repeatedly for reading similar files (if the column types are unchanged). You can use the dtype parameter in various pandas reading functions to specify the expected data types.

Here is boilerplate code for accomplishing this task. The function csv_read() accepts a filename (string) argument and returns a DataFrame. Internally, it does so by first reading a sample data of the first 20 rows (nrows=20), determining the data types (df_sample.dtypes), creating a dictionary of those types, and then reading the full dataset with explicit type mention by passing that dictionary (dtype = dt):

```
def csv_read(filename):
    """

    Reads a CSV file with explicit data types
    """

    # Reads only the first 20 rows
    df_sample = pd.read_csv(filename, nrows=20)
    # Constructs data type dictionary
    dt = {}
    for col,dtyp in zip(df_sample.columns, df_sample.dtypes):
        dt[col] = dtyp
    # Full read with explicit data type
    df1 = pd.read_csv(filename, dtype = dt)

    return df1
```

Figure 3-4 shows a visual illustration of the idea of reading sample data first, determining the data type, and then utilizing it for the full reading of the data.

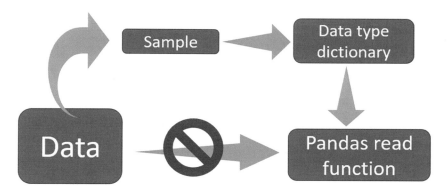

***Figure 3-4.*** *Reading large data files in pandas first by determining the data types and then specifying them explicitly while reading*

**As a practical example,** imagine that every morning your data processing pipeline must read a large CSV file from all the business transactions that were put into a data warehouse last night. The column names and types are unchanged, and only the raw data changes every day. You do a lot of data cleaning and processing on the new raw data every day to pass it on to some cool machine learning algorithm. In this situation, you should have your data type dictionary ready and pass it on to your file reading function every morning. You should still run an occasional check to determine if the data types have changed somehow (e.g., int to float, string to Boolean).

# Iterating Over a DataFrame

It is a quite common situation where you are given a large pandas DataFrame and are asked to check some relationships between various fields in the columns, in a row-by-row fashion. The check could be some logical operation or some conditional logic involving a sophisticated mathematical transformation on the raw data.

Essentially, it is a simple case of *iterating over the rows of the DataFrame* and doing some processing at each iteration. You can choose from the following approaches. Interestingly, some of the approaches are much more efficient than others.

## Brute-Force *For Loop*

The code for this naïve approach will go something like this:

```
for i in range(len(df)):
    if (some condition is satisfied):
        do some calculation with df.iloc[i]
```

Essentially, you are iterating over each row (df.iloc[i]) using a generic for loop and processing them one at a time. There's nothing wrong with the logic and you will get the correct result at the end.

But this is quite inefficient. As you increase the number of columns or the complexity of the calculation (or of the condition checking done at each iteration), you will see that they quickly add up. Therefore, *this approach should be avoided as much as possible for building scalable and efficient data science pipelines.*

## Better Approaches: df.iterrows and df.values

Depending on the situations at hand, you may have choices of two better approaches for this iteration task.

pandas offers a dedicated method for iterating over rows called `iterrows()` (`https://pandas.pydata.org/pandas-docs/stable/reference/api/pandas.DataFrame.iterrows.html`), which might be handy to use in this particular situation. Depending on the DataFrame size and complexity of the row operations, this may reduce the total execution time by ~10X over the `for` loop approach.

You already saw the pandas method for obtaining a NumPy representation of the DataFrame: `df.values()`. This can significantly speed things up (even better than `iterrows`). However, this method removes the axis labels (column names) and so you must use the generic NumPy array indexing like 0, 1 to process the data. The pseudocode will look like the following:

```
for row in df.values:
    if function(row) satisfies some condition:
        do some calculation with row
```

---

A clear, worked-out example on this topic of comparing the efficiencies of multiple pandas methods can be found in the article cited below. It also shows how the speed improvement depends on the complexity of the specific operation at each iteration. "Faster Iteration in pandas," (`https://medium.com/productive-data-science/faster-iteration-in-pandas-15cac58d8226`), *Towards Data Science*, July 2021.

---

# Using Modern, Optimized File Formats

CSV is a flat-file format used widely in data analytics. It is simple to work with and performs decently in small to medium data regimes. However, as you do data processing with bigger files (and also, perhaps, pay for the cloud-based storage of them), there are some excellent reasons to move towards file formats using the columnar data storage principle (www.stitchdata.com/columnardatabase/). The basic idea of columnar data storage (vs. the traditional row-based storage) is illustrated in Figure 3-5.

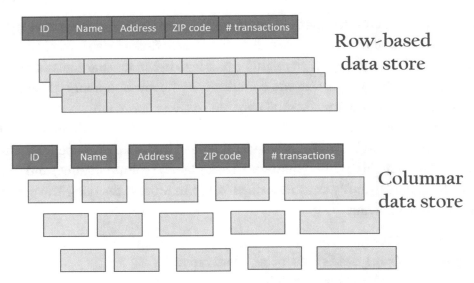

***Figure 3-5.*** *Columnar (vs. traditional row-based) data format illustration*

**Apache Parquet** is one of the most popular of these columnar file formats. It's an excellent choice in the situation when you have to store and read large data files from disk or cloud storage. Parquet is intimately related to the Apache Arrow framework. But what is Apache Arrow?

As per their website, https://arrow.apache.org/, "*Apache Arrow is a development platform for in-memory analytics. It contains a set of technologies that enable big data systems to process and move data fast. It specifies a standardized language-independent columnar memory format for flat and hierarchical data, organized for efficient analytic operations on modern hardware.*"

Therefore, to take advantage of this columnar storage format, you need to use some kind of Python binding or tool to read data stored in Parquet files into the system memory and possibly transform that into a pandas DataFrame for the data analytics tasks. This can be accomplished by using the PyArrow framework.

# Impressive Speed Improvement

PyArrow is a Python binding (API) for the Apache Arrow framework. Detailed coverage of Apache Arrow or PyArrow (`https://arrow.apache.org/docs/python/`) is far beyond the scope of this book, but interested readers can refer to the official documentation at `https://arrow.apache.org/` to get started.

Using the PyArrow function `read_table`, you can demonstrate considerable improvement of the reading speed of large data files over the commonly used pandas `read_csv` method. For example, Figure 3-6 shows the ratio of pandas and PyArrow reading times of the same data, stored in CSV and Parquet, respectively. The ratio goes up as the data size increases; PyArrow performs considerably better with larger file sizes.

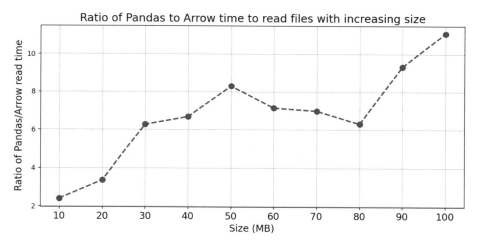

***Figure 3-6.*** *pandas vs. PyArrow reading time ratio for CSV (and Parquet) files. Source: https://towardsdatascience.com/how-fast-is-reading-parquet-file-with-arrow-vs-csv-with-pandas-2f8095722e94, author permission granted*

This is something truly astonishing to ponder. pandas is based on the fast and efficient NumPy arrays, yet it cannot match the file-reading performance shown by the Parquet format. If we think about it deeply, the reason becomes clear that the file-reading operation has almost nothing to do with how pandas optimize the in-memory organization of the data *after it is loaded* into the memory. Therefore, while pandas can be a fast and efficient package for in-memory analytics, we don't have to stay dependent upon traditional file formats like CSV or Excel to work with pandas. Instead, we should move towards using more modern and efficient formats like Parquet.

## Read Only What Is Needed

Often, you may not need to read all the columns from a columnar storage file. For example, you may apply some filter on the data and choose only selected data for the actual in-memory processing. With CSV files or regular SQL databases, this means you are choosing specific rows out of all the data. However, for the columnar database, this effectively means choosing specific columns. Therefore, you do have an advantage in terms of reading speed when you are reading only a small fraction of columns from the Parquet file.

Figure 3-7 shows the reading advantage as the number of columns increases for the same CSV vs. Parquet comparison. When you read a very small fraction of columns, say < 10 out of 100, the reading speed ratio becomes as large as > 50 (i.e., you get 50X speedup compared to the regular pandas CSV file reading). The speedup tapers off for large fractions of columns and settles down to a stable value.

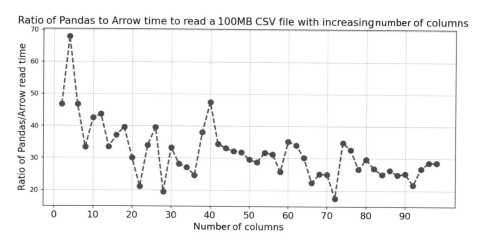

**Figure 3-7.** *pandas vs. PyArrow reading time ratio for CSV (and Parquet) files as the number of columns vary. Source:* `https://towardsdatascience.` `com/how-fast-is-reading-parquet-file-with-arrow-vs-csv-with-` `pandas-2f8095722e94,` *author permission granted*

**Reading selected columns from a large dataset is an extremely common scenario** in data analytics and machine learning tasks. Often, subject matter experts advise data scientists with domain knowledge and can preselect a few features from a large dataset although the default data collection mechanism may store a file with many columns/features. In these situations, it makes logical sense to read only what is needed and process those columns for the ML workload. Storing the data in a columnar data format like Parquet pays handsomely for these cases.

## PyArrow to pandas and Back

While the results shown above are impressive, the central question is about how to take advantage of this fast and efficient file format for pandas-based data analytics tasks. This has been made extremely simple by PyArrow utility methods, as this simple boilerplate code illustrates:

```
import pyarrow as pa
import pandas as pd
```

```
df = pd.DataFrame({"a": [1, 2, 3],
                   "b":[2.7,-1.2,5.4],
                   "c": ['abc','xyz','pqr']})
# Convert from pandas to Arrow
table = pa.Table.from_pandas(df)
# Convert back to pandas
df_new = table.to_pandas()
```

So, there are ready functions to convert PyArrow tables and pandas DataFrame back and forth. You can take advantage of this in the scenario illustrated in Figure 3-8.

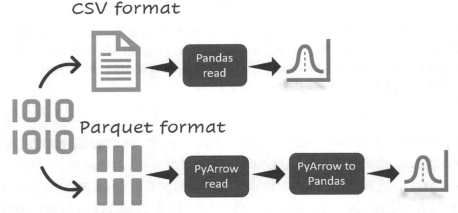

*Figure 3-8.* *Storing large datasets in Parquet (vs. CSV) may offer overall speed advantage for many processing tasks with pandas*

Suppose you have a large CSV file of numeric quantities with ~1 million rows and 14 columns, and you want to calculate the basic descriptive stats on this dataset. Not so surprisingly, **if you only use pandas code, the majority of the time will be taken by the file reading operation, not by the statistical calculation**. You can make this task efficient by storing the file in the Parquet format instead of CSV, reading it using the read_table method, converting to pandas using the to_pandas method, doing the statistical calculation, and then just storing the result back in CSV or Parquet. The output consists of only a few rows/columns as it is just the descriptive stats, so the file format does not matter much. A demo example with speed comparison is shown in the accompanying Jupyter notebook with this book.

# Other Miscellaneous Ideas

pandas is such a vast and storied library that there are thousands of ways to improve upon inefficient and non-productive code patterns while using it. A few miscellaneous suggestions are mentioned here.

## Remove Orphan DataFrames Regularly

A very common programming pattern is the following:

- Create a DataFrame from an in-memory object or a file on the disk.

- Drop or fill Null or NaN values.

- Apply a user-defined function on certain columns.

- Group the final dataset by some specific column.

- Further processing on the grouped object…

Often, data scientists create intermediate DataFrames while executing this pipeline and don't remove them from the active memory space, thereby piling up orphan or unused DataFrames as large memory-hogging garbage.

```
df1 = pd.read_csv("A large file")
df2 = df1.dropna()
df3 = df2.apply(user_function, columns = [...])
df4 = df3.groupby([column_1, column_2])
df_final = ...
```

If the only in-memory object that matters is df_final, then you must actively track and delete all intermediate DataFrames as soon as their utility is over:

```
df1 = pd.read_csv("A large file")
df2 = df1.dropna()
del(df1)
df3 = df2.apply(user_function, columns = [...])
del(df2)

df4 = df3.groupby([column_1, column_2])
del(df3)
df_final = ...
```

# Chaining Methods

Continuing from the example above, it makes perfect sense to let the system handle all the active tracking and deleting of intermediate DataFrame objects for a productive codebase. pandas allows chaining methods, which makes this a relatively easy approach to implement. The code can read something like this:

```
df_final = pd.read_csv("A large file").dropna().apply(user_function,
columns = [...]).groupby([column_1, column_2])
```

As long as the methods and the chained code are readable, this is a perfectly sensible approach.

# Using Specialized Libraries to Enhance Performance

There are, in fact, quite a few external libraries that can help speed up pandas tasks significantly. They include, but are not limited to, the following:

> Using a specialized pipeline building library
>
> Using libraries to utilize just-in-time compilation (https://en.wikipedia.org/wiki/Just-in-time_compilation) and other numerical tricks
>
> Using parallel processing and Big Data helper frameworks to spread the pandas workload over multiple computing cores and in out-of-memory spaces
>
> Use GPU-accelerated computing (https://medium.com/dataseries/gpu-powered-data-science-not-deep-learning-with-rapids-29f9ed8d51f3as) an alternative to pandas with minimal changes in API and codebase

Each of these ideas needs a significant space to discuss at any reasonable details. Therefore, I cover them separately in later chapters.

# Efficient EDA with Matplotlib and Seaborn

Matplotlib and Seaborn are two widely used visualization libraries for data science tasks in the Python ecosystem. Together, they offer unparalleled versatility, rich graphics options, and deep integration with the Python data science ecosystem for doing any kind of visual analytics you can think of.

However, there are a few common situations where you can end up using these fantastic packages in an inefficient manner. Additionally, you may also waste valuable time writing unnecessary code or using additional tools to make your visual analytics end products more presentable, which could have been accomplished with simple modifications in the settings of Matplotlib and Seaborn. In this section, I cover tips and tricks that can come handy to make your data science and analytics tasks productive when using either of these libraries.

## Embrace the Object-Oriented Nature of Matplotlib

Matplotlib is built in a thoughtful manner (`www.aosabook.org/en/matplotlib.html`) following multiple layers of abstractions and object-oriented design hierarchy (as shown in Figure 3-9). Almost always, a data scientist deals with the scripting layer to draw quick plots (e.g., `plt.scatter(x,y)`) and change the look and feel of that graphical output (e.g., `plt.xlabel("The x-axis variable", fontsize=15)`). Sometimes, they venture into the middle artistic layer, creating custom `Axes` and setting the properties of `Figure` objects. Usually, a data scientist does not need to work directly with the backend layer for regular data analytics tasks.

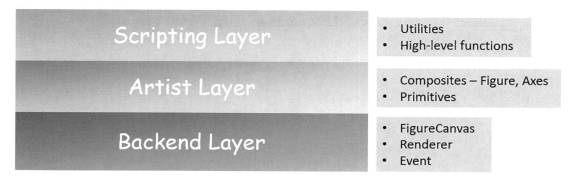

***Figure 3-9.*** *Matplotlib layers and core abstractions/objects*

However, it is a great education for a data scientist to have deep knowledge about this layered architecture and follow the best practices that leverage the strength of a solid object-oriented design. In particular situations such as those involving subplots, this becomes prominent.

## Two Approaches for Creating Panels with Subplots

A simple example of a good practice is to **not to use the following old style of code** to create two subplots or panels stacked vertically:

```
# Create the main figure
plt.figure()
# The first of two panels
plt.subplot(2, 1, 1) # (rows, columns, panel number)
plt.plot(x, np.sin(x))
# The second panel
plt.subplot(2, 1, 2)
plt.plot(x, np.cos(x));
```

A better alternative is to use the following code:

```
# Create an array of two Axes objects
fig, ax = plt.subplots(2)
# Call plot() method on the appropriate object
ax[0].plot(x, np.sin(x))
ax[1].plot(x, np.cos(x))
```

They produce identical graphical output, as shown in Figure 3-10.

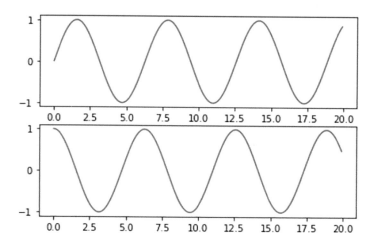

***Figure 3-10.*** *Matplotlib subplots panel example*

But why is the second approach *better* or *more productive*? Think about the cognitive load you might have to carry if it were 5 or 15 plots instead of 2 and the chances of bugs that could have been introduced writing code like `plt.subplot(3, 1, 3)` or `plt.subplot(4, 4, 13)`. How would you keep track of all those parameters inside the `plt.subplot()` function? The second approach frees you from these considerations by allowing it to pass in a single number like 2 or 15 and repeat the plot statement that many times.

However, an even better approach is to put this code in a proper function that has a little more intelligence to handle any number of plots and that refactors the plotting statements using a loop.

## A Better Approach with a Clever Function

Consider the following code defining a function that can produce a panel with an arbitrary number of plots (always in a three-column format respecting the natural width of the webpage or a book), dynamically adjusting the number of rows with the number of total subplots:

```
def plot_panels(n):
    """

    Produce a panel consisting of variable number of rows and 3 columns
    """

    if n%3==0:
        nrows =  int(n/3)
```

```
    else:
        nrows = n//3+1
    ncols = 3
    fig, ax = plt.subplots(nrows, ncols, figsize=(15,nrows*3))
    axes = ax.ravel()
    for i in range(n):
        axes[i].plot(x, np.sin(x))
```

Here, you can change the variable n to any value. Internally, the function will always calculate the appropriate number of rows with the logic in the code and set ncols = 3. Here, ax is a (multi-dimensional) list of Matplotlib Axes objects (https://matplotlib.org/stable/api/axes_api.html) and therefore can be indexed with axes[i] within a loop after you flatten the list with an axes = ax.ravel() statement.

When you call this function with plot_panels(5), you get the result shown in Figure 3-11.

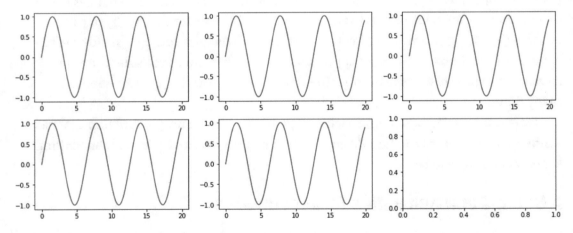

***Figure 3-11.*** *Matplotlib panel function output with five plots*

Note the blank canvas in the last row. This is because the plots must be arranged in a rectangular grid and for placing five plots on a 3 x 2 grid, so the last one will be left blank. When you call the same function with plot_panels(15), you get the result shown in Figure 3-12.

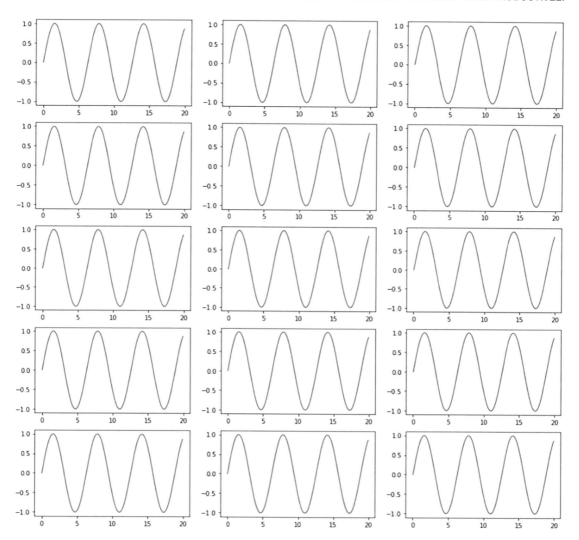

***Figure 3-12.*** *Matplotlib panel function output with 15 plots*

It is the **object-oriented style of programming pattern** you embraced in your function definition that resulted in this scalable and efficient mechanism of generating any number of plots without worrying about potential bugs. This type of practice makes the codebase productive in the long run.

# Set and Control Image Quality

Matplotlib interacts with the user's graphical output system (web browser or stand-alone window) in a complex manner and optimizes the output image quality with a balanced set of internal settings. However, it is possible to tweak those settings as per the user's preference to get the most optimum quality that they desire.

This becomes particularly important for using Matplotlib in the Jupyter notebook environment, which is an extremely common scenario. The quality of the default image, rendered in a Jupyter notebook web browser, may not be good enough for publication in a book or further processing. Data scientists often spend additional time and effort enhancing the quality of the visualizations they produce as part of the data science tasks. However, Matplotlib provides a simple and intuitive workaround to accomplish the same.

## Setting DPI Directly in plt.figure()

Setting the dots per inch is easily done with just one parameter:

```
plt.figure(figsize=(6,4),dpi=150)
plt.plot(x,y)
```

In a Jupyter notebook, the default DPI value is quite low. Depending on your system settings, it is generally between 70 and 100. When you increase it, your figure also gets bigger, so you have to be mindful of not clipping the image in your browser window.

## Setting DPI and Output Format for Saving Figures

In addition to, or alternatively, you may also want to save the plot as a file object on your local disk for later use. You can choose the DPI and output format:

```
plt.figure(figsize=(6,4))
plt.plot(x,y)
plt.title("Parabola", fontsize=16)
plt.xlabel('x-axis')
plt.ylabel('y-axis')
plt.savefig("Parabola.png",
            dpi=300,
            format = 'png')
```

When you choose JPEG as the output format, you can control a host of other settings related to the JPEG compression. However, PNG or PDF are better in terms of publication-worthy quality since they are lossless formats.

---

**What is a good DPI to choose?**   It depends on the intended usage, of course. For print, 150dpi is considered low-quality printing, even though 72dpi is considered the standard for the web (which is why it's not easy printing quality images straight from the web). Low-resolution images will have blurring and pixelation (https://en.wikipedia.org/wiki/Pixilation) after printing. Medium-resolution images have between 200dpi - 300dpi. The industry standard for quality photographs and image is typically 300dpi.

---

# Adjust Global Parameters

The Matplotlib back end provides the ultimate flexibility in terms of setting global parameters that control the look and feel of your visualization. The rcParams settings (https://matplotlib.org/stable/api/matplotlib_configuration_api. html#matplotlib.RcParams) have all the possible varieties you can think of. Here is a code example:

```
import matplotlib as mpl
# Data
x = np.arange(-10,10,0.1)
y = x**2
# Set all backend parameters
mpl.rcParams['lines.linewidth'] = 3
mpl.rcParams['text.color'] = 'red'
mpl.rcParams['lines.linestyle'] = '--'
mpl.rcParams['axes.facecolor'] = '#c3e2e6'
mpl.rcParams['figure.dpi'] = 120
mpl.rcParams['font.style'] = 'italic'
mpl.rcParams['font.weight'] = 'heavy'
# Plot
plt.plot(x,y)
```

```
plt.title("Parabola", fontsize=16)
plt.xlabel('x-axis')
plt.ylabel('y-axis')
```

Note how you had to import the Matplotlib module itself with the statement `import matplotlib as mpl` and not just use the `matplotlib.pyplot as plt`. Also note the `figure.dpi` as one of the many settings you set in this code. A typical result from this setting is shown in Figure 3-13.

If you have decided on a set of image quality and styling settings, you can store them in a local config file and just read the values at the beginning of your Jupyter notebook or Python script while importing Matplotlib. That way, every image produced by that script or in that Jupyter session will have the same look and feel. The output of the code above should look something like Figure 3-13.

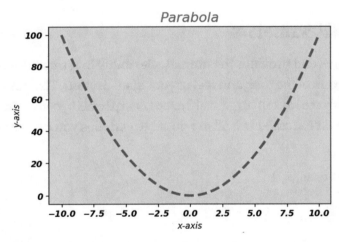

***Figure 3-13.*** *Matplotlib global rcParams change illustration*

---

Did you notice that the `axes.facecolor` was set to a **hex string** #c3e2e6 in the code above? Matplotlib accepts regular color names like red, green, or blue, or hex strings in its various internal settings. You can simply use an online color picker tool (`https://imagecolorpicker.com/`) and copy-paste the hex code for better styling of your image.

---

# Tricks with Seaborn

Seaborn is a Python library built on top of Matplotlib with a concentrated focus on statistical visualizations like boxplots, histograms, and regression plots. Naturally, for data scientists, it is a great tool to use in a typical exploratory data analysis (EDA) phase. However, using Seaborn with a couple of simple tricks can improve the productivity of your EDA tasks.

## Use Sampled Data for Large Datasets

Seaborn provides excellent APIs/methods to generate beautiful visualizations on all features/variables of your dataset:

- Pairwise plots (relating every variable in a dataset to another one)

- Histograms

- Boxplots

It might be tempting to generate all these plots for all the features and their pairwise combination (for the pair plot). However, depending on the amount of data and possible combination for the pairwise plot, the number of raw visual elements can be overwhelming for your system to handle.

One quick fix to this situation is to **use random sample (a small fraction) of the dataset for generating all these plots**. If the data is not too skewed, then by looking at a random sample (or a few of them), you should get a good feeling about the pattern and distributions from a typical EDA anyway.

A boilerplate code will look like the following:

```
N = 100
df_sample = df.sample(N)
plot_seaborn(df_sample)
<more code ...>
```

Here you pass on only 100 samples from the original DataFrame to the plotting function. Note that to maintain readability and data structure integrity, you should not randomly sample 100 rows from the DataFrame but use a built-in function to return another DataFrame and pass that along to the plotting function.

# Use pandas Correlation with Seaborn heatmap

This is a trick to **quickly visualize the correlation strengths between multiple features** of your dataset with just two lines of code. This kind of trick should be standard part of your efficient data science toolkit.

Here is a code snippet:

```
df_mpg = sns.load_dataset('mpg')
mpg_corr = df_mpg.corr()
sns.heatmap(mpg_corr,cbar=True,cmap='plasma')
plt.show()
```

This loads the famous Auto MPG dataset (https://archive.ics.uci.edu/ml/datasets/auto+mpg) and produces the correlation heatmap shown in Figure 3-14, demonstrating the positive and negative correlation strengths between various numerical features of the dataset. The bright colors and italic/bold axis names of this plot are the result of the Matplotlib style settings you did in the previous section. Unless you change them explicitly or start a new Jupyter notebook session, they remain in effect.

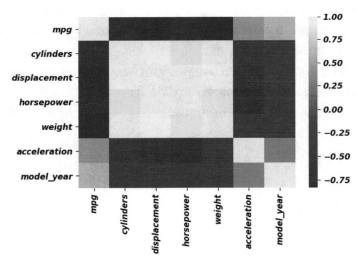

***Figure 3-14.***  *Using the pandas correlation function with a Seaborn heatmap to get the correlation visualization quickly for any dataset*

## Use Special Seaborn Methods to Reduce Work

Seaborn provides some special method/plotting utilities that can reduce the work for a data scientist in common tasks and thereby improve productivity. These utilities should be put to use at every opportunity. Examples include

- Doing a linear regression and creating the plots of residuals with `residplot`

- Counting the occurrence of categorical variables and plotting them using `countplot`

- Using `clustermap` to create a hierarchical colored diagram from a matrix dataset

# Summary

In this chapter, I started by describing how NumPy is faster than native Python code and enumerated its speed efficiency in simple scenarios. I talked about the pros and cons of converting Python objects like lists and tuples to NumPy arrays before doing numerical processing. Then, I discussed the importance of vectorizing operations as much as possible for efficient data science pipelines. I also discussed some of the reading utilities that NumPy offers and how they can make your code compact and productive.

Next, I delved into the efficient use of the pandas framework by discussing various methods to iterate over DataFrames and accessing or setting values. Usage of modern, optimized file storage formats like Parquet (in the context of Apache Arrow and column-oriented data storage) were discussed at length. Some miscellaneous ideas like chaining and cleaning up orphan DataFrame were talked about next.

Finally, I showed some tips and tricks to be used with popular visualization libraries Matplotlib and Seaborn. The object-oriented layered structure of Matplotlib was shown to be a strong foundation for building efficient data science code for plotting. I also demonstrated various methods of controlling image quality and plot settings in a global manner (i.e., for a Python or Jupyter session). Sampled data was discussed as an idea to control the explosion of plots that can happen with large datasets.

These kind of tips and tricks are developed over time based on data analysis, numerical computing, and exploratory data visualization needs that arise from handling real-life datasets in projects that need to be efficient and productive from time and computing resources points of view. As a regular practitioner of data science, you will also develop your own tricks and make your data analysis and modeling code efficient. The ideas in this chapter are just introductory guiding pointers to get you to think in that direction.

# CHAPTER 4

# Writing Machine Learning Code More Productively

Data scientists often come from a background quite far removed from traditional computer science/software engineering, such as physics, biology, statistics, economics, and electrical engineering. Unfortunately, there are not a lot of tutorials geared towards data scientists and machine learning practitioners who do not come from a software engineering background.

Data scientists use Python a lot for their work. Why? Because it's awesome for ML and the data science community. It is the most widely used major language for modern data-driven analytics and artificial intelligence apps. However, it is also used for simple scripting purposes, to automate stuff, to test a hypothesis, to create interactive plots for brainstorming, to control lab instruments, and so on. But Python for software development and Python for scripting are not the same beast, at least in the domain of data science.

**Scripting is (mostly) the code you write for yourself. Software is the assemblage of code you (and other teammates) write for others**. It's wise to admit that when (a majority of) data scientists who do not come from a software engineering background write Python programs for AI/ML models and statistical analysis, they tend to write such code *mostly for themselves.*

Writing high-quality, production-level code is a skill to be learned and honed over a lifetime. It's the bread and butter of software engineers and developers. Not all data scientists will have the motivation and drive to acquire these skills. However, some simple good practices can be learned and applied in your everyday work.

This chapter will take you through that journey with some hands-on examples using the scikit-learn library. Chapters 5 and 6 will build on and expand the same concept.

T. Sarkar, *Productive and Efficient Data Science with Python*, https://doi.org/10.1007/978-1-4842-8121-5_4

# Why (and How) to Modularize Code for Machine Learning

Writing modular and well-organized code almost always comes with long-term rewards. This habit can **save you time and cognitive effort** when debugging and troubleshooting. Well-planned, modular code looks elegant. It is often simple to read, and it automatically welcomes other team members to help you and contribute to your work in a collaborative fashion. This, of course, improves the overall quality and robustness of the product/service.

But how do you decide what to modularize? How do you even start thinking about it? Here are some questions that you can ask yourself while working on any data science project.

---

**Spaghetti code is to be avoided at all costs**   Hastily written code that gets the job done but does not scale properly, is the prime example of 'bad code' or 'spaghetti code' that is littered everywhere in data science practice. This type of code can also result from poor planning, not following well-designed coding style, non-adherence to any object-oriented programming pattern, etc. Fundamentally, such spaghetti code is error-prone, extremely difficult to scale and debug, and counter-productive for production-level usage.

---

## Questions to Ask Yourself

Even if you have never had a software engineering course in your life, some ideas may come naturally to you. All you have to do is to put yourself in someone else's shoes and think about how that person will use your code in a constructive manner.

- If you have a code block that appears more than once in your analysis (in the exact same form or in slight variations), can you **make a function out of it**?

- When you make such a function, which parameters will be passed on? Which can be optional? What are the default values?

- If you encounter a situation where you don't know how many parameters need to be passed on, are you using the **\*args** and **\*\*kwargs** that Python offers?

- Did you write a **docstring** for that function to let others know what the function does and what parameters it expects as well plus an example?

- When you have collected a bunch of such utility functions, are you still working on the same notebook, or switching over to a new, clean notebook and just calling `from my_utility_script import func1, func2, func3`? (Did you create a `my_utility_script` as a simple Python file rather than a Jupyter notebook?)

- Did you put the `my_utility_script` in a directory, put an `__init__.py` file (even a blank one) in the same directory, and **make it a Python module** to be importable just like NumPy or Pandas?

- Are you thinking about not merely importing classes and methods from packages like NumPy and TensorFlow but **adding your own methods to them** and extending their functionality?

# Start Simple with a Standard Data Science Flow

For starters, let's consider a standard data science task flow so you can organize your coding approach to follow modularization thinking. Even before writing a single line of code, you can mentally organize (*modularize*) the tasks and plan for separate modules, as shown in Figure 4-1.

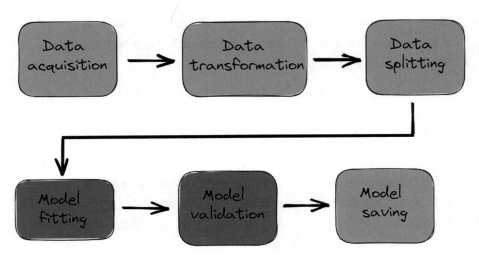

***Figure 4-1.*** *A standard data science flow organized in a modular fashion (in your head) to be implemented in your code*

Why those three colors (orange, blue, and green)? They simply represent the three main flavors of the tasks: data-related, algorithm-related, and deployment-related, respectively. The deployment portion is highly compressed and represented with this single model saving task here. In a real-life production scenario, there will be a host of modules related to it but all of them can start with this module, where you can save and output the validated model as a software artifact (e.g., a Python pickle).

The main idea of Figure 4-1 is, however, to emphasize the scope and need for modularization of these tasks. As data science practitioners, you perform these tasks regularly inside a Jupyter notebook. To embrace productive data science, you need to organize and even think beyond the notebook towards this modularization.

Let's see how with a familiar scikit-learn example.

## A Scikit-learn Task Flow Example

In this example, you will work with the famous breast cancer dataset (`https://archive.ics.uci.edu/ml/datasets/breast+cancer`) and build a simple logistic regression classifier for the same. The task is simple, but the key learning will be how to approach the flow with a modularized coding practice.

# The Monolithic Example

The opposite to modular code is *monolithic code*: all code in a single file or Jupyter notebook. You could have written this monolithic code in a single shot:

```
from sklearn.datasets import load_breast_cancer
from sklearn.linear_model import LogisticRegression
<...>

# Data load
data = load_breast_cancer()
X, y = data['data'], data['target']

# Some visual exploration
features_avg = []
for i in range(30):
    features_avg.append(X[:,i].mean())
plt.figure(figsize=(4,6),dpi=100)
plt.barh(y=['Feature-'+str(i) for i in range(30)],width=features_avg)
plt.xlabel("Feature average")
plt.show()

# Model build
clf = LogisticRegression(random_state=0,
                         max_iter=500,
                         class_weight='balanced').fit(X, y)
clf.score(X, y)

# Cross-validation
scores = cross_val_score(clf, X, y, cv=5)
scores

print(f"Accuracy {scores.mean()} with a standard deviation of {scores.
std()}")

# Model save
<...>
```

**Everything is kind of mixed in the monolithic code above**: import, data loading, model building, validation, and saving. It has some standalone code like `clf.score(X, y)` that **makes sense only inside a Jupyter notebook cell**. It has a print statement, which is fine for the exploration and experiment phase but may not be suitable for an efficient codebase. It runs fine in a notebook but is hard to troubleshoot if bugs creep in or the model needs tuning.

Let's see how to clearly compartmentalize the code and build a modular code base for the same task.

## Little Boxes, Little Boxes...

Compartmentalizing or boxing is important for software development. This also increasingly applies to productive data science work as well. For the code snippet above, you can make these boxes easily. You start by copying the code blocks for different tasks into separate Python scripts or standalone files from the Jupyter notebook. The idea is shown in Figure 4-2.

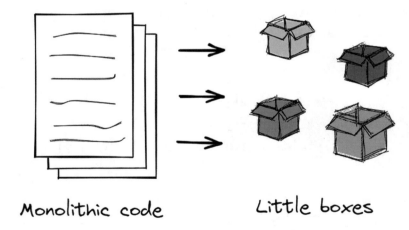

*Figure 4-2.* *From monolithic code to constructing little boxes*

To start, this code is for **data loading** only:

```
from sklearn.datasets import load_breast_cancer

def load_data():
    """

    Loads the data and returns Numpy arrays
    """
```

```
data = load_breast_cancer()

X = data['data']
y = data['target']

return X,y
```

That's it. **A single function to do only one job**. It is saved in a file called load_data.
py. Modularizing code highly encourages the use of single-purpose functions instead of
standalone code statements in the script. This is what is demonstrated here.

Next, **data splitting** into test and training sets:

```
from sklearn.model_selection import train_test_split

def data_split(X,y,
               test_size=0.3,
               random_state=42):
    """
    Randomly splits in test and train sets
    and returns them as Numpy arrays
    """
    X_train, X_test, y_train, y_test = train_test_split(
        X, y, test_size=test_size, random_state=random_state)

    return  X_train, X_test, y_train, y_test
```

Note the use of default variables test_size and random_state in case you want to
play with a test set fraction or different random initializations for experimental purposes.

Next, **model fitting** code:

```
from sklearn.linear_model import LogisticRegression
import numpy as np

def model_fit(X_train,y_train,
              max_iter=500):
    """
    Fits the model with training data.
    Returns the fitted estimator.
    """
```

```
class_zero, class_one = np.bincount(y_train)
class_ratio = class_zero/class_one

if class_ratio > 1.25 or class_ratio < 0.8:
    clf = LogisticRegression(max_iter=max_iter,
                        class_weight='balanced')
else:
    clf = LogisticRegression(max_iter=max_iter)

clf.fit(X_train,y_train)
return clf
```

You have to do some cross-validation with the test set data before you save this fitted model. So, the **cross-validation** code is as follows:

```
from sklearn.model_selection import cross_val_score

def cross_validate(clf,X_train,y_train,cv=10):
    """
    Cross validates the model.
    Returns an array of scores.
    """
    scores = cross_val_score(clf,X_train,y_train, cv=cv)
    return scores
```

You get back a NumPy array of cross-validation scores. Finally, you have to save/ package the model. But you may want to save the model only if the average of the cross-validated scores is above a certain threshold. Otherwise, you can go back to tune the model or look for more data (the dataset is fixed in this example, but the general idea is valid).

Therefore, your final **model saving** code looks like the following:

```
from joblib import dump, load

def model_save(clf,scores,threshold=0.9):
    """
    Saves a model depending on the CV scores
    """
```

```
if scores.mean() > threshold:
    dump(clf, 'logistic_model.joblib')
    return 1
else:
    return 0
```

Note that instead of using pickle, you use the **joblib** library for more efficient and compact storage of the scikit-learn estimator. This is described here: `https://scikit-learn.org/stable/model_persistence.html`.

OK, you created modularized code for your data science task. Now what?

## How to Use the Modular Code

After creating these modules, the directory structure may look like Figure 4-3. Note the Jupyter notebook at the bottom (circled). This is what you get as the fruit of the modularization of your code.

Your notebook looks **much cleaner and more readable** than the spaghetti code you had earlier. If you examine that Jupyter notebook, you may see something like Figure 4-4.

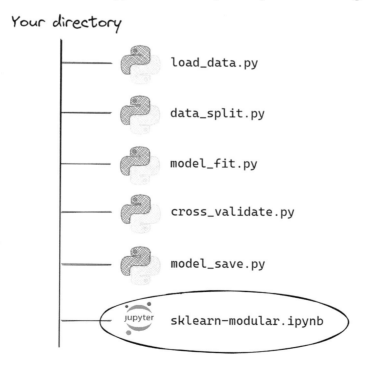

***Figure 4-3.*** *Python script/modules in the directory for various ML tasks*

## Imports (your own modules)

```
[1]: # Importing your modules
     from load_data import load_data
     from data_split import data_split
     from model_fit import model_fit
     from cross_validate import cross_validate
     from model_save import model_save
```

## Loading data

```
[2]: X, y = load_data()
```

## Splitting data

```
[3]: X_train, X_test, y_train, y_test = data_split(X,y,
                                              random_state=101)
```

## Fitting model

```
[4]: fitted_model = model_fit(X_train,y_train,
                             max_iter=5000)
```

```
[5]: type(fitted_model)
```

```
[5]: sklearn.linear_model._logistic.LogisticRegression
```

## Cross-validation scores

```
[6]: scores = cross_validate(fitted_model,X_test,y_test)
```

```
[7]: scores
```

```
[7]: array([0.94444444, 0.94117647, 0.88235294, 0.94117647, 0.94117647,
            1.        , 0.88235294, 0.94117647, 0.94117647, 0.82352941])
```

## Could the model be saved?

### With a high threshold of 0.95

```
[8]: if model_save(fitted_model,scores,threshold=0.95):
         print("Model saved successfully")
     else:
         print("Model did not pass cross-validation")
```

```
Model did not pass cross-validation
```

### With a lowered threshold of 0.9

```
[9]: if model_save(fitted_model,scores,threshold=0.9):
         print("Model saved successfully")
     else:
         print("Model did not pass cross-validation")
```

```
Model saved successfully
```

***Figure 4-4.*** *Typical Jupyter notebook (cleaner and compact) after modularizing the code*

The key benefit of this approach is that you can play with the following aspects of the task **independently and without touching the main notebook code**:

- Data source (just modify the `load_data.py` file)

- Data splitting options (just modify the `data_split.py` file)

- Choice of model and hyperparameters (just modify the `model_fit.py` file)

- Cross-validation strategy and options (just modify the `cross_validate.py` file)

- The decision to save the model (just modify the `model_save.py` file)

Also, note how the input and output of each module is controlled through a focused and targeted function definition. This gives you the **opportunity to validate and check the expected outcome from each of the modules**. This means if for some reason the data or model is corrupted, you can catch it mid-flight before it goes to the model fitting or saving stage. This saves infrastructure costs and enhances the robustness of the ML platform as a whole.

Figure 4-5 demonstrates the idea of separate test/validation blocks for each of the core modules. It also shows a `system_config.json` file that may store the cross-validation threshold and the `model_save.py` file to check the current model's performance against that criterion before saving the model.

Can you imagine all this flexibility and possibilities with a monolith Jupyter notebook?

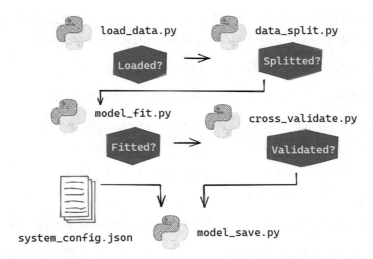

***Figure 4-5.*** *Modular code used along with data/model validation checks and system configuration files*

# Systematic Evaluation of ML Algorithms in an Automated Fashion

As discussed in the beginning of this chapter, apart from modularization, another central pillar of efficient data science code is automation. We often write repetitive code that can introduce bugs and inefficiency.

One of the most common tasks for a typical DS workflow is to run the same data through multiple ML algorithms and choose the best one (according to some predetermined metric). In this section, you will examine a hands-on example of automating this evaluation task.

## List of Classifiers

At the beginning, you have to pick the scikit-learn estimators (along with their hyperparameters) for this evaluation. You can define a list with these objects:

```
classifiers = [
    LogisticRegression(C=0.1,n_jobs=-1),
    KNeighborsClassifier(10,n_jobs=-1),
    SVC(kernel="linear", C=0.1),
    SVC(gamma='scale', C=1),
```

```
DecisionTreeClassifier(max_depth=10,min_samples_leaf=10),
RandomForestClassifier(max_depth=3, n_estimators=50,       max_features=5,
min_samples_leaf=10,n_jobs=-1),
    MLPClassifier(hidden_layer_sizes=(50,50),alpha=0.2,activation='relu',
    max_iter=200,learning_rate_init=0.01,learning_rate='adaptive',
    early_stopping=True,validation_fraction=0.2),
    AdaBoostClassifier(base_estimator=DecisionTreeClassifier(max_depth=3),
    n_estimators=50,learning_rate=0.1),
    BaggingClassifier(base_estimator=DecisionTreeClassifier(max_depth=3),
    n_estimators=50, max_features=5,n_jobs=-1),

GaussianNB(),
QuadraticDiscriminantAnalysis(reg_param=0.1)]
```

You can also define a list of names (strings) for plotting and enumeration purposes:

```
names = ["Logistic Regression","Nearest Neighbors", "Linear SVM",
"RBF SVM", "Decision Tree", "Random Forest", "Neural Net", "AdaBoost",
"Bagging","Naive Bayes", "QDA"]
```

# Function to Automate Model Fitting

At the heart of this approach is the function that runs through the given list of estimators and fits the data to them one by one. It also encapsulates the usual data splitting and scorekeeping. Optionally, you can also record the time it takes to fit each model so that you can do a trade-off analysis of model performance and computational cost later on.

So, the function starts like this:

```
def run_classifiers(X,y,
                    clf_lst = [LogisticRegression(C=0.1,n_jobs=-1)],
                    names=None,
                    num_runs=10,
                    test_frac=0.2,
                    scaling=True,
                    metric='accuracy',
                    runtime=True,
                    verbose=0):
```

```
"""
Runs through the list of classifiers for a given number of times.
Returns a DataFrame with scores (and, optionally, running times).
"""
```

Note that it only needs some training data (X and y vectors) to run. Everything else is optional and has default values, even the classifier list. It features essential arguments like test_frac for the training/test set split, scaling for deciding whether to scale the training data, metric for comparing the algorithms against a single performance metric, and runtime to record computation time for each algorithm's run.

However, the most important argument is num_runs, which ensures that the ML algorithms run multiple times and all the performance metrics and running times are saved to a Pandas DataFrame. This is the final DataFrame that is returned by the function.

For example, if scaling is True, then it performs scaling:

```
if scaling:
    X_train= StandardScaler().fit_transform(X_train)
    X_test = StandardScaler().fit_transform(X_test)
```

If the runtime Boolean is enabled, then it computes and stores the running times:

```
if runtime:
    t1 = time.time()
    clf.fit(X_train, y_train)
    t2 = time.time()
    delta_t = round((t2-t1)*1000,3)
    rt.append(delta_t)
```

Finally, it returns either a single DataFrame of scores or two DataFrames if the runtime is also asked for:

```
if runtime:
    return df_scores, df_runtimes
else:
    return df_scores
```

The complete code for the function and other details are provided in the accompanying Jupyter notebook.

# How Does Automation Help?

Fundamentally, the automation approach makes your exploration and experimentation code cleaner and compact. You can start a Jupyter notebook, load some data into two vectors, X and y, and execute the function right away. You can get all the results (accuracy scores) at the same time with a single execution, as shown in Figure 4-6.

|  | 0 | 1 | 2 | 3 | 4 |
|---|---|---|---|---|---|
| LogisticRegression | 0.585000 | 0.614634 | 0.600985 | 0.636132 | 0.587065 |
| KNeighborsClassifier | 0.751295 | 0.733154 | 0.747253 | 0.748052 | 0.744304 |
| SVC | 0.579345 | 0.621212 | 0.583541 | 0.585752 | 0.604167 |
| SVC_1 | 0.816832 | 0.823834 | 0.789610 | 0.811594 | 0.797927 |
| DecisionTreeClassifier | 0.593176 | 0.627160 | 0.556150 | 0.668305 | 0.649077 |
| RandomForestClassifier | 0.648101 | 0.625954 | 0.602041 | 0.613811 | 0.635870 |
| MLPClassifier | 0.734584 | 0.785542 | 0.785714 | 0.776699 | 0.757033 |
| AdaBoostClassifier | 0.647343 | 0.716346 | 0.655340 | 0.656934 | 0.671835 |
| BaggingClassifier | 0.653061 | 0.607595 | 0.649289 | 0.652174 | 0.632432 |
| GaussianNB | 0.586735 | 0.646914 | 0.625917 | 0.643216 | 0.621891 |
| QuadraticDiscriminantAnalysis | 0.828283 | 0.814070 | 0.794595 | 0.819588 | 0.812500 |

***Figure 4-6.*** *Typical DataFrame output of an automated run of multiple ML algorithms*

```
d1 = run_classifiers(X,y,
                 clf_lst=classifiers,
                 metric='f1',
                 num_runs=5,
                 runtime=False,
                 verbose=1)
```

Since you have verbose=1, you will see this kind of status message printed:

```
Finished 5 runs for LogisticRegression algorithm
------------------------------------------------------------
Finished 5 runs for KNeighborsClassifier algorithm
------------------------------------------------------------
Finished 5 runs for SVC algorithm
------------------------------------------------------------
Finished 5 runs for SVC_1 algorithm
------------------------------------------------------------
Finished 5 runs for DecisionTreeClassifier algorithm
------------------------------------------------------------
Finished 5 runs for RandomForestClassifier algorithm
------------------------------------------------------------
Finished 5 runs for MLPClassifier algorithm
------------------------------------------------------------
Finished 5 runs for AdaBoostClassifier algorithm
------------------------------------------------------------
Finished 5 runs for BaggingClassifier algorithm
------------------------------------------------------------
Finished 5 runs for GaussianNB algorithm
------------------------------------------------------------
Finished 5 runs for QuadraticDiscriminantAnalysis algorithm
------------------------------------------------------------
```

Thereafter, with simple plotting code, you can visualize the average performance of all of the algorithms and their variances (Figure 4-7).

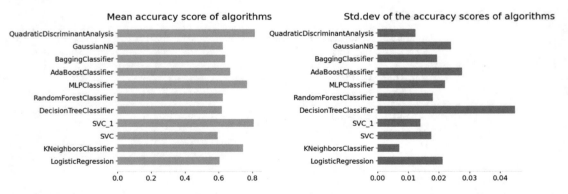

***Figure 4-7.*** *Mean accuracy scores and their standard deviation for an automated run of multiple ML algorithms*

Note that you had two support vector classifiers with a different kernel and penalty coefficients, and they are recorded as SVC and SVC_1 in the table.

You can experiment with various hyperparameter tuning with minimal code change. For example, to record decision tree performance for various tree depths, you can create a list:

```
clf_lst = [DecisionTreeClassifier(max_depth=i) for i in range(2,16)]
```

You can then pass this list to the automation function. You get the DataFrame back and simple averaging of the results yields the plot shown in Figure 4-8.

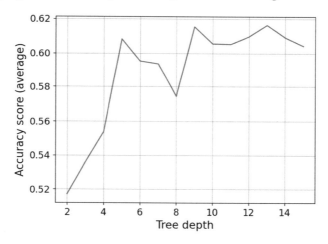

***Figure 4-8.*** *Mean accuracy scores of decision tree classifiers with varying depth*

Basically, once you have an automated way to run a multitude of ML algorithms in a single shot and compare their performance, you can think of a host of practical applications for this utility in the experimental and production phases.

---

## Automation and modularization naturally lead to a low-code environment

In Chapter 12, we talk about low-code libraries and frameworks that abstract away a lot of manual data science work and generate results with only a few lines of code. One of the main driving forces behind such low-code tools is the kind of modularization that you did here. Effectively, you reduced the code for repeated experimentation to only a few lines by utilizing the custom modules. This makes the overall codebase leaner and more efficient to maintain and debug.

---

# Decision Boundary Visualization

For many classification problems in the domain of supervised ML, you may want to go beyond the numerical prediction (of the class or of the probability) and visualize the actual decision boundary between the classes. This is, of course, particularly suitable for binary classification problems and for a pair of features: the visualization is displayed on a 2D plane. For example, Figure 4-9 shows a visualization of the decision boundary for a Support Vector Machine (SVM) tutorial from the official scikit-learn documentation (`https://scikit-learn.org/stable/modules/svm.html`).

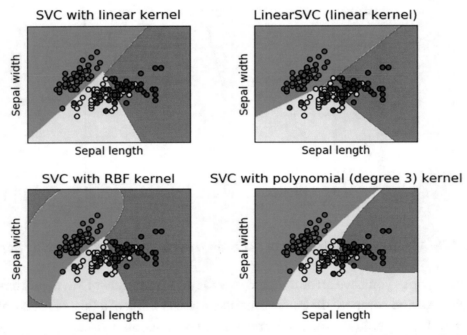

***Figure 4-9.*** *Decision boundaries are visualized for SVMs with different kernels*

Now the problem is that scikit-learn does not offer a ready-made, accessible method for doing this kind of visualization. However, you can create custom code to achieve this so that the data science task can be more efficient when it comes to visualizing decision boundaries.

# The Custom Function

The full description and the code for the function are provided in the accompanying Jupyter notebook. The code starts like this:

```
def plot_decision_boundaries(X, y,
                             model_class,
                             **model_params):
    """
    Function to plot the decision boundaries of a classification model.
This uses just the first two columns of the data for fitting the model as
we need to find the predicted value for every point in scatter plot.

    Arguments:
            X: Feature data as a Numpy-type array.
            y: Label data as a Numpy-type array.
            model_class: A Scikit-learn ML estimator class
            e.g. GaussianNB or LogisticRegression
            **model_params: Model parameters to be passed on to the ML
            estimator
    """
```

Note the use of the **model_params unpacking operator to allow the user to pass on any number and variety of parameters to the function corresponding to the model in question. Internally, it works by creating a 2D mesh grid and plotting colored contour regions corresponding to the predicted classes.

Here the model class denotes the exact scikit-learn estimator class that you call in to instantiate your ML estimator object. Note that you don't have to pass on the specific ML estimator that you are working with. Just the class name will suffice. This function will internally fit the data and predict to create the appropriate decision boundary (considering the model parameters that you also pass on).

---

**What is this unpacking operator?**   You might have seen the arguments *args and **kwargs in the API documentation of many functions. They allow you to pass multiple arguments or keyword arguments to a function when you don't even know the precise number and order of the arguments beforehand and must decide that dynamically, at runtime. This article presents an excellent tutorial.

---

# Example Results

For the demonstration, let's use a divorce classification dataset. This dataset is about participants who completed the personal information form and a divorce predictors scale. The data is a modified version of the publicly available data at the UCI portal (`https://archive.ics.uci.edu/ml/datasets/Divorce+Predictors+data+set`) after injecting some noise. There are 170 participants and 54 attributes (or predictor variables) that are all real-valued.

You'll compare the performance of multiple ML estimators on the same dataset:

- Naive Bayes

- Logistic regression

- K-nearest neighbor (KNN)

Because the binary classes of this dataset are easily separable, as shown in Figure 4-10, all the ML algorithms perform almost equally well. However, their respective decision boundaries look different from each other and this is what you are interested in visualizing through this utility function.

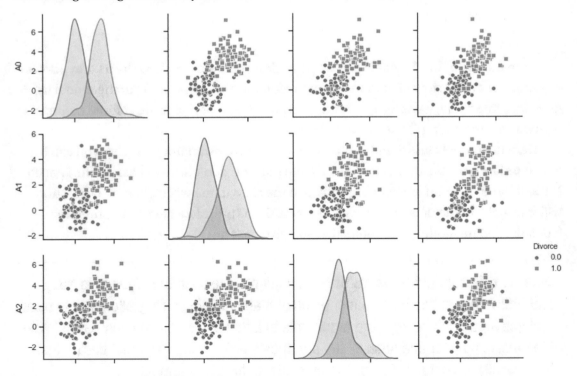

***Figure 4-10.*** *Class separability of the divorce dataset*

The decision boundary from the Naive Bayes algorithm is smooth and slightly nonlinear, as shown in Figure 4-11. You achieve this with only four lines of code:

```
plt.figure()
plt.title("Naïve Bayes decision boundary",fontsize=16)
plot_decision_boundaries(X_train,y_train,GaussianNB)
plt.show()
```

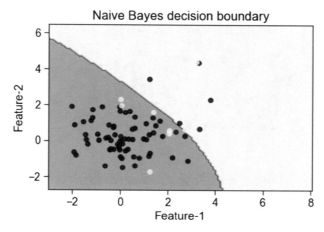

***Figure 4-11.***  *Decision boundary of the Naïve Bayes algorithm*

As expected, the decision boundary from the logistic regression estimator is visualized as a linear separator, as shown in Figure 4-12.

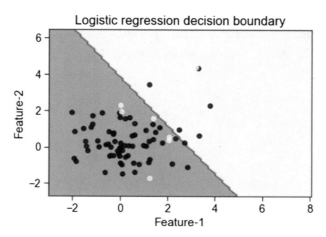

***Figure 4-12.***  *Decision boundary of the logistic regression algorithm*

The K-nearest neighbor decision boundary comes up as nonlinear and non-smooth, as shown in Figure 4-13. This is because KNN is an algorithm based on the local geometry of the distribution of the data on the feature hyperplane (and their relative distance measures).

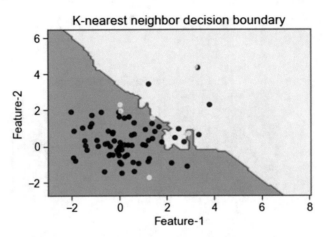

***Figure 4-13.*** *Decision boundary of the KNN algorithm*

The function works with any scikit-learn estimator, even a neural network. Here is the decision boundary with the **MLPClassifier** estimator of scikit-learn, which models a densely connected neural network with user-configurable parameters (`https://scikit-learn.org/stable/modules/generated/sklearn.neural_network.MLPClassifier.html`). Note that in the code, you pass on the hidden layer settings, the learning rate, and the optimizer (Stochastic Gradient Descent or SGD; `https://towardsdatascience.com/stochastic-gradient-descent-clearly-explained-53d239905d31`). The decision boundary generated by the code is shown in Figure 4-14.

```
plot_decision_boundaries(X_test,y_test,MLPClassifier,hidden_layer_sizes=(5,2),
                         solver='sgd',learning_rate_init=0.001,max_iter=1000)
plt.show()
```

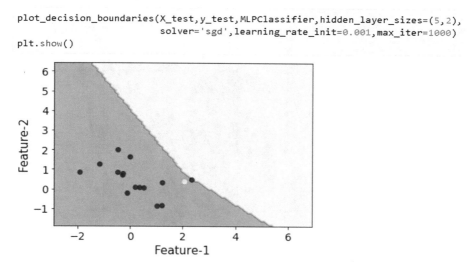

***Figure 4-14.***  *Decision boundary and code for the MLP algorithm*

# Parametric Experimentation

As mentioned, you can pass on any model parameters that you want to the utility function. In the case of the KNN classifier, as you increase the number of neighboring data points, the decision boundary becomes smoother. This can be readily visualized using this utility function, as shown in Figure 4-15.

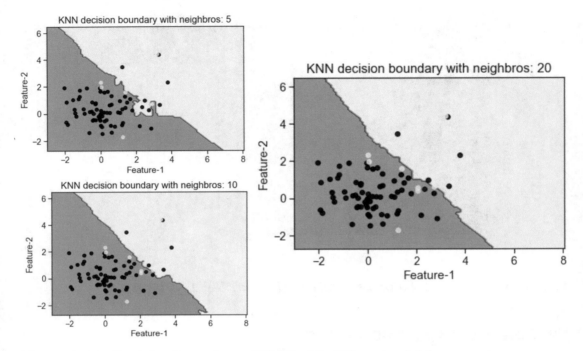

***Figure 4-15.*** *Decision boundary of KNN with different neighbor counts –*
*experimentation with the algorithm*

# Other Scikit-learn Utilities and Techniques

Scikit-learn provides many other tools and utilities to make your ML code more
productive. An exhaustive treatment of them is beyond the scope of this book. However,
here I briefly mention some of the most useful ones that you can readily utilize in your
data science code.

## Hyperparameter Search Utilities

In scikit-learn, hyperparameters are passed as arguments to the constructor of the
estimator classes. They often need to be tuned meticulously in order to achieve good
ML model performance. However, this task can be exhaustive and inefficient if done
manually or without a systematic plan. Fortunately, scikit-learn provides efficient grid
search utilities that behave similarly to standard ML estimators and let you run a large
number of experiments (with varying hyperparameters) with just a few lines of code.

A search consists of the following:

- An estimator (a regressor or classifier such as `sklearn.svm.SVC()`)

- A parameter space

- A method for searching or sampling candidates

- A cross-validation scheme

- A score function

Check out the official documentation of scikit-learn at `https://scikit-learn.org/stable/modules/grid_search.html` to see the options and their usage. For increasing the productivity of your data science code, they can come in handy.

# Parallel Job Runner

Not all scikit-learn estimators can take advantage of multi-core CPUs natively, but some do have the ability to parallelize costly numerical operations using the backend supporting libraries:

- Using the `joblib` library. In this case, the number of threads or processes can be controlled with the `n_jobs` parameter.

- Using `OpenMP`, used in C or Python code.

`Joblib` is able to support both multiprocessing and multithreading. Whether `joblib` chooses to spawn a thread or a process depends on the back end it's using. You can make the choice in the code as follows:

```
from joblib import parallel_backend

with parallel_backend('threading', n_jobs=2):
    # estimator.fit(X,y)
    < ... >
```

Generally, `joblib` uses the `locy` back end. But there are other, more powerful alternatives. For example, **Dask** can scale scikit-learn algorithms out to a cluster of machines by providing an alternative `joblib` back end:

```
from dask.distributed import Client
import joblib
```

```
client = Client(processes=False) # create local cluster
# or connect to remote cluster
# client = Client("scheduler-address:8786")

with joblib.parallel_backend('dask'):
    # Scikit-learn code
```

In general, this type of **parallel processing is highly suitable for ML models that match the parallelism natively** (e.g., Random Forest with multiple trees or AdaBoost with multiple base estimators). We will revisit this in more detail in Chapter 11 when we discuss Dask-based parallelism.

## Out-of-the-box Visualization Methods

Visualization of ML models' output and performance metrics is a vast and complex topic. Every data scientist has their own choice and style of visualizing data and model outputs. However, for efficient data science practice, it is often beneficial to have a set of out-of-the-box routines that can take an ML model and output standard visualizations such as a ROC curve, learning curve, precision-recall curve, and confusion matrix.

Scikit-learn provides a uniform API than can accept an estimator object, test or predicted data, and draw out these visualizations using the Matplotlib back end. This comes in handy for quick prototyping and productive data science workflow.

More details can be found on the scikit-learn visualization API's page at `https://scikit-learn.org/stable/visualizations.html#visualizations`.

## Synthetic Data Generators

Scikit-learn provides a host of synthetic data generators for quickly evaluating and experimenting with ML algorithms. While a data science problem with a real dataset does not directly benefit from these generators, they often come in handy to gauge the relative strength and weakness of various ML algorithms and test out various coding approaches.

A somewhat detailed discussion about these methods can be found in this article along with a list of benefits for synthetic data generation in general: "Synthetic data generation — a must-have skill for new data scientists" (`https://towardsdatascience.com/synthetic-data-generation-a-must-have-skill-for-new-data-scientists-915896c0c1ae`).

# Summary

In this chapter, you started by learning about the utility and benefits of modularizing ML code. You took a typical data science workflow of building out a classification model with a well-known dataset and applied this principle of modular code. You compared the monolithic (or spaghetti) code in a Jupyter notebook to the short Python scripts/modules you wrote and saw the utility of the approach in a cleaner Jupyter notebook. You also saw how this approach played well with software testing and platform-level decision making.

Next, you explored an approach of systematic evaluation of ML algorithms with automation code where you constructed a function that can run through a list of any scikit-learn estimators, fit models, evaluate performance metrics and running times, and save everything in a nice dataset for later evaluation. This kind of automation is the first step towards learning how to do large-scale ML experimentation in a systematic and productive manner.

Next, you explored another productive technique of visualizing decision boundaries for arbitrary classification models using a unified function. This leads to efficient visual analytics of classification boundaries when you need to examine such characteristics.

Finally, you learned utilities and techniques embedded in the scikit-learn library that can improve the efficiency of your ML code and data science tasks. This included hyperparameter search, parallel job running, ready-made visualization routines, and synthetic data generators.

In the next chapters, you will build upon the concept of modular and object-oriented coding approaches and explore their utility and application for deep learning and classical ML tasks.

# CHAPTER 5

# Modular and Productive Deep Learning Code

In the previous chapter, I explored the idea that most data scientists often come from a background that is quite far removed from traditional computer science/software engineering. Consequently, they produce code that is perfectly suitable for great exploratory data analysis, statistical modeling, or innovative ML experiments but not robust enough for the production phase of a large business platform. Data scientists often think in terms of the next analysis script but not along the lines of the next software module that integrates into a larger system.

Scripting is (mostly) the code you write for yourself. Software is the assemblage of code you (and other teammates) write for others. It is an undeniable fact that most data scientists, not having a traditional software development background and training, tend to write AI/ML analysis code *mostly for themselves*.

They just want to get to the heart of the pattern hidden in the data. Fast. Without thinking deeply about normal mortals (users). They write a block of code to produce a rich and beautiful plot. But they don't create a function out of it to use later. They import lots of methods and classes from standard libraries. But they don't create a subclass of their own by inheritance and add methods to it for extending the functionality.

In the previous chapter, you explored some of these issues through scikit-learn code and a typical classical ML task, fitting a logistic regression model. In this chapter, you will explore how similar principles can help you write better code for deep learning tasks with some hands-on examples using Keras/TensorFlow.

© Dr. Tirthajyoti Sarkar 2022
T. Sarkar, *Productive and Efficient Data Science with Python*, https://doi.org/10.1007/978-1-4842-8121-5_5

# Modular Code and Object-Oriented Style for Productive DL

*Functions, inheritance, methods, classes*: they are at the heart of robust object-oriented programming (OOP). But you may not want to delve deeply into them if all you want to do is create a Jupyter notebook with your exploratory data analysis and plots.

You can avoid the initial pain of using OOP principles, but this almost always renders your notebook code non-reusable and non-extensible. More precisely, that piece of code serves only you (until you forget what exact logic you coded) and no one else. But readability (and, thereby, reusability) is critically important for any good software product/service. That is the true test of the merit of what you produce. Not for yourself. But for others.

Data science involving deep learning models and code is no exception. These days, powerful and flexible frameworks like TensorFlow or PyTorch make the actual coding of a complex neural network architecture relatively simple and brief. However, if the overall DS code is not modularized and well-organized (following much of the style discussed in Chapter 4 in the section "Why (and How) to Modularize Code for Machine Learning"), then it is plagued by the same issues of non-reproducibility and non-reusability. Let's see some examples of how you can organize and modularize DL code in your data science work.

## Example of a Productive DL Task Flow

Deep learning makes it easy to train ML models for highly nonlinear (and even noisy) datasets and phenomena. Modern frameworks like Keras/TensorFlow/PyTorch offer powerful and flexible APIs to build these models with relative ease and a surprisingly small amount of code. However, an end-to-end DS flow can be made much more productive if you follow some simple guidelines on how you build, manage, and utilize DL code. An approach of building compact modules and a systematic flow (shown in Figure 5-1) can help. Some examples of related guidelines are discussed below in the form of questions.

> One of the most common and repetitive tasks for DL analysis is to **build out a deep neural network (DNN) object**. Data scientists routinely use non-modularized code to just add layers (e.g., from Keras (`https://keras.io/api/layers/`) or PyTorch `https://`

pytorch.org/tutorials/recipes/recipes/defining_a_neural_
network.html) APIs) and build this as a local variable in their
Jupyter notebook. Wouldn't it be a much better idea to create a
custom function for this task?

After building an (untrained) model, you must **compile** (set
learning rate, batch size, etc.) and **run** the model with data. Would
a custom function help make this task modularized as well?

When you make such a **DNN builder** function, which parameters
will be passed on? Which ones can be optional? What are the
default values? If you encounter a situation where you don't know
how many parameters need to be passed on, are you using the
*args and **kwargs that Python offers?

Did you write a **docstring** for that function to let others know
what the function does and what parameters it expects plus an
example?

Can you also modularize the code used to **create the visual
analytics** based on the output of those model functions?

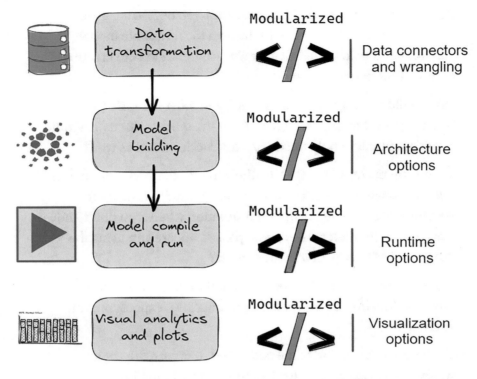

**Figure 5-1.** *Deep learning task flow organized in modular fashion*

# Wrappers, Builders, Callbacks

Fundamentally, in the subsection above I described **wrapping up** the most essential tasks in a DL-based workflow inside custom functions and using them as the core building blocks of your data science code. Additionally, you can wrap up the tasks related to data formatting/transformation and prediction/inference in a similar fashion.

It is to be noted that wrapper functions for regression and classification tasks can have separate sets of architecture and parameters. So, it makes sense to keep their build customized. The choice of the default parameter values in the wrapper functions is of critical importance, too.

Apart from a simple functional wrapper, you can also utilize a powerful construct called a ***callback*** that caters to the dynamic nature of DNN training. Essentially, a callback is an object that can perform actions at various stages of DNN training (e.g., at the start or end of an epoch or before starting a single batch). You can use callbacks for various scenarios, including but not limited to the following:

- **Early stopping** based on some error or computation criterion

- **Periodically saving the model** to disk (making the system robust against unexpected failure)

- Obtaining an overview on various internal states and statistics of a model in mid-flight (i.e., while the training is going on)

Finally, if you want to extend this approach all the way to the full OOP paradigm, you can build out classes and utility modules incorporating all these wrappers as special methods. You can call this a DL utility module, which you can call upon in any data science task where supervised ML modeling is needed.

# Modular Code for Fast Experimentation

Let's demonstrate the ideas discussed above using a simple case: a DL image classification problem with the Fashion MNIST (`https://github.com/zalandoresearch/fashion-mnist`) dataset. The core ML task is simple: build a classifier for this dataset, which is a funny spin on the original famous MNIST hand-written digit dataset. Fashion MNIST consists of 60,000 training images of 28 x 28-pixel size of objects related to fashion (e.g., hats, shoes, trousers, t-shirts, dresses, etc.). It also consists of 10,000 test images for model validation and testing. A slice of the dataset is shown in Figure 5-2 for illustration.

*Figure 5-2.  A slice of the Fashion MNIST dataset*

# Business/Data Science Question

The basic ML task for this dataset seems straightforward. But what if there is a higher-order optimization or visual analytics question around this core ML task: *how does the model architecture complexity impact the minimum epochs it takes to reach the desired accuracy*?

It should be clear to you why we even bother about such a question: because this is related to the overall business optimization. Training a neural net is not a trivial computational matter (www.technologyreview.com/s/613630/training-a-single-ai-model-can-emit-as-much-carbon-as-five-cars-in-their-lifetimes/). Therefore, it makes sense to **investigate what minimum training effort** must be spent to achieve a target performance metric and how the choice of architecture impacts it.

The image classification accuracy could be related to a broader business outcome such as a fashion recommendation or clothing identification in a store. The core data science task helps optimize the cost of running that business task—to use the image database with the optimal expenditure of computing resources using the ML code as the underlying nuts and bolts.

In this example, you will not even use a convolutional neural network (CNN; https://towardsdatascience.com/a-comprehensive-guide-to-convolutional-neural-networks-the-eli5-way-3bd2b1164a53), which are commonly used for image classification tasks. This is because, for this dataset, a simple densely connected neural net can accomplish reasonably high accuracy, and, in fact, a sub-optimal performance is required to illustrate the main point of the higher-order optimization question posed above.

So, you must solve two problems:

- What the *minimum number of epochs* for reaching the *desired accuracy* target and how do you determine this?

- How does the *specific architecture of the model* impact this number or training behavior?

To achieve the goals, you will use two simple OOP principles:

- Creating an inherited class from a base class object

- Creating utility functions and calling them from a compact code block that can be presented to an external user for higher-order optimization and analytics

## Inherit from the Keras Callback

You inherit a Keras callback class (as the base) and write your own subclass by adding a method that checks the training accuracy and takes an action based on that value. The code snapshot and some explanations are shown in Figure 5-3. More details on this can be found in the official TensorFlow article "Writing your own callbacks" at www.tensorflow.org/guide/keras/custom_callback.

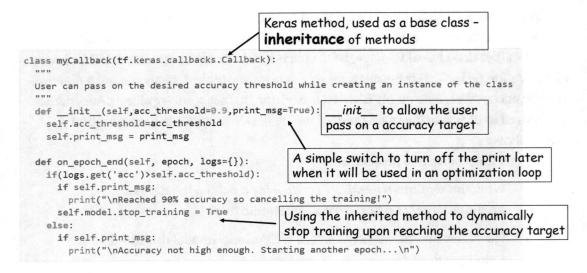

```
class myCallback(tf.keras.callbacks.Callback):
  """
  User can pass on the desired accuracy threshold while creating an instance of the class
  """
  def __init__(self,acc_threshold=0.9,print_msg=True):
    self.acc_threshold=acc_threshold
    self.print_msg = print_msg

  def on_epoch_end(self, epoch, logs={}):
    if(logs.get('acc')>self.acc_threshold):
      if self.print_msg:
        print("\nReached 90% accuracy so cancelling the training!")
      self.model.stop_training = True
    else:
      if self.print_msg:
        print("\nAccuracy not high enough. Starting another epoch...\n")
```

**Keras method, used as a base class – inheritance of methods**

**__init__ to allow the user pass on a accuracy target**

**A simple switch to turn off the print later when it will be used in an optimization loop**

**Using the inherited method to dynamically stop training upon reaching the accuracy target**

***Figure 5-3.***  *A custom class built on top of a Keras callback*

Basically, this simple callback results in **dynamic control of the epochs**; the training stops automatically when the accuracy reaches the desired threshold. Figure 5-4 shows a snapshot of an example run.

```
60000/60000 [==============================] - 5s 89us/sample - loss: 0.2954 - acc: 0.8900
Epoch 6/10
59360/60000 [==========================>.] - ETA: 0s - loss: 0.2816 - acc: 0.8970
Accuracy not high enough. Starting another epoch...
60000/60000 [==============================] - 6s 97us/sample - loss: 0.2816 - acc: 0.8968
Epoch 7/10
59584/60000 [==========================>.] - ETA: 0s - loss: 0.2699 - acc: 0.9000
Accuracy not high enough. Starting another epoch...

60000/60000 [==============================] - 6s 92us/sample - loss: 0.2701 - acc: 0.9000
Epoch 8/10
59456/60000 [==========================>.] - ETA: 0s - loss: 0.2580 - acc: 0.9048
Reached 90% accuracy so cancelling the training!
60000/60000 [==============================] - 6s 93us/sample - loss: 0.2585 - acc: 0.9046
<tensorflow.python.keras.callbacks.History at 0x297567e9208>
```

**Print message to indicate accuracy not high enough yet**

**The code asked for 10 epochs of training but callback stopped it at 8**

**Print message to indicate accuracy reached target**

***Figure 5-4.***  *Snapshot of an example run with the callback enabled*

# Model Builder and Compile/Train Functions

Next, you put the Keras model construction code in a utility function so that a model of an arbitrary number of layers and architecture (as long as they are densely connected) can be generated using simple user input in the form of some function arguments. The code snapshot and the associated explanations are shown in Figure 5-5.

Define a function which generates a Keras model from some user input

```python
def build_model(num_layers=1, architecture=[32],act_func='relu',
                input_shape=(28,28), output_class=10):
    """
    Builds a densely connected neural network model from user input
    num_layers: Number of hidden layers
    architecture: Architecture of the hidden layers (densely connected)
    act_func: Activation function. Could be 'relu', 'sigmoid', or 'tanh'.
    input_shape: Dimension of the input vector
    output_class: Number of classes in the output vector
    """
    layers=[tf.keras.layers.Flatten(input_shape=input_shape)]
    if act_func=='relu':
        activation=tf.nn.relu
    elif act_func=='sigmoid':
        activation=tf.nn.sigmoid
    elif act_func=='tanh':
        activation=tf.nn.tanh

    for i in range(num_layers):
        layers.append(tf.keras.layers.Dense(architecture[i], activation=tf.nn.relu))
    layers.append(tf.keras.layers.Dense(output_class, activation=tf.nn.softmax))
```

Docstring with detailed description and explanation of expected arguments

Any number of hidden layers with arbitrary number of neurons (and choice of activation function) can be added

***Figure 5-5.*** *Snapshot of a model builder function*

You also put the compilation and training code into a utility function to use those hyperparameters in a higher-order optimization loop conveniently. The code snapshot and the associated explanations are shown in Figure 5-6.

Before going further, we define a simple function to compile and train a given model (to use later)

```
def compile_train_model(model,x_train, y_train, callbacks=None,
                   learning_rate=0.001,batch_size=1,epochs=10,verbose=0):
    """
    Compiles and trains a given Keras model with the given data.
    Assumes Adam optimizer for this implementation.

    learning_rate: Learning rate for the optimizer Adam
    batch_size: Batch size for the mini-batch optimization
    epochs: Number of epochs to train
    verbose: Verbosity of the training process
    """

    model_copy = model
    model_copy.compile(optimizer=tf.keras.optimizers.Adam(lr=learning_rate),
            loss='sparse_categorical_crossentropy',
            metrics=['accuracy'])

    model_copy.fit(x_train, y_train, epochs=epochs, batch_size=batch_size,
            callbacks=[callbacks],verbose=verbose)
    return model_copy
```

Turn the hyperparameters into arguments of an utility function so that they can be used in higher order analytics

Docstring with detailed description and explanation of expected arguments

When you are modifying an argument, it's best to make a copy and work on it

*Figure 5-6.* *Snapshot of a model compiling and training function*

# Visualization Function

Next, it's time for visualization. Generic plot functions take raw data as input. However, if you have a specific purpose of plotting the evolution of training set accuracy (and showing how it compares to the target), then your plot function should just accept the (trained) deep learning model as the input and generate the desired plot. The code snapshot and the associated explanations are shown in Figure 5-7.

Let's define a plot utility function to use it later ┌─────────────────────┐
│ Accepts a Keras model │
│ object as argument │
└─────────────────────┘

```
def plot_loss_acc(model,target_acc=0.9, title=None):
    """
    Takes a deep learning model and plots the loss ans accuracy over epochs
    Users can supply a title if needed
    target_acc: The desired/ target acc. This parameter is needed for this function to show a horizontal bar
    """

    e=np.array(model.history.epoch)+1 # Add one to the List of epochs which is zero-indexed
    l=np.array(model.history.history['loss'])
    a=np.array(model.history.history['acc'])

    fig, ax1 = plt.subplots()

    color = 'tab:red'
    ax1.set_xlabel('Epochs',fontsize=15)
    ax1.set_ylabel('Loss', color=color,fontsize=15)
    ax1.plot(e, l, color=color,lw=2)
```

┌─────────────────────────────────────┐
│ A custom title option for │
│ proper display when you │
│ run higher order analytics │
└─────────────────────────────────────┘

┌────────────────────────────────────────────┐
│ It extracts the relevant metrics from the model │
│ object and uses them in the generic plotting method │
└────────────────────────────────────────────┘

***Figure 5-7.*** *Snapshot of the visualization function*

A typical result (loss-accuracy plot) is shown in Figure 5-8.

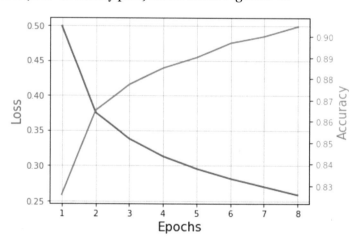

***Figure 5-8.*** *A typical loss-accuracy plot from the trained DL model*

# Final Analytics Code, Compact and Simple

Thus far you have modularized the core DL code. Now you can take advantage of all the functions and classes you defined earlier and bring them together to accomplish the higher-order optimization task. Consequently, your final code will be highly compact, but it will generate the same interesting plots of loss and accuracy over epochs for a variety of accuracy threshold values and DNN architectures (neuron counts).

This will give you the ability to use a minimal amount of code to produce visual analytics about the choice of performance metric (classification accuracy in this case) and DNN architecture. This is the first step towards building an optimized machine learning system.

Generate a few cases for investigation:

```python
from itertools import product

accuracy_desired = [0.85,0.9,0.95]
num_neurons = [16,32,64,128]
cases = list(product(accuracy_desired,num_neurons))

print("So, the cases we are considering are as follows...\n")

for i,c in enumerate(cases):
    print("Accuracy target {}, number of neurons: {}".format(c[0],c[1]))
    if (i+1)%4==0 and (i+1)!=len(cases):
        print("-"*50)
```

This code generates the cases shown in Figure 5-9.

```
So, the cases we are considering are as follows...

Accuracy target 0.85, number of neurons: 16
Accuracy target 0.85, number of neurons: 32
Accuracy target 0.85, number of neurons: 64
Accuracy target 0.85, number of neurons: 128
--------------------------------------------------
Accuracy target 0.9, number of neurons: 16
Accuracy target 0.9, number of neurons: 32
Accuracy target 0.9, number of neurons: 64
Accuracy target 0.9, number of neurons: 128
--------------------------------------------------
Accuracy target 0.95, number of neurons: 16
Accuracy target 0.95, number of neurons: 32
Accuracy target 0.95, number of neurons: 64
Accuracy target 0.95, number of neurons: 128
```

***Figure 5-9.*** *Some representative cases are generated for the optimization task*

The final analytics/optimization code is succinct and easy to follow for a high-level user who does not need to know the complexity of Keras model building or callbacks classes. This is the core principle behind OOP, the **abstraction of the layers of complexity**, which you are able to accomplish for your deep learning task.

Note how you pass on the `print_msg=False` to the class instance. While you need basic printing of the status for the initial check/debug, you should execute the analysis silently for the optimization task. If you did not have this argument in your class definition, you would not have a way to stop printing debugging messages:

```
for c in cases:
    # A mycallback class with the specific accuracy target
    callbacks = myCallback(c[0], print_msg=False)

    # Build a model with a specific number of neurons
    model = build_model(num_layers=1,architecture=[c[1]])

    # Compile and train the model with the callback class.
    # Choose suitable batch size and a max epoch limit
    model = compile_train_model(model, x_train,y_train,callbacks=callbacks,
                                batch_size=32,epochs=30)

    # A suitable title string
    title = "Loss and accuracy over the epochs for\naccuracy threshold \
    {} and number of neurons {}".format(c[0],c[1])

    # Use the plotting function, pass on the accuracy target,
    # trained model, and the custom title string
    plot_loss_acc(model,target_acc=c[0],title=title)
```

Some representative results are shown in Figure 5-10; they are automatically generated by executing the code block above. It clearly shows how with a minimal amount of high-level code you can generate visual analytics to judge the relative performance of various neural architectures for various levels of performance metrics. This enables a user, without tweaking the lower-level functions, to easily make a judgment on the choice of a model as per the desired accuracy and complexity.

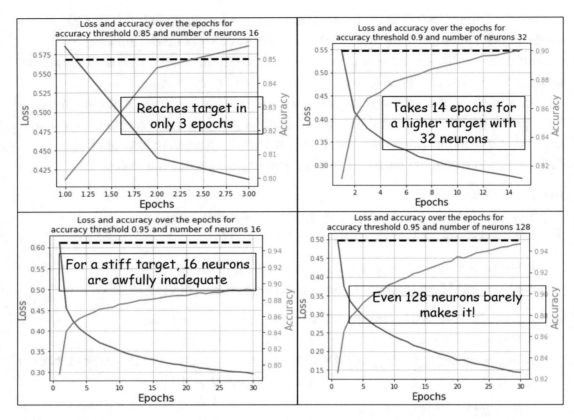

***Figure 5-10.*** *Representative results for various model architecture (neuron counts per hidden layer) and accuracy targets*

Also, note the custom titles for each plot. These titles clearly enunciate the target performance and the complexity of the neural net, thereby making the analytics easy. It was a small addition to the plotting utility function, but this shows the need for careful planning while creating such functions. If you had not planned for such an argument to the function, it would not have been possible to generate a custom title for each plot. **This careful planning of the API (application program interface) is part and parcel of good OOP**.

# Turn the Scripts into a Utility Module

So far, you may be working with a Jupyter notebook, but you may want to turn this exercise into a neat Python module that you can import from any time you want. Just like you write `from matplotlib import pyplot`, you can import these utility functions (Keras model build, train, and plotting) anywhere. The idea is shown in Figure 5-11.

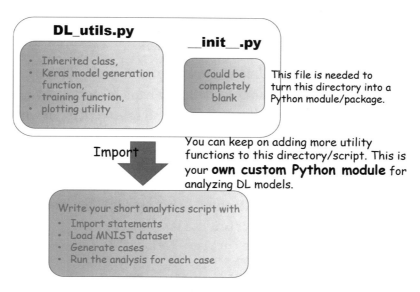

*Figure 5-11. Building a deep learning utility module (for your own use)*

## Summary of Good Practices

You just learned some good practices, borrowed from OOP, to apply to a DL analysis task. Almost all of them may seem trivial to seasoned software developers. However, this chapter is designed for budding data scientists who may not have that structured programming background but need to understand the importance of imbuing these good practices in their ML workflow.

At the risk of repeating myself, let me summarize the good practices here:

> Whenever you get a chance, turn repetitive code blocks into **utility functions.**

> Think very carefully about the **API of the function** (i.e., the minimal set of arguments required and how they will serve a purpose for a higher-level programming task).

> Don't forget to write a **docstring** for a function, even if it is a one-liner description.

> If you start accumulating many utility functions related to the same object, consider turning that object to a **class** and the utility functions as **methods.**

> **Extend class functionality** whenever you get a chance to accomplish complex analysis using inheritance.

> Don't stop at Jupyter notebooks. Turn them into executable scripts and put them in a small **module**. Build the habit of modularizing your work so that it can be easily **reused and extended** by anyone, anywhere.

In the next chapter, you will try your hand at building your own ML estimator class based on these principles. For a taste of DL utility functions and a neural net trainer class, please read "Deep learning with Python" at `https://github.com/tirthajyoti/Deep-learning-with-Python/tree/master/utils`.

# Streamline Image Classification Task Flow

Image classification is one of the most common tasks in a data science workflow involving deep learning tools. Streamlining or automating such a task is, therefore, a prime example of the automation and modularization that I have been preaching thus far.

For this specific task, a data scientist may desire a single function to automatically pull images from a specified directory on the disk (or from a network address) and give back a fully trained neural net model, ready to be used for prediction. Therefore, in this section, you will explore how to use a couple of utility methods from the Keras (TensorFlow) API to streamline the training of such models (specifically for a classification task) with built-in data preprocessing.

Put simply, you want to

- Grab some data.

- Put it inside a directory/folder arranged by classes.

- Train a neural net model with minimum code/fuss.

In the end, you aim to write a **single utility function** that can accept just the name/ address of the folder where the training images are stored and give back a fully trained CNN model. The idea is visually illustrated in Figure 5-12.

*Figure 5-12.* *Streamlining (and simplifying) the image classification task*

# The Dataset

Let's use a dataset consisting of 4000+ images of flowers for this demo. The dataset can be downloaded from the Kaggle website here: . The data collection is based on Flickr, Google, and Yandex images. The pictures are divided into five classes:

- Daisy

- Tulip

- Rose

- Sunflower

- Dandelion

For each class, there are about 800 photos. The photos are not particularly high resolution (about 320 x 240 pixels each). They are not reduced to a single size since they have different proportions. However, they come organized neatly in five directories named with the corresponding class labels. You can take advantage of this organization and apply the Keras methods to streamline the training of your convolutional network.

The full Jupyter notebook is in the GitHub repository. I will use selected snapshots of the code in this section to show the important parts for illustration.

**Should you use a GPU?**    It is recommended to run this script on a GPU. You will build a convolutional neural net (CNN) with five convolutional layers; consequently, the training process with thousands of images can be computationally intensive and slow if you are not using some sort of GPU. For the Flowers dataset, a single epoch took ~1 minute on my laptop with a NVidia GTX 1060 Ti GPU (6GB Video RAM), Core i-7 8770 CPU, and 16GB DDR4 RAM.

For illustration, Figure 5-13 shows how they are stored on a local hard disk. Some sample images are in Figure 5-14.

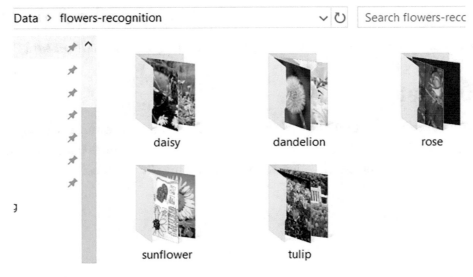

***Figure 5-13.*** *Stored Flowers image data*

Daisy flower images

Rose flower images

***Figure 5-14.***  *Sample flower images. Note the difference is shape and resolution*

# Building the Data Generator Object

This is where the actual magic happens. The official description of the ImageDataGenerator class says "*Generate batches of tensor image data with real-time data augmentation. The data will be looped over (in batches).*"

Basically, it can be used to augment image data with a lot of built-in preprocessing such as scaling, shifting, rotation, noise, whitening, etc. Right now, you'll just use the rescale attribute to scale the image tensor values between 0 and 1. Here is a useful article on this aspect of the class: "How to increase your small image dataset using Keras ImageDataGenerator"(https://medium.com/@arindambaidya168/https-medium-com-arindambaidya168-using-keras-imagedatagenerator-b94a87cdefad).

But the real utility of this class for the current demonstration is the super useful method named flow_from_directory, which can pull image files one after another from the specified directory. Note that this directory must be the top-level directory where all the subdirectories of individual classes can be stored separately. The flow_from_directory method automatically scans through the subdirectories and sources the images along with their appropriate labels.

You can specify the class names (as you did here with the classes argument) but this is optional. However, you will later see how this can be useful for selective training from a large trove of data.

Another useful argument is the target_size, which lets you resize the source images to a uniform size of 200 x 200, no matter the original size of the image. This is some cool image-processing right there with a simple function argument.

You can also specify the batch size. If you leave batch_size unspecified, by default, it will be set to 32. Choose the class_mode as categorical since you are doing a multi-class classification here. Here is the code snippet:

```
batch_size = 128

from tf.keras.preprocessing.image import ImageDataGenerator

# All images will be rescaled by 1./255
train_datagen = ImageDataGenerator(rescale=1/255)

# Flow training images in batches of 128
# All images will be resized to 200 x 200
train_generator = train_datagen.flow_from_directory(
        '../Data//flowers-recognition',
        target_size=(200, 200),
        batch_size=batch_size,
        classes = ['daisy','dandelion','rose','sunflower','tulip'],
        class_mode='categorical')
```

When you run this code, the Keras function scans through the top-level directory, finds all the image files, and automatically labels them with the proper class (based on the subdirectory they were in). The working of this utility is shown in Figure 5-15 with respect to the flowers' dataset.

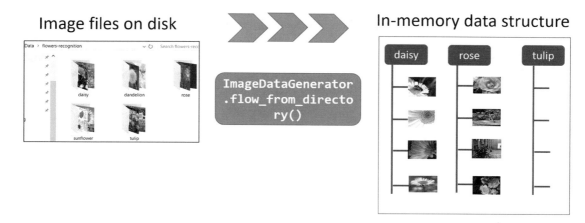

**Figure 5-15.** *The ImageDataGenerator object working on the Flower dataset*

What's more interesting is that this is also a Python generator object (`https://realpython.com/introduction-to-python-generators/`). That means it will be used to *yield data one by one* during the training. This significantly reduces the problem of dealing with a very large dataset whose contents cannot be fitted into memory at one go.

# Building the Convolutional Neural Net Model

For the sake of brevity, I will not delve deep into the code behind the CNN model. In brief, it consists of five convolutional layers/max-pooling layers and 128 neurons at the end followed by a 5-neuron output layer with a **SoftMax** activation for the multi-class classification. You use the **RMSprop optimizer** with an initial learning rate of 0.001. The model summary is shown in Figure 5-16. It has in excess of 200,000 trainable parameters.

| Layer (type) | Output Shape | Param # |
|---|---|---|
| conv2d_1 (Conv2D) | (None, 198, 198, 16) | 448 |
| max_pooling2d_1 (MaxPooling2 | (None, 99, 99, 16) | 0 |
| conv2d_2 (Conv2D) | (None, 97, 97, 32) | 4640 |
| max_pooling2d_2 (MaxPooling2 | (None, 48, 48, 32) | 0 |
| conv2d_3 (Conv2D) | (None, 46, 46, 64) | 18496 |
| max_pooling2d_3 (MaxPooling2 | (None, 23, 23, 64) | 0 |
| conv2d_4 (Conv2D) | (None, 21, 21, 64) | 36928 |
| max_pooling2d_4 (MaxPooling2 | (None, 10, 10, 64) | 0 |
| conv2d_5 (Conv2D) | (None, 8, 8, 64) | 36928 |
| max_pooling2d_5 (MaxPooling2 | (None, 4, 4, 64) | 0 |
| flatten_1 (Flatten) | (None, 1024) | 0 |
| dense_1 (Dense) | (None, 128) | 131200 |
| dense_2 (Dense) | (None, 5) | 645 |

```
Total params: 229,285
Trainable params: 229,285
Non-trainable params: 0
```

***Figure 5-16.***  *Summary of the CNN model used for flower classification*

# Training with the fit_generator Method

I discussed the cool things the train_generator object does with the flow_from_
directory method and with its arguments. Let's utilize this object in the fit_generator
method of the CNN model, defined above.

Note the steps_per_epoch argument to fit_generator. Since train_generator
is a generic Python generator, it never stops and therefore the fit_generator will not
know where a particular epoch ends and the next one starts. You have to let it know the
steps in a single epoch. This is, in most cases, the length of the total training sample
divided by the batch size. In the previous section, you found out the total sample size

as `total_sample`. Therefore, in this particular case, the `steps_per_epoch` is set to `int(total_sample/batch_size)`, which is 34, so you will see 34 steps per epoch in the training log below.

```
history = model.fit_generator(
        train_generator,
        steps_per_epoch=int(total_sample/batch_size),
        epochs=epochs,
        verbose=1)
```

When you execute, the model trains and you can check the accuracy/loss with the usual plot code (Figure 5-17).

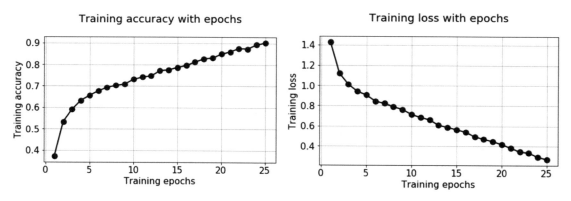

***Figure 5-17.*** *Representative loss/accuracy plots of the CNN training task*

# Encapsulate All of This in a Single Function

What have you accomplished so far?

You have been able to utilize the Keras `ImageDataGenerator` and `fit_generator` methods to pull images automatically from a single directory, label them, resize and scale them, and flow them one by one (in batches) for training a neural network.

Can you encapsulate all of this in a single function?

One of the central goals of making useful software/computing systems is abstraction (i.e., hiding the gory details of internal computation and data manipulation, and presenting a simple and intuitive working interface/API to the user). Towards that goal, let's encapsulate the process you followed above into a single function. Figure 5-18 shows the idea.

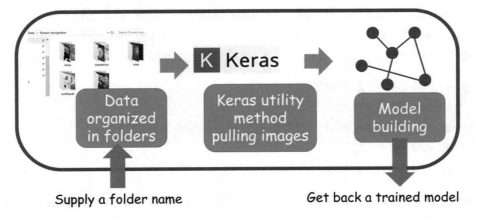

***Figure 5-18.*** *Encapsulate the core components in a single function. The user supplies a directory name and gets back a trained model*

When you are designing a high-level API, you should aim for more generalization than what is required for a particular demo. With that in mind, you can think of providing additional arguments to this function to make it applicable to other image classification cases (you will see an example soon).

Specifically, you provide the following arguments in the function:

- `train_directory`: The directory where the training images are stored in separate folders. These folders should be named as per the classes.

- `target_size`: Target size for the training images. A tuple such as (200,200).

- `classes`: A Python list with the classes for which you want the training to happen. This forces the generator to choose specific files from the `train_directory` and not look at all the data.

- `batch_size`: Batch size for training

- `num_epochs`: Number of epochs for training

- `num_classes`: Number of output classes to consider

- `verbose`: Verbosity level of the training, passed to the `fit_ generator` method

Of course, you could have provided additional arguments corresponding to the whole model architecture or optimizer settings. This chapter is not focused on such issues, so let's keep it compact. The full code is in the GitHub repo. Figure 5-19 shows the docstring portion to emphasize on the point of making it a flexible API.

```
def train_CNN(train_directory,target_size=(200,200), classes=None,
            batch_size=128,num_epochs=20,num_classes=5,verbose=0):
    """

    Trains a conv net for the flowers dataset with a 5-class classifiction output
    Also provides suitable arguments for extending it to other similar apps

    Arguments:
            train_directory: The directory where the training images are stored in separate folders.
                            These folders should be named as per the classes.
            target_size: Target size for the training images. A tuple e.g. (200,200)
            classes: A Python list with the classes
            batch_size: Batch size for training
            num_epochs: Number of epochs for training
            num_classes: Number of output classes to consider
            verbose: Verbosity level of the training, passed on to the `fit_generator` method
    Returns:
            A trained conv net model

    """
    from tensorflow.keras.preprocessing.image import ImageDataGenerator
    import tensorflow as tf
    from tensorflow.keras.optimizers import RMSprop
```

***Figure 5-19.*** *Snapshot of the single utility function that streamlines the classification task*

# Testing the Utility Function

You test the train_CNN function by simply supplying a folder/directory name and getting back a trained model that can be used for predictions. Suppose that you want to train only for daisy, rose, and tulip classes and ignore the other two flowers' data. You simply pass on a list to the classes argument. In this case, you must set the num_classes argument to 3.

You will notice how the steps per epoch are automatically reduced to 20 as the number of training samples is less than the case above. Also, note that verbose is set to 0 by default in the function above, so you need to specify explicitly verbose=1 if you want to monitor the progress of the training epoch-wise.

Basically, you can **get a fully trained CNN model with two lines of code** now!

```
# Define the folder
train_directory = "../Data//flowers-recognition/"

# Get the model
```

```
trained_model=train_CNN(train_directory=train_directory,
                        classes=['daisy','rose','tulip'],
                        num_epochs=30,
                        num_classes=3,
                        verbose=1)
```

# Does It Work (Readily) for Another Dataset?

This is an acid test for the utility of such a function: *can we just take it and apply to another dataset without much modification*? Let's find out.

A rich yet manageable image classification dataset is Caltech-101 (www.vision.caltech.edu/Image_Datasets/Caltech101/). By manageable, I mean not as large as the famous ImageNet (www.image-net.org/about.php) database, which requires massive hardware infrastructure to train (and is therefore out of bounds for testing ideas quickly on your laptop), yet diverse enough for practicing and learning the tricks of convolutional neural networks. It is an image dataset of diverse types of objects belonging to 101 categories. There are 40 to 800 images per category. Most categories have about 50 images. The size of each image is roughly 300 x 200 pixels. Some categories are shown in Figure 5-20.

COMPUTATIONAL VISION AT CALTECH

## Caltech 101

🌸 Caltech256 🌸

[Description ][ Download ][ Discussion [Other Datasets]

*Figure 5-20.* *The Caltech-101 image dataset*

---

**Who built Caltech-101?**    The Caltech-101 dataset was built by none other than famous Stanford professor Dr. Fei Fei Li (https://profiles.stanford.edu/fei-fei-li) and her colleagues (Marco Andreetto and Marc Aurelio Ranzato) at Caltech in 2003 when she was a graduate student there. We can surmise, therefore, that Caltech-101 was a direct precursor for her work on ImageNet.

---

Download the dataset and uncompress the contents in the same Data folder as before. The directory should look like Figure 5-21.

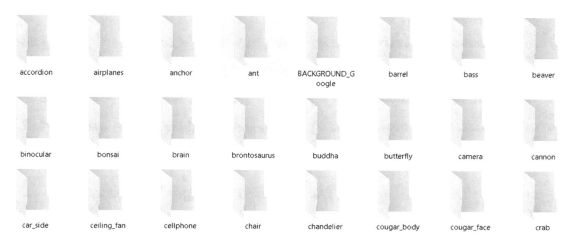

accordion    airplanes    anchor    ant    BACKGROUND_G oogle    barrel    bass    beaver

binocular    bonsai    brain    brontosaurus    buddha    butterfly    camera    cannon

car_side    ceiling_fan    cellphone    chair    chandelier    cougar_body    cougar_face    crab

***Figure 5-21.*** *Directory of the stored Caltech-101 images*

So, you have what you want: a top-level directory with subdirectories containing training images. And then, the same two lines as before:

```
# Define the folder
train_directory = "../Data/101_ObjectCategories/"

# Get the model
model_caltech101 = train_CNN(train_directory=train_directory,
                             classes=['crab','cup'],
                             batch_size=4,
                             num_epochs=25,
                             num_classes=2,
                             verbose=1)
```

All you did is to pass on the address of this directory to the function and choose the categories of the images you want to train the model for. Let's say you want to train the model for classification between *cup* and *crab*. You can just pass their names as a list to the classes argument as before.

Also, note that you may have to reduce the batch_size significantly for this dataset as the total number of training images will be much lower compared to the Flowers dataset, and if the batch_size is higher than the total sample, you will have steps_per_ epoch equal to 0 and that will create an error during training.

Voila! The function finds the relevant images (130 of them in total) and trains the model, 4 per batch, so 33 steps per epoch. The result is shown in Figure 5-22.

```
Found 130 images belonging to 2 classes.
Epoch 1/25
33/33 [==============================] - 1s 26ms/step - loss: 0.7573 - acc: 0.5769
Epoch 2/25
33/33 [==============================] - 0s 9ms/step - loss: 0.6901 - acc: 0.5538
Epoch 3/25
33/33 [==============================] - 0s 9ms/step - loss: 0.6779 - acc: 0.6231
Epoch 4/25
33/33 [==============================] - 0s 9ms/step - loss: 0.6212 - acc: 0.7538A:
Epoch 5/25
33/33 [==============================] - 0s 9ms/step - loss: 0.5458 - acc: 0.7923
Epoch 6/25
```

*Figure 5-22.* *Training happening with Caltech-101 images (two classes, cup and crab)*

You saw how easy it was to just pass on the training images' directory address to the function and train a CNN model with your chosen classes. But is the model any good? Let's find out by testing it with random pictures downloaded from the Internet. Let's say you downloaded images of crabs and cups. You do some rudimentary image processing (resizing and dimension expansion) to match the model and get the output objects, img_crab and img_cup. Then you test the model with these images.

```
model_caltech101.predict(img_crab)
>> array([[1., 0.]], dtype=float32)
```

The model predicted the class correctly for the crab test image.
And for the cup image,

```
model_caltech101.predict(img_cup)
>> array([[0., 1.]], dtype=float32)
```

You can download any random image and test the performance of your model. If not satisfied, you should train the model by changing the architecture and hyperparameters using the modularized function.

The main point, however, is that **you were able to train a CNN model with just the same two lines of code for a completely different dataset** than you started with. This is the power of modularizing code and building a generic API that works with a wide variety of data sources. This saves valuable time and makes the code reusable. The edifice of productive data science stands on these foundational elements.

# Other Extensions

So far, inside the `fit_generator` you only had a `train_generator` object for training. But what about a validation set? It follows exactly the same concept as a `train_generator`. You can randomly split from your training images a validation set and set it aside in a separate directory (the same subdirectory structures as the training directory) and you should be able to pass that on to the `fit_generator` function.

Want to directly work with a pandas DataFrame that stores your image? No problem. There is a method called `flow_from_dataframe` for the `ImageDataGenerator` class where you can pass on the names of the image files as contained in a pandas DataFrame and the training can proceed.

You are strongly encouraged to check out and extend these ideas as you see fit for your applications.

# Activation Maps in a Few Lines of Code

DL models use millions of parameters and create extremely complex and highly nonlinear internal representations of the images or datasets that are fed to these models. They are, therefore, often called the perfect black-box ML techniques (`www.wired.com/story/inside-black-box-of-neural-network/`) (Figure 5-23). We can get highly accurate predictions from them after we train them with large datasets, but we have little hope of understanding the internal features and representations (`www.technologyreview.com/s/604087/the-dark-secret-at-the-heart-of-ai/`) of the data that a model uses to classify a particular image into a category. In short, the *black-box problem of deep learning* is a powerful predictive power without an intuitive and easy-to-follow explanation.

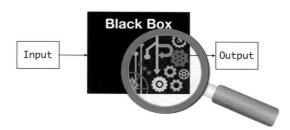

***Figure 5-23.***  *The black-box problem of deep learning (source: CMU ML blog,*
*https://blog.ml.cmu.edu/2019/05/17/explaining-a-black-box-using-deep-*
*variational-information-bottleneck-approach/).*

This does not bode well because we humans are visual creatures (`www.seyens.com/humans-are-visual-creatures/`). Millions of years of evolution have gifted us an amazingly complex pair of eyes (`www.relativelyinteresting.com/irreducible-complexity-intelligent-design-evolution-and-the-eye/`) and an even more complex visual cortex (`www.neuroscientificallychallenged.com/blog/know-your-brain-primary-visual-cortex`), and we use these organs to make sense of the world. The scientific process starts with observation, and that is almost always synonymous with vision. In business, only what we can observe and measure can we control and manage effectively. Seeing/observing is how we start to make mental models (`https://medium.com/personal-growth/mental-models-898f70438075`) of worldly phenomena, classify objects around us, separate a friend from a foe, and so on.

Activations maps have been proposed to help visualize the inner workings of complex CNN models. Let's talk about them.

# Activation Maps

Several approaches for understanding and visualizing CNNs have been developed in the literature, partly as a response to the common criticism that the learned internal features in a CNN are not interpretable. The most straightforward visualization technique is to show the activations of the network during the forward pass.

At a simple level, activation functions help decide whether a neuron should be activated. This helps determine whether the information that the neuron is receiving is relevant for the input. The activation function is a non-linear transformation that happens over an input signal, and the transformed output is sent to the next neuron.

Activation maps are just a visual representation of these activation numbers at various layers of the network as a given image progresses through as a result of various linear algebraic operations. One can deduce the workings of the network and design limitations from these maps. For ReLU activation-based networks, the activations usually start out looking relatively blobby and dense, but as the training progresses the activations usually become sparser and more localized. One design pitfall that can be easily caught with this visualization is that some activation maps may be all zero for many different inputs, which can indicate dead filters and can be a symptom of high learning rates.

However, visualizing these activation maps is a non-trivial task, even after you have trained your neural net well and are making predictions out of it. *How do you easily visualize and show these activation maps for a reasonably complicated CNN with just a few lines of code?*

# Activation Maps with a Few Lines of Code

In the previous section, I showed how to write a single compact function to obtain a fully trained CNN model by reading image files one by one automatically from the disk. Now you'll you use this function along with a nice little library called **Keract**, which makes the visualization of activation maps very easy. It is a high-level accessory library of Keras to show useful heatmaps and activation maps on various layers of a neural network.

Therefore, for this code, you need to use a couple of utility functions from the module you built earlier, `train_CNN_keras` and `preprocess_image`, to make a random RGB image compatible for generating the activation maps.

You'll use the same Caltech-101 dataset discussed in the last section. However, you are training only with five categories of images: *crab*, *cup*, *brain*, *camera*, and *chair*.

## Training

Training is done with a few lines of code only:

```
train_directory = "../Data/101_ObjectCategories/"
target_size=(512,512)
batch_size=4
classes = ['crab','cup','brain','camera','chair']
num_classes = len(classes)
num_epochs=10

model = train_CNN_keras(train_directory=train_directory,
                    num_epochs=num_epochs,
                    target_size=target_size,
                    classes = classes,
                    batch_size=batch_size,
                    num_classes=num_classes)
```

To generate the activations, you can choose a random image of a human brain from the Internet or any other source. Store the test image as the file `brain-1.jpg`.

## Activation

Another couple of lines of code generate the activation:

```
from keract import get_activations

# The image path
img_path = '../images/brain-1.jpg'
# Preprocessing the image for the model
img = preprocess_image(img_path=img_path,
                       model=model,
                       resize=target_size)
# Generate the activations
activations = get_activations(model, img)
```

You get back a dictionary with layer names as the keys and NumPy arrays as the values corresponding to the activations. Figure 5-24 shows where the activation arrays have varying lengths corresponding to the size of the filter maps of that particular convolutional layer.

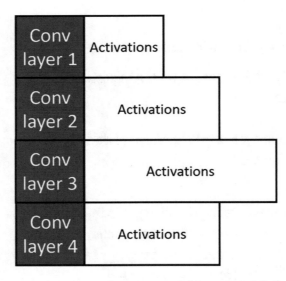

***Figure 5-24.*** *Activation map arrays are stored (the variable length corresponding to the size of the convolutional filter at that layer)*

Thereafter, two lines of code for displaying the activation maps:

```
from keract import display_activations
display_activations(activations, save=False)
```

You get to see activation maps layer by layer. Figure 5-25 shows first convolutional layer (the 16 images corresponding to the 16 filters). Your actual image may look different based on what you use as the test image, but the idea of activation layers visualization is clearly demonstrated.

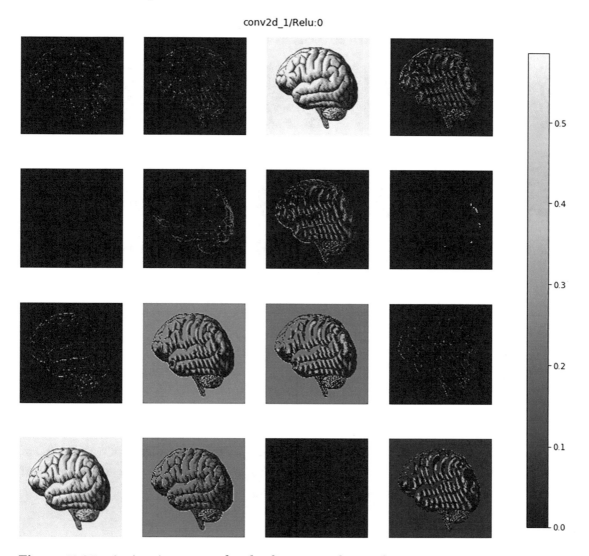

***Figure 5-25.*** *Activation maps for the first convolution layer*

Figure 5-26 shows layer number 2 (the 32 images corresponding to the 32 filters).

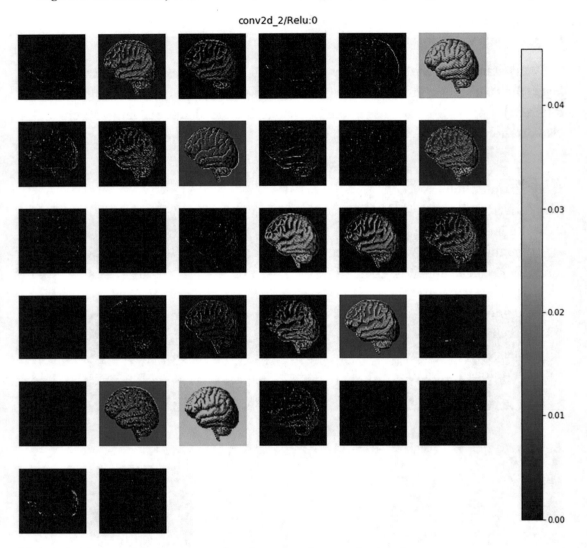

***Figure 5-26.*** *Activation maps for the second convolution layer*

For this model, there are 5 convolutional layers (followed by max pooling layers), so you get back 10 sets of images. For brevity, I won't show the rest, but you are encouraged to explore and see them by playing with the Jupyter notebook.

## Another Library for Web-Based UI

Another beautiful library for activation visualization is called **Quiver**. However, this one is built on the Python microserver framework Flask and displays the activation maps on a browser port rather than inside your Jupyter Notebook. It also needs a fully trained Keras model as input. So, you can easily use the utility function described in the previous section and try this library for interactive visualization of activation maps.

## How Is This Productive Data Science?

In this chapter, you learned how by using only a few lines of code (utilizing compact functions from a special module and a nice little accessory library to Keras) you can train a CNN, generate activation maps, and display them layer by layer—from scratch. This gives you the ability to train CNN models (simple to complex) from any image dataset (as long as you can arrange them in a simple directory format) and look inside their guts for any test image you want.

And once you build the necessary utility modules and the activation map scripts, you can reuse and apply them to a wide variety of image data. This leads to a fast and efficient exploration of a large set of images for all kinds of applications. This is why this kind of approach integrates with the story of productive and efficient data science.

# Hyperparameter Search with Scikit-learn

Keras is one of the most popular go-to Python libraries/APIs for beginners and professionals in deep learning. Although it started as a stand-alone project by François Chollet, it has been integrated natively into TensorFlow starting in version 2.0. Read more about it here (`https://keras.io/about/`):. As per its own official doc, it is "*an API designed for human beings, not machines*" as it "*follows best practices for reducing cognitive load.*"

Now, hyperparameter tuning is one of the situations where the cognitive load is sure to increase. DL models have a great many hyperparameters to begin with: learning rate, decay rate, activation function, dropout rate, momentum, batch size, and more. Optimizing a DL model for best performance and computing cost depends critically on the right choice of these hyperparameters. Therefore, data scientists spend a lot of time and effort tuning them manually or via some automated script or optimization strategy/framework.

Although there are many supporting libraries and frameworks for handling it, for simple grid searches, Keras offers a beautiful API to integrate with our favorite scikit-learn library. In this section, we will talk about it.

## Scikit-learn Enmeshes with Keras

Almost every Python machine-learning practitioner is intimately familiar with the scikit-learn library and its beautiful API with simple methods (www.tutorialspoint.com/scikit_learn/scikit_learn_estimator_api.htm) like fit, get_params, and predict. The library also offers extremely useful methods for **cross-validation**, **model selection**, **pipelining**, and **grid search** abilities. Data scientists use these tools for classical ML problems every day. But can you use the same APIs for a deep learning problem?

It turns out that Keras offer a couple of special wrapper classes, both for regression and classification problems, to utilize the full power of these APIs that are native to scikit-learn. In this section, you will work using a simple k-fold cross-validation (https://medium.com/datadriveninvestor/k-fold-cross-validation-6b8518070833) and exhaustive grid search with a Keras classifier (www.tensorflow.org/api_docs/python/tf/keras/wrappers/scikit_learn/KerasClassifier) model. It utilizes an implementation of the scikit-learn classifier API for Keras.

## Data and (Preliminary) Keras Model

First, you create a simple function to synthesize and compile a Keras model with some tunable arguments built in:

```
from tf.keras.models import Sequential
from tf.keras.layers import Dense

def create_model():
    # create model
    model = Sequential()
    model.add(Dense(30, input_dim=8, activation='relu'))
    model.add(Dense(15, activation='relu'))
    model.add(Dense(1, activation='sigmoid'))
    # Compile model
    model.compile(loss='binary_crossentropy',
```

```
              optimizer='adam',
              metrics=['accuracy'])
    return model
```

You tackle a simple binary classification task using the popular Pima Indians Diabetes dataset (`www.kaggle.com/uciml/pima-indians-diabetes-database`). This dataset is originally from the National Institute of Diabetes and Digestive and Kidney Diseases (`www.niddk.nih.gov/`). The objective of the dataset is to diagnostically predict whether or not a patient has diabetes, based on certain diagnostic measurements included in the dataset.

You do some minimal data preprocessing including scaling the feature data with `MinMaxScaler` from scikit-learn. You can pass this `X_scaled` vector to the special wrapper class you will create.

## The KerasClassifier Class

This is the special wrapper class from Keras that enmeshes the scikit-learn classifier API with Keras parametric models. You can pass on various model parameters corresponding to the `create_model` function, and other hyperparameters like epochs and batch size to this class. Here is the code:

```
from tf.keras.wrappers.scikit_learn import KerasClassifier

model = KerasClassifier(build_fn=create_model,
                        epochs=10,
                        batch_size=32,
                        verbose=0)
```

Note how you pass on your model creation function as the `build_fn` argument. This is an example of using a function as a first-class object in Python (`https://dbader.org/blog/python-first-class-functions`) where you can pass on functions as regular parameters to other classes or functions.

For now, you have fixed the batch size and the number of epochs you want to run your model for because you just want to run cross-validation on this model. Later, you will treat them as hyperparameters and do a full grid search over them to find the best combination.

# Cross-Validation with the Scikit-learn API

Here is the code to build a 10-fold cross-validation sweep with the Keras model. First, you must import the estimators from the `model_selection` module of scikit-learn. Thereafter, you can simply run the model with this code, where you pass on the `KerasClassifier` object you built earlier along with the feature and target vectors. The important parameter here is the `cv` where you pass the `kfold` object. This tells the `cross_val_score` estimator to run the Keras model with the data provided, in a 10-fold stratified cross-validation setting.

```
from sklearn.model_selection import StratifiedKFold
from sklearn.model_selection import cross_val_score

num_folds = 10
kfold = StratifiedKFold(n_splits=num_folds,
                        shuffle=True)
cv_results = cross_val_score(model,
                             X_scaled, Y,
                             cv=kfold,
                             verbose=2)
```

The output variable `cv_results` is a NumPy array consisting of all of the accuracy scores. Accuracy is the metric you coded in your model compiling process. Obviously, you could have chosen any other classification metric like precision or recall, and in that case, that metric would have been calculated and stored in the `cv_results` array.

You can easily calculate the average and standard deviation of the 10-fold CV run to estimate the stability of the model predictions. This is one of the primary utilities of a cross-validation run and now you can gauge the stability of any Keras model using this approach.

# Grid Search with a Updated Model

In this example, you will search over the following hyperparameters:

- Activation function

- Optimizer type

- Initialization method

- Batch size

- Number of epochs

However, for this to work, you must integrate the first three of these parameters into your model definition code:

```
def create_model_grid(activation = 'relu',
                      optimizer='rmsprop',
                      init='glorot_uniform'):
    # create model
    model = Sequential()

    if activation=='relu':
        model.add(Dense(12, input_dim=8,
                        kernel_initializer=init, activation='relu'))
        model.add(Dense(8, kernel_initializer=init, activation='relu'))
    if activation=='tanh':
        model.add(Dense(12, input_dim=8,
                        kernel_initializer=init, activation='tanh'))
        model.add(Dense(8, kernel_initializer=init, activation='tanh'))
    if activation=='sigmoid':
        model.add(Dense(12, input_dim=8,
                        kernel_initializer=init, activation='sigmoid'))
        model.add(Dense(8, kernel_initializer=init, activation='sigmoid'))
    model.add(Dense(1, kernel_initializer=init, activation='sigmoid'))

    # Compile model
    model.compile(loss='binary_crossentropy',
                  optimizer=optimizer,
                  metrics=['accuracy'])
    return model
```

Then, you create the same KerasClassifier object as before but call it model_grid:

```
model_grid = KerasClassifier(build_fn=create_model_grid, verbose=0)
```

Make the exhaustive hyperparameter search space size as **3 × 3 × 3 × 3 × 3 = 243**. Note that the actual number of Keras runs will also depend on the number of cross-validation you choose, as cross-validation will be used for each of these combinations. In total, there will be 729 fittings of the model, 3 cross-validation runs for each of the 243 parametric combinations. If you don't like the full grid search, you can always try a randomized grid search.

Figure 5-27 shows the choices for this exhaustive grid search.

```
activations = ['tanh','relu','sigmoid']
optimizers = ['rmsprop', 'adam','sgd']
initializers = ['glorot_uniform', 'normal', 'uniform']
epochs = [5,10,25]
batches = [8,16,64]
```

***Figure 5-27.*** *Exhaustive grid search options*

You must create a dictionary of search parameters and pass it on to the scikit-learn GridSearchCV estimator:

```
from sklearn.model_selection import GridSearchCV

param_grid = dict(activation =  activations,
                  optimizer = optimizers,
                  epochs = epochs,
                  batch_size = batches,
                  init = initializers)

grid = GridSearchCV(estimator = model_grid,
                    param_grid = param_grid,
                    cv = 3,
                    verbose = 2,)
```

You set the cv = 3 to reduce the time for the run. By default, it will be set to 5 by scikit-learn if you leave out that argument.

**What verbosity levels to choose?**    It is advisable to set the verbosity of
`GridSearchCV` to 2 to keep visual track of what's going on. Remember to keep
`verbose=0` for the main `KerasClassifier` class, though, as you probably don't
want to display all the gory details of training individual epochs.

After this, just fit with the scaled feature data and labels!

```
grid_result = grid.fit(X_scaled, Y)
```

How does the result look? It is just as expected from a standard scikit-learn estimator,
with all the parameters internally stored for exploration (Figure 5-28).

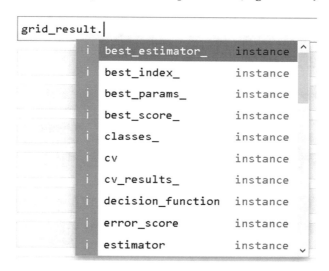

***Figure 5-28.*** *Fitted grid search estimator with all the parameters*

You can find out the best combination with the `best_score_` and `best_params_`
attributes from the fitted estimator. A snapshot is shown in Figure 5-29.

```
print("Best accuracy: {}\nBest combination: {}".format(grid_result.best_score_,
                          grid_result.best_params_))

Best accuracy: 0.75390625
Best combination: {'activation': 'tanh', 'batch_size': 8, 'epochs': 25, 'init': 'glor
ot_uniform', 'optimizer': 'rmsprop'}
```

***Figure 5-29.*** *Snapshot of best hyperparameter choice printed*

You did the initial 10-fold cross-validation using ReLU activation and Adam optimizer and got an average accuracy of 0.691. After doing an exhaustive grid search, you discover that a tanh activation and a rmsprop optimizer could have been better choices for this problem.

It is also quite straightforward to create a pandas DataFrame from the grid search results and analyze them further. You include the mean and standard dev scores in this table.

```
import pandas as pd

params = grid_result.cv_results_['params']
d = pd.DataFrame(params)
d['Mean'] = grid_result.cv_results_['mean_test_score']
d['Std. Dev'] = grid_result.cv_results_['std_test_score']
```

The DataFrame looks like Figure 5-30.

| | activation | batch_size | epochs | init | optimizer | Mean | Std. Dev |
|---|---|---|---|---|---|---|---|
| 0 | tanh | 8 | 5 | glorot_uniform | rmsprop | 0.652344 | 0.022999 |
| 1 | tanh | 8 | 5 | glorot_uniform | adam | 0.648438 | 0.011500 |
| 2 | tanh | 8 | 5 | glorot_uniform | sgd | 0.651042 | 0.024774 |
| 3 | tanh | 8 | 5 | normal | rmsprop | 0.651042 | 0.024774 |
| 4 | tanh | 8 | 5 | normal | adam | 0.651042 | 0.024774 |
| ... | ... | ... | ... | ... | ... | ... | ... |
| 238 | sigmoid | 64 | 25 | normal | adam | 0.651042 | 0.024774 |
| 239 | sigmoid | 64 | 25 | normal | sgd | 0.651042 | 0.024774 |
| 240 | sigmoid | 64 | 25 | uniform | rmsprop | 0.651042 | 0.024774 |
| 241 | sigmoid | 64 | 25 | uniform | adam | 0.651042 | 0.024774 |
| 242 | sigmoid | 64 | 25 | uniform | sgd | 0.651042 | 0.024774 |

243 rows × 7 columns

***Figure 5-30.*** *DataFrame created from the grid search parameters*

You can create targeted visualizations from this dataset to examine which hyperparameters improve the performance and reduce the variation in the accuracy metric. Figure 5-31 shows some examples.

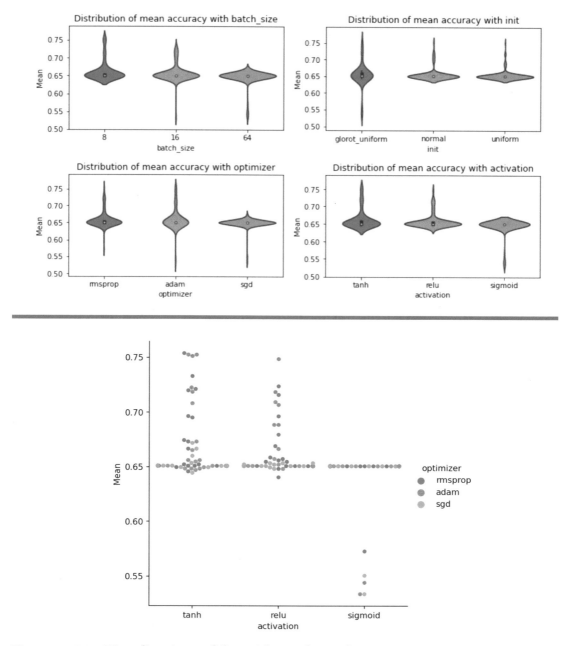

***Figure 5-31.*** *Visualizations of the grid search results*

# Summary

This chapter covered a variety of topics centered on the idea of making commonly used deep learning code and tasks more productive and efficient. I carried over the idea of modularizing the code from the previous chapter and showed hands-on examples with useful model building and plot functions with the Keras framework. A powerful construct called the Keras callback was also discussed in this context.

Next, I discussed the idea of streamlining one of the most common DL tasks that a data scientist can encounter: image classification. The goal was to arrive at a single utility function that presents a very simple API to the user. You just pass on a folder name to this function, and it will return a fully trained conv net model by processing all the images in that folder. Not only did you build this function step by step, but you also demonstrated the utility of such an API by applying it to a completely different dataset.

In the next section, you further utilized this function and integrated it with a special library that can extract and visualize activation maps for the various convolution layers of the DL model. Basically, you demonstrated how to visualize the inner workings of a complex DL model with only a few lines of code. Together, these two sections embodied the true journey towards productive and efficient data science involving deep learning.

Finally, you explored the topic of making hyperparameter search easy and seamless. Although there are many dedicated libraries and frameworks for this task, you saw a simple and intuitive approach using the grid search tool from scikit-learn and some special wrapper classes from Keras. It also demonstrated how two of the most popular ML libraries, Keras and scikit-learn, can work together in a seamless manner.

Making deep learning code and products fast and efficient is a huge topic by itself. There are countless approaches and research directions focusing on this. This chapter only aims to induce some fundamental ideas so that you can explore them further.

# CHAPTER 6

# Build Your Own ML Estimator/Package

I start this chapter with the same assertion as in Chapter 4: *data scientists often come from a background quite removed from traditional computer science/software engineering*, such as physics, biology, statistics, economics, and electrical engineering. Figure Figure 6-1 confirms this.

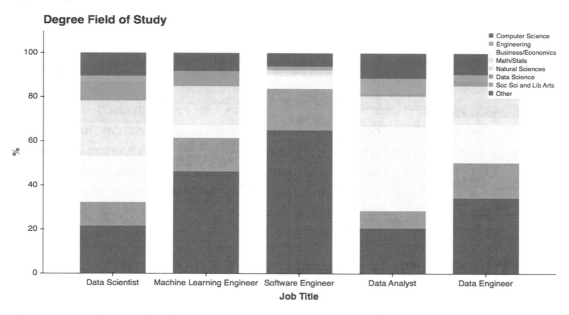

***Figure 6-1.*** *Data scientists come from a wide variety of fields and professional experience. Source: "Where do Data Scientists Come From?" (https://medium.com/indeed-engineering/where-do-data-scientists-come-from-fc526023ace)*

But ultimately data scientists are expected to pick up enough programming/software engineering skills to be truly impactful for their organization and business. Even if data scientists are not writing the final production code for the ML platform/service, they are

T. Sarkar, *Productive and Efficient Data Science with Python*, https://doi.org/10.1007/978-1-4842-8121-5_6

expected to work in a highly integrated fashion with seasoned software development teams. This is essential to ensure a smooth delivery experience, flawless execution of the ML product, and, of course, achieve the desired business outcome.

This means that data scientists must learn how to write machine learning code (whether it is the final model or just some experimental prototype) efficiently.

> There must be proper **organization** and **modularization** in their code so that it can interface well with the standard software engineering tools and techniques.

> There must be some amount of **automation** in their code to reduce the time to explore, evaluate, and experiment with data and models.

> Data scientists must be comfortable with writing **functional and module tests**, **incorporating object-oriented principles**, and so on.

> Data scientists must also develop the habit of producing good **documentation** for their code so that it can be reusable and readable by other developers.

In Chapters 4 and 5, I touched upon some of these concepts, especially modularization and OOP principles. This chapter will take you through the journey of developing a lightweight but useful ML package of your own, so that you can experience many aspects of producing a complete piece of software for data science. In my experience, this exercise of writing (and publishing) an ML package teaches several valuable lessons to any upcoming data scientist.

# Why Develop Your Own ML Package?

There is a very succinct answer to the question posed above: *so that others (anywhere in the world) can use your work and benefit from it.*

Imagine that feeling. Your code is not restricted to a standalone Jupyter notebook. It is properly structured and modularized first, so that you can call the useful methods just like you do with your favorite Python libraries (e.g., NumPy and pandas). Going beyond that, you are packaging the code in the form of a downloadable Python library, so that anybody in the world can install it with a single `pip` command and start getting a benefit from your work. The idea is simply illustrated in Figure 6-2.

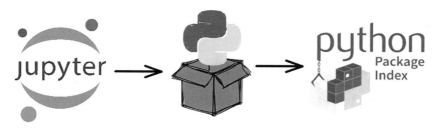

***Figure 6-2.*** *From a Jupyter notebook to a PyPi installer package*

Some of the steps (and associated learnings) of going through this process are as follows:

**Code organizational thinking**: Publishing an open-source Python package forces a data scientist to plan and organize their code and modules meticulously.

**Writing docstrings**: Docstrings are an essential good practice in a high-quality open-source package where collaboration is highly welcome. The data scientist will learn the value of the same in this process. Good docstrings may even lead to high-quality documentation for the package (generally maintained in websites such as `readthedoc.io`).

**Unit and functional tests**: The importance of tests for good software development cannot be overemphasized. For data science, testing brings its own challenges. Package development will usually include writing a basic suite of test cases. This will add a fundamentally valuable skill to the data scientist's repertoire.

**GitHub commit and actions**: Although not strictly necessary for publishing an open-source package, it is highly advisable to set up a GitHub repository and GitHub actions (commands that trigger based on a code change or commit, for example) for maintaining and updating the package (e.g., releasing new version or bug fix) in the long run.

Discussing all of these aspects is beyond the scope of this book. Therefore, I will mainly focus on developing the code structure from the ground up. However, there are plenty of good tutorials on how to write good docstrings or set up GitHub actions for open-source packages that you are encouraged to explore.

# A Data Scientist's Example

There are a few tutorials and guides that deal with teaching data scientists the principles of OOP and modular coding. However, almost all of them cover standard out-of-the-box OOP examples that do not appeal to a data scientist. Let me show you what I mean.

# An Arithmetic Example

If you are asked to write a program to implement addition, subtraction, multiplication, and division involving a couple of variables, a and b, what will you most likely do? You will most likely open up a Jupyter notebook and type the following in a cell, hit Shift-Enter, and get the result:

```
a+b
a-b
a*b
a/b
```

If you like to tidy things up by working with functions, then you may do the following as well:

```
def add(a,b):
    return a + b
def subtract(a,b):
    return a - b
...
```

But will you go as far as defining (complete with an initializer method) a `Calc` class and putting these functions inside that class as methods? These are all operations of a similar nature, and they work on similar data. Why not encapsulate them within a single higher-order object then? Why not the following code?

```
class Calc:
    def __init__(self,a,b):
        self.a = a
        self.b = b
    def add(self):
        return self.a+self.b
    def sub(self):
        return self.a-self.b
    def mult(self):
        return self.a*self.b
    def div(self):
        return self.a/self.b
```

No, most probably you won't do this. It does not make sense to do it for this problem either. But the idea is valid: if you have data and functions (methods, as they are called in the parlance of OOP) that can be combined logically, then they should be encapsulated in a class.

But it looks like too much work just to get quick answers to some simple numerical computations. So, what's the point? Data scientists are often valued on whether they can get the right answer to the data problem, not on what elaborate programming constructs they use in their code.

These kinds of examples are used to teach data scientists about OOP principles. They are perfectly valid examples and cover all the necessary know-how of writing good object-oriented Python code. However, the spark is missing as the final product can be rather pedantic, like an arithmetic calculator.

# Data Scientists Use OOP All the Time

If data scientists are not coding this way, is it not the case that they really don't need to use these elaborate programming constructs?

Wrong.

Without consciously being aware, data scientists make heavy use of the benefits of the OOP paradigm. All the time.

Do you remember `plt.plot` after `import matplotlib.pyplot as plt`? Those `.` **symbols**? You have a dash of object-oriented programming right there.

Or do you remember being happy to learn the cool trick in the Jupyter notebook of hitting Tab after putting a DOT (.), thereby showing all the functions that can be associated with an object (Figure 6-3)?

**Figure 6-3.** *The OOP paradigm makes it easy to access methods and parameters*

This example shows adherence to a logical consistency. Without following an OOP paradigm, we might have to name functions like `linear_model_linear_regression_fit`, `linear_model_linear_regression_predict`, and so on. They wouldn't be grouped under a common logical unit.

Why? Because they are different functions and work on a different set of data. While the `fit` function expects both training features and targets, `predict` needs only a test data set. The `fit` function is not expected to return anything, while `predict` is expected to return a set of predictions.

So, why are they visible under the same drop-down? In spite of being different, they have the commonality that they can both be imagined to be essential parts of the overall linear regression process. We expect a linear regression to fit some training data and then be able to predict for future unseen data. We also expect the linear regression model to provide some indication about how good the fit was, generally in the form of a single numeric quantity or score called the coefficient of regression or $R^2$. As expected, we see a function score, which returns exactly that $R^2$ number, also hanging around `fit` and `predict`. It is neat and clean. *Data, functions, and parameters are cohabitating inside a single logical unit* (Figure 6-4).

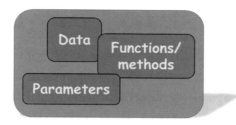

***Figure 6-4.*** *Data, functions, and parameters cohabitating inside a single logical unit*

## How Was It Made?

It was possible because somebody (the developers at the scikit-learn project) thought about the linear regression as a high-level process and decided what essential actions it should serve and what critical parameters it should inform its users about. Somebody made a high-level class called LinearRegression under which all those apparently disparate functions can be grouped together for easy bookkeeping and enhanced usability.

As data scientists, once you import this class from the library, you just have to create an instance of the class (called lm). That's it. All the functions, grouped under the class, became accessible to you through that newly defined instance. If you are not satisfied with some of the internal implementation of the functions, you can work on them and reattach them to the main class after modification. Only the code of the internal function changes, nothing else. The idea is visually illustrated in Figure 6-5.

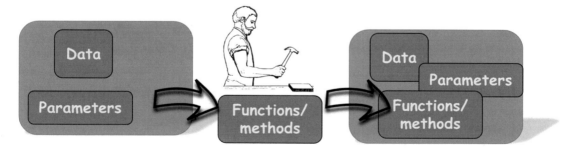

***Figure 6-5.*** *Attaching functions and methods to the class as needed*

In the following sections, you will examine the step-by-step process and thinking that goes into making such a useful ML estimator from scratch. You will start with basic data and parameters, attach methods as needed, and group them under suitable logical units.

# Linear Regression Estimator—with a Twist

A traditional introduction to OOP will have plenty of examples using classes such as animals, sports, and geometric shapes. But for data scientists, why not illustrate the concepts using the example of an object they use every day in their code: an ML estimator? It's just like the LinearRegression object from the scikit-learn library, shown in the picture above.

Next, you will go through the steps of building a simple linear regression (single or multivariate) estimator class following the OOP paradigm. Yes, it is the good ol' linear regression class. It has the usual fit and predict methods as in the LinearRegression class from scikit-learn. But it has a twist: *it provides many more functionalities*. Figure 6-6 shows a sneak peek.

***Figure 6-6.*** *A linear regression estimator with extra statistical functions and plot utilities*

As shown above, this estimator is richer than the scikit-learn estimator in the sense that it has, in addition to standard fit, predict, and $R^2$ score functions, a host of other utilities that are essential for a linear regression modeling task, especially for data scientists and statistical modeling folks who not only want to predict but also would like to

- Measure the goodness of the fit

- Verify the assumptions of the linear regression

- Check for multicollinearity in the data

- Detect outliers

Let's see how to start building this.

# How Do You Start Building This?

In this section, I will show how to start with the ML estimator and add essential methods. The next sections will cover adding more utility functions, grouping them, and so on. I want to note, however, that much of the actual code will be skipped for brevity purposes and only the essential concepts will be shown with the code snippets. For the complete code, you can check the Jupyter notebook or the Python script files provided with the book.

## Base Class Definition

Let's start with a simple code snippet to define the base class: `MyLinearRegression`. Here, `self` denotes the object itself and `__init__` is a special function that is invoked when an instance of the class is created somewhere in the code. As the name suggests, `__init__` can be used to initialize the class with necessary parameters (if any). Let's also add a simple descriptor with the `__repr__` method.

```
import numpy as np
class MyLinearRegression:

    def __init__(self, fit_intercept=True):
        self.coef_ = None
        self.intercept_ = None
        self._fit_intercept = fit_intercept

    def __repr__(self, fit_intercept=True):
        return "I am a Linear Regression model!"
```
These methods with double underscores (`__init__` and `__repr__`) serve special purpose inside a Python class and are called *dunder methods*.

**What are Dunder methods?**   They are magic methods inside a Python class definition that can help override functionality for built-in functions for custom classes. They are called so because of the presence of the double underscores in their names. Some common ones are

__init__ : Initializes the class with default parameters and states

__repr__ : A generic description of the class

__str__ : A string description of some property of the class when one prints it with the print function.

__len__ : Returns the length of the class/object when it makes sense (e.g., if the class represents some kind of collection or array)

Here is a nice article about them: "Dunder/Magic Methods in Python" (www.section.io/engineering-education/dunder-methods-python/).

Basically, you can now instantiate an object and print it:

```
mlr = MyLinearRegression()
print(mlr)
>> I am a Linear Regression model!
```

# Adding Useful Methods

So far, you have a correct but useless class definition because it does not do any machine learning. In this section, you start adding some useful methods and see how to test them.

## The Fitting Method

First, let's add the most useful method for an ML estimator: the fit method that executes the training/fitting with the given data. Here is the code. Note that this function definition will go inside the base class.

```
def fit(self, X, y):
    """
    Fit model coefficients.

    Arguments:
    X: 1D or 2D numpy array
    y: 1D numpy array
```

```
"""
# Data type check and conversion
if type(X) is not np.ndarray:
    try:
        X = np.array(X)
    except:
        print("Could not convert features to Numpy array")
        return None
if type(y) is not np.ndarray:
    try:
        y = np.array(y)
    except:
        print("Could not convert labels to Numpy array")
        return None
# check if X is 1D or 2D array
if len(X.shape) == 1:
    X = X.reshape(-1,1)

# add bias if fit_intercept is True
if self._fit_intercept:
    X_biased = np.c_[np.ones(X.shape[0]), X]
else:
    X_biased = X

# closed form solution
xTx = np.dot(X_biased.T, X_biased)
inverse_xTx = np.linalg.inv(xTx)
xTy = np.dot(X_biased.T, y)
coef = np.dot(inverse_xTx, xTy)

# set attributes
if self._fit_intercept:
    self.intercept_ = coef[0]
    self.coef_ = coef[1:]
else:
    self.intercept_ = 0
    self.coef_ = coef
```

The code is long but self-explanatory with the help of docstrings and carefully added comments. You use the NumPy matrix inversion (np.linalg.inv) to solve the linear regression problem from an ordinary least-square (https://en.wikipedia.org/wiki/Ordinary_least_squares) point of view and obtain the best-fitting coefficients. Also, note the rudimentary checks (if type(X) is not np.ndarray) and transformation of the data shape (X = X.reshape(-1,1)) that you put in the beginning to make sure that the linear algebra calculations are done without any error.

## Testing the Method

Let's test the method by generating some random data:

```
X = 10*np.random.random(size=(20,2))
y = 3.5*X.T[0]-1.2*X.T[1]+np.random.randn(20)
```

So, you have a linear relationship between the 2D vector X and the 1D vector y. You can visualize the linear relationship in Figure 6-7 (note the intentional noise added to the data)

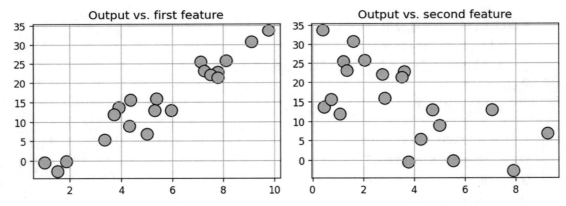

***Figure 6-7.*** *Plot of the test (randomly generated) data*

Create a fresh instance:

```
mlr = MyLinearRegression()
```

You can try to print the coefficients (`mlr.coef_`) but with a check on the `mlr.fitted_` state. If not fitted, you print that message.

```
if mlr.fitted_:
    print("Regression coefficients:", mlr.coef_)
else:
    print("Not fitted yet")
```

```
>> Not fitted yet
```

Then you fit, as follows:

```
mlr.fit(X,y)
```

Now, for the same code for printing the coefficients, you get the expected results:

```
if mlr.fitted_:
    print("Regression coefficients:", mlr.coef_)
else:
    print("Not fitted yet")
```

```
>> Regression coefficients: [ 3.40807972 -1.23152211]
```

So, the actual coefficients are 3.5 and -1.2, but due to the random noise added, you get the best fit as approximately 3.4 and -1.23. You can also get the intercept as

```
print("The intercept term is given by: ", mlr.intercept_)
```

```
>> The intercept term is given by:  0.7673816772685598
```

Note that the **estimated coefficients and intercept will change every time you run** this code because of the random noise addition to the data generation process.

# Prediction Method

Now, let's add the predict method to the class:

```
def predict(self, X):
    """

    Output model prediction.

    Arguments:
    X: 1D or 2D numpy array
    """
    # check if X is 1D or 2D array
    if len(X.shape) == 1:
        X = X.reshape(-1,1)
    # Calculates only if already fitted
    if self.fitted_:
        self.predicted_ = self.intercept_ + np.dot(X, self.coef_)
    else:
        print("Not fitted yet")
        return None

    return self.predicted_
```

# Testing Prediction

You use the old (training) data for fitting and a set of new points for prediction. Here is sample code for testing:

```
num_new_samples = 10

X_new = 10*np.random.random(size=(num_new_samples,2))
y_new = 3.5*X_new.T[0]-1.2*X_new.T[1]+np.random.randn(num_new_samples)

mlr = MyLinearRegression()
mlr.fit(X,y)
y_pred=mlr.predict(X_new)
```

When you plot the predicted vs. true values, you get the result shown in Figure 6-8.

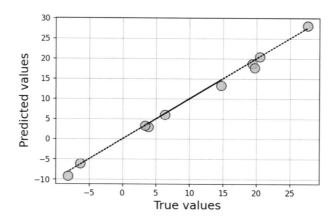

**Figure 6-8.** *Predicted vs. true values of the y-vector*

Now that you have sorted out the quintessential methods, let's discuss adding some utility methods like visualization and statistical analysis.

# Adding Utility Methods

At this point, you can start expanding your regression class and add stuff that is not even present in the standard scikit-learn class! For example, you always want to see how the fitted values compare to the ground truth. This is what was plotted above. But instead of having that code lying around in the Jupyter notebook, you can create a function for that and add it to the class.

## Method for Plotting True vs. Predicted Values

Let's call it `plot_fitted`. Note that a method is like a normal function. It can take additional arguments. Here, you have an argument `reference_line` (default set to `False`) that draws a 45-degree reference line on the fitted vs. true plot. Also, note the docstring description.

```
def plot_fitted(self,reference_line=False):
    """

    Plots fitted values against the
    true output values from the data

    Arguments:
    reference_line: A Boolean switch to
```

```
    draw a 45-degree reference line on the plot
    """
    if self.fitted_:
        y_pred = np.dot(X,self.coef_) + self.intercept_
        plt.title("True vs. fitted values",fontsize=14)
        plt.scatter(y,y_pred,
                        s=150,alpha=0.75,
                        color='orange',
                        edgecolor='k')
        if reference_line:
            plt.plot(y,y,c='k',linestyle='dotted')
        plt.xlabel("True values")
        plt.ylabel("Fitted values")
        plt.grid(True)
        plt.show()
    else:
        print("Not fitted yet")
        return None
```

Note that you have a prediction going on inside the plotting code (y_pred= np.dot(X,self.coef)+self.intercept) and then you use that vector for plotting. As always, you execute the plotting code only after ensuring that some data has been fitted (if self.fitted_).

Here is code to demonstrate the utility of this method. With just three lines of code, you create a brand new estimator, fit the data, and plot the ground truth vs. predicted values!

```
# A fresh estimator
mlr = MyLinearRegression()
# Fitting with the data
mlr.fit(X,y)
# Call the 'plot_fitted' method
mlr.plot_fitted()
```

Figure 6-9 shows the result. It's similar to Figure 6-8 but using a built-in method instead of standalone code.

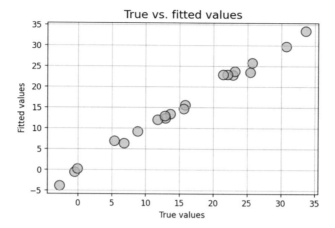

**Figure 6-9.** *Predicted vs. true values using the built-in plotting utility*

Here are many more useful plotting utilities to add:

- **Pairplots** (plots the pairwise relation between all features and outputs, much like the pairs function in the R language)

- **Fitted vs. residual plot** (this falls under diagnostic plots for the linear regression i.e., to check the validity of the fundamental assumptions of regression (https://towardsdatascience.com/how-do-you-check-the-quality-of-your-regression-model-in-python-fa61759ff685)

- **Histogram** and the **quantile-quantile (Q-Q)** plot of the residuals (this checks for the assumption of normality of the error distribution)

# All Kinds of Error Metrics

You can add a bunch of error metrics to the base class like this:

```
def sse(self):
        '''returns sum of squared errors (model vs actual)'''
        squared_errors = (self.resid_) ** 2
        self.sq_error_ = np.sum(squared_errors)
        return self.sq_error_

def sst(self):
    '''returns total sum of squared errors (actual vs. avg(actual))'''
```

```
    avg_y = np.mean(self.target_)
    squared_errors = (self.target_ - avg_y) ** 2
    self.sst_ = np.sum(squared_errors)
    return self.sst_

def r_squared(self):
    '''returns calculated value of r^2'''
    self.r_sq_ = 1 - self.sse()/self.sst()
    return self.r_sq_

# More metrics here

def pretty_print_stats(self):
    '''returns report of statistics for a given model object'''
    items = ( ('sse:', self.sse()), ('sst:', self.sst()),
              ('mse:', self.mse()), ('r^2:', self.r_squared()),
              ('adj_r^2:', self.adj_r_squared()))
    for item in items:
        print('{0:8} {1:.4f}'.format(item[0], item[1]))
```

For this to work, you must calculate one essential property called *residuals* (self.resid_) when fitting the data. So, add that code to the fit method, of course:

```
# features and data
self.features_ = X
self.target_   = y
< ... >
# Predicted/fitted y
self.predicted_ = np.dot(X,self.coef_) + self.intercept_
# Residuals
self.resid_ = self.target_ - self.predicted_
< ... >
```

However, instead of cluttering the base class with so many methods, let's go back to the idea of logical consistency and grouping and use more OOP principles to organize the code better. Let's see how in the following section.

# Do More in the OOP Style

As you enthusiastically plan utility methods to add to the class, you recognize that this approach may make the code of the main class very long and difficult to debug. To solve this conundrum, you can make use of another beautiful principle of OOP called inheritance (www.geeksforgeeks.org/inheritance-in-python/).

# Separate Plotting Classes

You recognize that all plots are not of the same type. Pairplots and fitted vs. true data plots are of similar nature as they can be derived from the data only. Other plots are related to the goodness-of-fit and residuals. Therefore, you can create two separate classes with those plotting functions: Data_plots and Diagnostic_plots. Furthermore, you can also define your main MyLinearRegression class in terms of these utility classes. That is an instance of inheritance. This whole approach is shown in Figure 6-10.

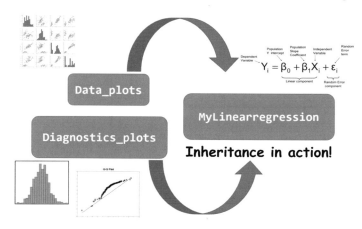

***Figure 6-10.***  *Define several distinct plotting classes and use them in the base class*

Partial code for the Diagnostic_plots is as follows:

```
class Diagnostics_plots:
    """

    Diagnostics plots and methods

    Arguments:
    fitted_vs_residual: Plots fitted values vs. residuals
    fitted_vs_features: Plots residuals vs all feature variables in a grid
```

```
    histogram_resid: Plots a histogram of the residuals (can be normalized)
    shapiro_test: Performs Shapiro-Wilk normality test on the residuals
    qqplot_resid: Creates a quantile-quantile plot for residuals comparing
    with a normal distribution
    """

    def __init__():
        pass

    def fitted_vs_residual(self):
        """Plots fitted values vs. residuals"""
<...>
```

And for the Data_plots:

```
class Data_plots:
    """

    Methods for data related plots

    pairplot: Creates pairplot of all variables and the target
    plot_fitted: Plots fitted values against the true output values from
    the data
    """

    def __init__():
        pass

    def pairplot(self):
        """Creates pairplot of all variables and the target using the
        Seaborn library"""
        if not self.is_fitted:
            print("Model not fitted yet!")
            return None
<...>
```

So, the definition of the main class changes slightly now:

```
class MyLinearRegression(Data_plots, Diagnostics_plots):

    def __init__(self, fit_intercept=True):
```

```
      self.coef_ = None
      self.intercept_ = None
      self._fit_intercept = fit_intercept
<...>
```

The class definition MyLinearRegression(Data_plots,Diagnostics_plots) allows the main class to inherit all the beautiful plotting methods defined in the plotting classes. Now you can check the quality of the regression fit by plotting the diagnostics and data plots with only three or four lines of code:

```
mlr = MyLinearRegression()
mlr.fit(X,y)
```

The fitted vs. residual plot is shown in Figure 6-11:

```
mlr.fitted_vs_residual()
```

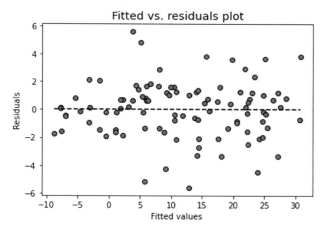

***Figure 6-11.*** *Fitted vs. residuals plot*

Histogram of the residuals (Figure 6-12):

```
mlr.histogram_resid()
```

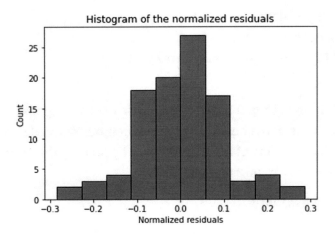

***Figure 6-12.*** *Histogram of the normalized residuals*

Q-Q plot of the residuals (Figure 6-13):

```
mlr.qqplot_resid()
```

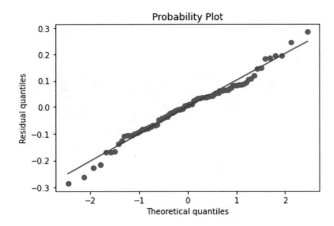

***Figure 6-13.*** *Quantile-quantile plot of the residuals*

The modularization of code is at work here. You can modify and improve the core plotting utilities without touching the main class. This is a highly flexible and less error-prone approach that increases the productivity and efficiency of the data scientist.

# More Supporting Classes and Syntactic Sugar

Just for completeness, consider the following:

- Metrics class for computing various regression metrics: SSE, SST, MSE, $R^2$, and Adjusted $R^2$.

- Outliers class to plot Cook's distance (https://en.wikipedia.org/wiki/Cook%27s_distance) leverage, and influence plots

- Multicollinearity class to compute variance inflation factors (VIF; https://en.wikipedia.org/wiki/Variance_inflation_factor)

All in all, the grand scheme looks like Figure 6-14.

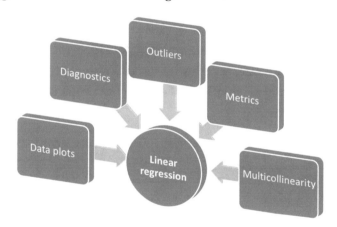

***Figure 6-14.*** *Linear regression estimator with all the supporting classes*

Once you inherit other classes, they behave just like the usual Python module you are familiar with. So, you can add utility methods to the main class to execute multiple methods from a sub-class together. For example, the following method runs all the usual diagnostics checks at once. Note how you are accessing the plot methods by putting a simple .DOT (i.e. Diagnostics_plot.histogram_resid), just like accessing a function from pandas or NumPy library.

```
def run_diagnostics(self):
    """Runs diagnostics tests and plots"""
    Diagnostics_plots.fitted_vs_residual(self)
    Diagnostics_plots.histogram_resid(self)
```

```
Diagnostics_plots.qqplot_resid(self)
print()
Diagnostics_plots.shapiro_test(self)
```

# Modularization: Importing the Class as a Module

Although not a canonical OOP principle, the essential advantage of following the OOP paradigm is to be able to modularize your code. You can experiment and develop all this code in a standard Jupyter notebook. But for maximum modularity, consider converting the notebook into a standalone executable Python script (with a .py extension). As a good practice, remove all the unnecessary comments and test code from this file and keep only the classes together.

Once you do that, you can import the MyLinearRgression class from a completely different notebook. This is often the preferred way of testing your code as this does not touch the core model but only tests it with various data samples and functional parameters. Figure 6-15 shows a snapshot of a clean notebook where you import the class from a separate module.

**Notebook to test the MyLinearRegression class and its methods**

```
from Class_MyLinearRegression import MyLinearRegression as mlr
import numpy as np
import matplotlib.pyplot as plt
```

**Generate random data with noise**

```
num_samples=100
num_dim = 5
X = 10*np.random.random(size=(num_samples,num_dim))
coeff = np.array([2,-3.5,1.2,4.1,-2.5])
y = np.dot(coeff,X.T)+2*np.random.randn(num_samples)
```

**Instantiate model and fit**

```
model = mlr()
model.fit(X,y)
```

**Model metrics**

```
print ("R-squared: ",model.r_squared())
print ("Adjusted R-squared: ",model.adj_r_squared())
print("MSE: ",model.mse())
```
```
R-squared:   0.9890652102512777
Adjusted R-squared:  0.9884835724986861
MSE:   4.447051771303101
```

***Figure 6-15.*** *Testing the ML estimator by importing it from a separate module*

# Publishing It as a Python Package

At this point, you can consider releasing this Python script as a standalone Python package (`https://towardsdatascience.com/build-your-first-open-source-python-project-53471c9942a7`) that does fitting, prediction, plotting, diagnostics, and more. Although you can host the package on your personal website or on the cloud, the most obvious place to put it is in the official Python package repository, **PyPI**. This is the place from where anybody in the world can download and install your package with the `pip` command. For example, if your package is named `my-ml-package`, then anybody can run `pip install my-ml-package` and the Python library will be installed on their machine.

## Special Instructions for PyPI Hosting

To host on PyPI, you must follow certain steps:

1. Create a `setup.py` file (`https://godatadriven.com/blog/a-practical-guide-to-using-setup-py/`).

2. Create the proper directory structure (if you have files other than the main script and `setup.py`, such as sample data and test scripts).

3. Put the files in a GitHub repository.

4. Set up GitHub actions for regular commits and updates.

5. Create documentation using a tool like Sphinx and link it to the GitHub Readmes.

6. And so on.

These specific instructions are already well explained in the link provided above, so I don't repeat them in this book.

Of course, you should a lot of docstring descriptions (`www.geeksforgeeks.org/python-docstrings/`), examples of usage of a function, assertion checks (`https://airbrake.io/blog/python/python-assertionerror`), and unit tests (`https://softwaretestingfundamentals.com/unit-testing/`) to make it a good package. But since you built the code from scratch (following some key OOP principles), you learned a lot of valuable lessons. You obtained a taste of developing a useful piece of software from the ground up.

**What is PyPI?**    The Python Package Index or PyPI is the official third-party software repository for the Python language. It is analogous to the CPAN repository for Perl or the CRAN repository for R. PyPI is run by the Python Software Foundation (PSF), which maintains and develops the official Python version release.

# GitHub Integration

My version of the open-source package is here: `https://github.com/tirthajyoti/mlr` (Figure 6-16). Although a GitHub repo is not mandatory for publishing a Python package on PyPI, it is highly recommended to create and maintain one. GitHub integration can make updating and version controlling of your package easy and painless. With a proper GitHub setup, all you have to do is to push/commit the latest updated files onto your GitHub and the PyPI version will be updated as well (after executing a set of special commands that tells PyPI to read the updated files from your GitHub repo). The documentation for the same can be found here: `https://mlr.readthedocs.io/en/latest/`.

| | | |
|---|---|---|
| ⌥ master ▾ | ⑂ 1 branch | ◇ 0 tags |
| tirthajyoti Update README.md | | |
| 📁 docs | Update examples_advanced.md | |
| 📁 images | Advanced examples page updated | |
| 📁 mlr | Update Data_plots.py | |
| 🗋 .gitignore | Initial commit | |
| 🗋 LICENSE | Initial commit | |
| 🗋 MANIFEST.in | Create MANIFEST.in | |
| 🗋 README.md | Update README.md | |
| 🗋 setup.py | Updated setup and added top image | |

***Figure 6-16.*** *GitHub repo snapshot of the linear regression package*

# Summary

In this chapter, you focused on building a linear regression estimator from the ground up. You aimed for a clean and simple API, like what is provided by a scikit-learn estimator. However, you added quite a few additional methods and utilities (e.g., for visualization and statistical inference) to this class than what is found in a standard scikit-learn estimator.

In the process, you learned how to plan and organize the code for building such an ML estimator and how to take advantage of the OOP paradigm using inheritance and encapsulation. The design was not meant to be set in stone, but rather act as a guide for you to plan and build your own data science APIs for various business and scientific applications.

You also learned additional steps that a data scientist must take to publish this code as a full-fledged Python package (on the PyPI server) and how this can teach you valuable skills.

# CHAPTER 7

# Some Cool Utility Packages

Python has an amazing ecosystem for data science work, starting from numerical analysis to advanced deep learning or reinforcement learning, with statistical modeling and visualization thrown in as well. A great open-source culture keeps new and exciting developments coming and thriving. Data scientists can learn, contribute code, share their experience, help debug, and support each other in this environment.

There are some predominant libraries and packages in this ecosystem that are used by almost all data scientists in their daily job. I touch upon them in the next section. However, there are also some little-known Python packages (the so-called *hidden gems,* as in Figure 7-1) that can help you do common data science jobs faster and more efficiently. They are not general-purpose large projects like NumPy or pandas. Instead, they focus on some niche aspects of similar data science tasks and do them well.

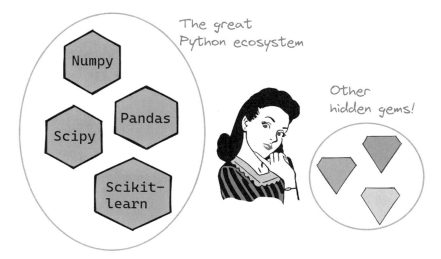

***Figure 7-1.*** *There are hidden gems beyond the great Python data science ecosystem*

© Dr. Tirthajyoti Sarkar 2022
T. Sarkar, *Productive and Efficient Data Science with Python*, https://doi.org/10.1007/978-1-4842-8121-5_7

To be highly productive in data science, you must stay abreast of these new developments and embrace these focused utility packages wherever they makes sense. In this chapter, I touch upon a few such nifty packages and show some hands-on examples of efficient data science. The goal is to introduce the idea of exploration to you so that you take full advantage of the great Python data science zoo.

# Build Pipelines Using pdpipe

pandas is an amazing library in the Python ecosystem for data analytics and machine learning. It forms the perfect bridge between the data world, where Excel/CSV files and SQL tables live, and the modeling world, where scikit-learn and TensorFlow perform their magic.

A data science flow is most often a sequence of steps: datasets must be cleaned, scaled, and validated before they can be used by that powerful machine learning algorithm. These tasks can, of course, be done with many single-step functions/methods that are offered by packages like pandas. However, an elegant alternative is to use a **pipeline**. In almost all cases, a pipeline reduces the chance of error and saves time by automating repetitive tasks. In the data science world, great examples of packages with pipeline features are dplyr (`https://dplyr.tidyverse.org/`) in the R language and the scikit-learn module composition and pipelines (`https://scikit-learn.org/stable/modules/compose.html`) in the Python ecosystem.

pandas also offer a `pipe` method that can be used for similar purposes with user-defined functions. However, in this section, I am going to discuss a wonderful little library called `pdpipe`, which specifically addresses this pipelining issue with pandas DataFrame and solves the problem in an elegant and intuitive way.

## The Dataset

You will use a dataset of US housing prices (downloaded from Kaggle at `www.kaggle.com/vedavyasv/usa-housing`). You can load the dataset in pandas. Its summary statistics are shown in Figure 7-2.

| | count | mean | std | min | 25% | 50% | 75% | max |
|---|---|---|---|---|---|---|---|---|
| Avg. Area Income | 5000.0 | 68583.11 | 10657.99 | 17796.63 | 61480.56 | 68804.29 | 75783.34 | 107701.75 |
| Avg. Area House Age | 5000.0 | 5.98 | 0.99 | 2.64 | 5.32 | 5.97 | 6.65 | 9.52 |
| Avg. Area Number of Rooms | 5000.0 | 6.99 | 1.01 | 3.24 | 6.30 | 7.00 | 7.67 | 10.76 |
| Avg. Area Number of Bedrooms | 5000.0 | 3.98 | 1.23 | 2.00 | 3.14 | 4.05 | 4.49 | 6.50 |
| Area Population | 5000.0 | 36163.52 | 9925.65 | 172.61 | 29403.93 | 36199.41 | 42861.29 | 69621.71 |
| Price | 5000.0 | 1232072.65 | 353117.63 | 15938.66 | 997577.14 | 1232669.38 | 1471210.20 | 2469065.59 |

*Figure 7-2.* *Summary statistics of the dataset used for the demo*

However, this is only a partial view. It also contains an Address field (Figure 7-3) that contains raw text data. This does not show up in the summary stats above because it is not a numeric column.

| Avg. Area Income | Avg. Area House Age | Avg. Area Number of Rooms | Avg. Area Number of Bedrooms | Area Population | Price | Address |
|---|---|---|---|---|---|---|
| 53029.35 | 4.29 | 6.74 | 2.40 | 34472.30 | 430088.25 | 58197 Anderson Squares Suite 899\nSarahburgh, … |
| 79566.92 | 5.50 | 7.11 | 5.06 | 49311.76 | 1608889.26 | 536 Thompson Turnpike\nWest Toddfurt, VT 33903… |
| 64927.65 | 5.74 | 6.59 | 4.34 | 29364.76 | 1138885.10 | USCGC Ashley\nFPO AE 25345 |
| 71306.46 | 5.77 | 6.69 | 2.04 | 43284.40 | 1335904.50 | 3890 Hunt Trail\nDavidhaven, OR 04793 |
| 87927.97 | 5.59 | 4.78 | 2.13 | 34724.16 | 1276259.02 | 01358 Barton Ranch\nLawrenceborough, SD 60884-… |

*Figure 7-3.* *The dataset contains an Address field with raw text*

Let's add a small transformation based on the Avg. Area Number of Bedrooms column. Here is the code:

```
def size(n):
    if n<=4:
        return 'Small'
    elif 4<n<=6:
        return 'Medium'
    else:
        return 'Big'
df['House_size']=df['Avg. Area Number of Rooms'].apply(size)
```

You define a function named `size` and apply it to the `Avg. Area Number of Rooms` column. The resulting dataset looks like Figure 7-4.

| | Avg. Area Income | Avg. Area House Age | Avg. Area Number of Rooms | Avg. Area Number of Bedrooms | Area Population | Price | Address | House_size |
|---|---|---|---|---|---|---|---|---|
| 3920 | 66749.57 | 7.16 | 6.10 | 3.37 | 46553.98 | 1394637.65 | 1630 Castillo Summit Apt. 619\nEast Karenborou... | Big |
| 2267 | 76992.82 | 6.53 | 6.05 | 4.46 | 24874.04 | 1212440.29 | 8188 Henry Gardens\nPort Rogerberg, OK 27962-5231 | Big |
| 4302 | 61877.55 | 5.55 | 6.80 | 3.25 | 28604.94 | 1083745.37 | 03529 Hull Mountains\nLake Zacharyshire, WY 94496 | Big |
| 4320 | 64426.87 | 5.50 | 8.95 | 3.31 | 18214.31 | 1055548.68 | Unit 4466 Box 0788\nDPO AP 45943 | Big |
| 1796 | 78159.95 | 5.12 | 6.18 | 4.08 | 31111.62 | 1264972.44 | 3276 Harris Pines Suite 433\nPort Paul, NY 662... | Big |

**Figure 7-4.** *Dataset after applying the house size transformation*

# Start Laying Pipes

Start with the simplest possible pipeline, consisting of just one operation. Let's say the machine learning team and the domain experts say that they think they can safely ignore the `Avg. Area House Age` data for modeling. Therefore, you can drop this column from the dataset. For this task, you create a pipeline object named `drop_age` with the `ColDrop` method from `pdpipe` and pass the DataFrame to this pipeline:

```
import pdpipe as pdp
drop_age = pdp.ColDrop('Avg. Area House Age')
df2 = drop_age(df)
```

That's it. The resulting DataFrame, as expected, looks like Figure 7-5.

| Avg. Area Income | Avg. Area Number of Rooms | Avg. Area Number of Bedrooms | Area Population | Price | Address | House_size |
|---|---|---|---|---|---|---|
| 64491.0 | 5.0 | 4.0 | 40359.0 | 718887.0 | 95198 Ortiz Key\nPort Sara, TN 24541-2855 | Medium |
| 64347.0 | 7.0 | 2.0 | 32338.0 | 959102.0 | 73554 Justin Springs Suite 074\nSouth Barbaram... | Big |
| 68387.0 | 7.0 | 2.0 | 37895.0 | 1389224.0 | USNS Beard\nFPO AA 45652-4890 | Big |
| 61503.0 | 7.0 | 3.0 | 37651.0 | 822432.0 | 18941 Ray Ports\nEast Nicoleland, OR 67363 | Big |
| 61677.0 | 9.0 | 4.0 | 38468.0 | 1328659.0 | 9423 Paige Unions Apt. 551\nValeriebury, AZ 96... | Big |

**Figure 7-5.** *Dataset after dropping the Age column using a pipe operation*

# Chain Stages of Pipeline Simply by Adding

Now, single pipes are fun, but pipelines are truly useful and practical only when they have **multiple (connected) stages**. There are multiple methods by which you can do that in pdpipe. However, the simplest and most intuitive approach is to use the + operator. It is like hand-joining pipes. Just add one to another.

Let's say, apart from dropping the Age column, you also want to one-hot-encode the House_size column so that a classification or regression algorithm can be run on the dataset easily. You can accomplish this simply by writing this code:

```
pipeline = pdp.ColDrop('Avg. Area House Age')
pipeline += pdp.OneHotEncode('House_size')
df3 = pipeline(df)
```

So, you created a pipeline object first with the ColDrop method to drop the Avg. Area House Age column. Thereafter, you simply added the OneHotEncode method to this pipeline object with the usual Python += syntax. The new pipeline now processes the DataFrame object. The resulting DataFrame is shown in Figure 7-6. Note the additional indicator columns House_size_Medium and House_size_Small created from the one-hot-encoding process.

| Avg. Area Income | Avg. Area Number of Rooms | Avg. Area Number of Bedrooms | Area Population | Price | Address | House_size_Medium | House_size_Small |
|---|---|---|---|---|---|---|---|
| 69606.0 | 7.0 | 3.0 | 35427.0 | 1588196.0 | 74421 Horton Manor Apt. 121\nLake Edward, SC 7... | 0 | 0 |
| 58841.0 | 7.0 | 4.0 | 39555.0 | 1496730.0 | 78312 Martin Terrace Suite 957\nNew Kimberly, ... | 0 | 0 |
| 43242.0 | 7.0 | 2.0 | 29479.0 | 629658.0 | 860 Graham Meadows Suite 412\nEast | 0 | 0 |

***Figure 7-6.*** *Dataset after one-hot-coding added to the pipeline*

## Dropping Rows Based on Their Values

Next, you may want to remove rows of data based on their values. Specifically, you may want to drop all the data where the house price is less than 250,000. You can use the ApplybyCol method to apply any user-defined function to the DataFrame. You can also use the method ValDrop to drop rows based on a specific value. You can easily chain these methods to your pipeline to selectively drop rows (you are still adding to your existing pipeline object which already does the other jobs of column dropping and one-hot-encoding). You accomplish this by creating a small user-defined function named price_tag and then using it inside the pipe:

```
def price_tag(x):
    if x>250000:
        return 'keep'
    else:
        return 'drop'
pipeline+=pdp.ApplyByCols('Price',price_tag,
                        'Price_tag',drop=False)
pipeline+=pdp.ValDrop(['drop'],'Price_tag')
pipeline+= pdp.ColDrop('Price_tag')
```

Note, in the code above, for the first operation, the second argument of the ApplyByCols method represents the user-defined function whereas the third argument named Price_tag represent the name of the resulting column. Figure 7-7 shows the dataset.

| Avg. Area Income | Avg. Area Number of Rooms | Avg. Area Number of Bedrooms | Area Population | Price | Price_tag | Address | House_size_Medium | House_size |
|---|---|---|---|---|---|---|---|---|
| 57358.62 | 7.10 | 3.14 | 22061.59 | 948279.94 | keep | 16028 Sarah Isle Suite 386\nEast Clifford, PW ... | 0 | |
| 73886.08 | 5.59 | 2.16 | 26038.51 | 987004.08 | keep | 85083 Combs Fort\nConnorhaven, AR 99906-2530 | 1 | |
| 96397.58 | 6.20 | 2.40 | 22681.93 | 1053966.43 | keep | 2499 Dalton Keys\nNicholasland, LA 68235 | 0 | |
| | | | | | | 63891 Rebecca | | |

*Figure 7-7.* *Dataset after the price tag function is applied*

Now the `ValDrop` method comes in and it looks for the string drop in the `Price_tag` column and drops those rows that match. Finally, the `ColDrop` method removes the `Price_tag` column, cleaning up the DataFrame. Essentially, this `Price_tag` column is only needed temporarily, to tag specific rows, and should be removed after it serves its purpose.

The efficient aspect is that all of this is accomplished by **simply chaining stages of operations on the same pipeline**. At this point, you can look back and see what your pipeline does to the DataFrame right from the beginning:

- Drops a specific column

- One-hot-encodes a categorical data column for modeling

- Tags data based on a user-defined function

- Drops rows based on the tag

- Drops the temporary tagging column

Six lines of code for all of these actions:

```
pipeline = pdp.ColDrop('Avg. Area House Age')
pipeline+= pdp.OneHotEncode('House_size')
pipeline+=pdp.ApplyByCols('Price',price_tag,
                          'Price_tag',drop=False)
pipeline+=pdp.ValDrop(['drop'],'Price_tag')
pipeline+= pdp.ColDrop('Price_tag')
df5 = pipeline(df) # Final DataFrame
```

Moreover, the latest version of the package implements another direct method to do all of this in a single line of code like this:

```
pdp.RowDrop({'Price': lambda x: x <= 250000})
```

## scikit-learn and NLTK Stages

There are many more useful and intuitive DataFrame manipulation methods available for in `pdpipe` that can make the data science tasks productive and efficient. Additionally, even some operations from the scikit-learn and NLTK packages are included in `pdpipe` for making awesome pipelines.

## Scaling Data with a scikit-learn Method

For example, one of the most common tasks for building ML models is the scaling of the data. scikit-learn offers a few different types of scaling such as min-max scaling or standardization-based scaling (where the mean of a data set is subtracted followed by division by standard deviation). You can directly chain such scaling operations in a pipeline. The following code demonstrates the use:

```
exclude = ['House_size_Medium','House_size_Small']
pipeline_scale = pdp.Scale('StandardScaler', exclude_columns=exclude)
df6 = pipeline_scale(df5)
```

Here you apply the `StandardScaler` estimator from the scikit-learn package to transform the data for clustering or neural network fitting. You can selectively exclude columns that do not need such scaling, as you have done here for the indicator columns `House_size_Medium` and `House_size_Small`. The resulting DataFrame shows the effect of scaling (Figure 7-8).

| Avg. Area Income | Avg. Area Number of Rooms | Avg. Area Number of Bedrooms | Area Population | Price | Address | House_size_Medium | House_size_Small |
|---|---|---|---|---|---|---|---|
| 2.067 | -1.195 | -1.379 | -0.128 | 1.366 | 06374 Martin Passage\nNew Shawnland, KS 59839-... | 1 | 0 |
| -0.183 | 0.504 | 0.840 | -1.328 | -1.849 | 827 Ferguson Isle\nRosebury, AL 61416-3167 | 0 | 0 |
| 0.044 | 0.062 | 1.164 | -0.352 | 0.300 | Unit 8410 Box 5521\nDPO AP 20914-6877 | 0 | 0 |

***Figure 7-8.*** *Dataset after standard normal scaling was applied to selected columns*

## Tokenizer from NLTK

The `Address` field in your DataFrame is useless right now. However, if you can extract ZIP codes or states from those strings, they might be useful for some form of visualization or machine learning task.

You can use a word tokenizer for this purpose. NLTK is a popular and powerful Python library for text mining and natural language processing (NLP) and it offers a range of tokenizer methods. Here, you can use one such tokenizer to split up the text in the Address field and extract the name of the state from that. You recognize that the name of the state is the penultimate word in the address string. Therefore, you can create the following chained pipeline for this job:

```
def extract_state(token):
    return str(token[-2])

pipeline_tokenize = pdp.TokenizeWords('Address')
pipeline_state = pdp.ApplyByCols('Address',extract_state,
result_columns='State')
pipeline_state_extract = pipeline_tokenize + pipeline_state
df7 = pipeline_state_extract(df6)
```

The resulting DataFrame is shown in Figure 7-9. Note the new State column.

| Avg. Area Income | Avg. Area Number of Rooms | Avg. Area Number of Bedrooms | Area Population | Price | State | House_size_Medium | House_size_Small |
|---|---|---|---|---|---|---|---|
| 0.614 | -0.391 | -0.553 | -0.420 | 0.830 | AA | 0 | 0 |
| -0.624 | 0.691 | 0.897 | -0.020 | -0.883 | KS | 0 | 0 |
| -2.871 | 0.769 | 0.921 | 0.189 | -0.956 | NV | 0 | 0 |
| -0.080 | -0.014 | -1.468 | 0.713 | 0.179 | NM | 0 | 0 |
| -0.098 | 0.761 | 1.893 | -1.456 | -0.181 | MH | 0 | 0 |

**Figure 7-9.** *Dataset after NLTK tokenizer method was applied to the Address column*

## All Together

Figure 7-10 summarizes all the operations shown in this demo.

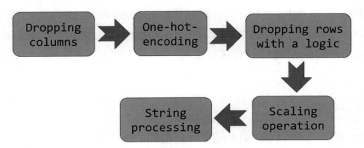

***Figure 7-10.*** *Dataset after a NLTK tokenizer method was applied to the Address column*

All of these operations may be used as frequently as needed on similar types of datasets. Having a simple set of sequential code blocks to execute as a preprocessing operation enhances the productivity of the data scientist. Pipelining is the key to achieving that uniform set of sequential code blocks. pandas is the most widely used Python library for such data preprocessing tasks in a data science team, and pdpipe provides a simple yet powerful way to build pipelines with pandas-type operations.

# Speeding Up NumPy and pandas

NumPy and pandas are probably the two most widely used core Python libraries for DS and ML tasks. Obviously, the speed of evaluating numerical expressions is critically important for these DS/ML tasks and these two libraries do not disappoint in that regard.

Under the hood, they use fast and optimized vectorized operations (as much as possible) to speed up mathematical operations. Plenty of articles have been written about how NumPy is much superior (especially when you can vectorize your calculations) over plain-vanilla Python loops or list-based operations. In this section, I show how using a simple extension library called NumExpr can improve the speed of the mathematical operations that the core NumPy and pandas yield.

## What Is This Library?

First, install it with the pip command:

```
pip install numexpr
```

The project is hosted on GitHub at https://github.com/pydata/numexpr. It is from the PyData (https://pydata.org/) stable, the organization under NumFocus, (https://numfocus.org/), which also gave rise to Numpy and pandas.

As per the official source,

> "NumExpr is a fast numerical expression evaluator for NumPy. With it, expressions that operate on arrays are accelerated and use less memory than doing the same calculation in Python. In addition, its multi-threaded capabilities can make use of all your cores—which generally results in substantial performance scaling compared to NumPy."

Here is the detailed documentation for the library and examples of various use cases: https://numexpr.readthedocs.io/projects/NumExpr3/en/latest/.

# Speeding It Up

Let's start with a very simple mathematical operation of adding a scalar number, say 1, to a NumPy array. To use the Numexpr package, all you need to do is to wrap the same calculation under a special method named evaluate in a symbolic expression. The following code illustrates the usage clearly:

```
import numpy as np
import numexpr as ne

a = np.arange(1e6)
b = np.arange(1e6)

%%timeit -n200 -r10
c = a+1
```

>> **3.55 ms ± 52.1 µs per loop** (mean ± std. dev. of 10 runs, 200 loops each)

```
%%timeit -n200 -r10
c = ne.evaluate("a + 1")
```

>> **1.94 ms ± 86.5 µs per loop** (mean ± std. dev. of 10 runs, 200 loops each)

That was magical! All you had to do was to write the familiar a+1 NumPy code in the form of a symbolic expression "a+1" and pass it on to the ne.evaluate() function. And you got a significant speed boost from **3.55 ms to 1.94 ms on average**.

Note that, for consistency purposes, you ran the same computation 200 times in a 10-loop test to calculate the execution time. Of course, the exact results are somewhat dependent on the underlying hardware. You are welcome to evaluate this on your machine and see what improvement you got.

## Arithmetic Involving Two Arrays

Let's dial it up a little and involve two arrays. Here is the code to evaluate a simple linear expression using two arrays:

```
%%timeit -n100 -r10
c = 2*a+3*b
```

>> **11.7 ms ± 177 µs per loop** (mean ± std. dev. of 10 runs, 100 loops each)

```
%%timeit -n100 -r10
c = ne.evaluate("2*a+3*b")
```

>> **2.14 ms ± 130 µs per loop** (mean ± std. dev. of 10 runs, 100 loops each)

For two-array operation, there's an even bigger improvement than the simple scalar addition **from 11.7 ms to 2.14 ms on the average**.

## A Somewhat More Complex Operation

Now, let's notch it up further by involving more arrays in a somewhat complicated rational function expression. Suppose you want to evaluate the expression in Figure 7-11 involving five Numpy arrays, each with one million random numbers (drawn from a Normal distribution).

$$c = \frac{a_1^2 + 2a_2 + (3/a_3)}{\sqrt{a_4^2 + a_5^2}}$$

where $a_1, a_2, a_3, a_4, a_5$ are arrays with
1 million Normally distributed random numbers

***Figure 7-11.*** *A complex rational function involving multiple NumPy arrays*

Here is the code. You create a NumPy array of the shape (1000000, 5) and extract five (1000000,1) vectors from it to use in the rational function. Also note how the symbolic expression in the Numexpr method understands the string symbol 'sqrt' natively (you just write sqrt).

```
a = np.random.normal(size=(1000000,5))
a1,a2,a3,a4,a5 = a[:,0],a[:,1],a[:,2],a[:,3],a[:,4]

%%timeit -n100 -r10
c = (a1**2+2*a2+(3/a3))/(np.sqrt(a4**2+a5**2))

>> 47 ms ± 220 µs per loop (mean ± std. dev. of 10 runs, 100 loops each)

%%timeit -n100 -r10
ne.evaluate("(a1**2+2*a2+(3/a3))/(sqrt(a4**2+a5**2))")

>> 3.96 ms ± 218 µs per loop (mean ± std. dev. of 10 runs, 100 loops each)
```

This shows a huge speed boost from 47 ms to ~4 ms on average. In fact, this is a trend; you will notice that *the more complicated the expression becomes and the greater number of arrays it involves, the higher the speed boost* becomes with Numexpr.

## Logical Expressions/Boolean Filtering

Furthermore, you are not limited to the simple arithmetic expressions shown above. One of the most useful features of NumPy arrays is to use them directly in an expression involving logical operators such as > or < to create Boolean filters or masks. You can do the same with Numexpr and speed up the filtering process. Here is an example of checking whether the Euclidean distance measure involving four vectors is greater than a certain threshold:

```
x1 = np.random.random(1000000)
x2 = np.random.random(1000000)
y1 = np.random.random(1000000)
y2 = np.random.random(1000000)

%%timeit -n100 -r10
c = np.sqrt((x1-x2)**2+(y1-y2)**2) > 0.5

>> 23.2 ms ± 143 µs per loop (mean ± std. dev. of 10 runs, 100 loops each)
```

```
%%timeit -n100 -r10
c = ne.evaluate("sqrt((x1-x2)**2+(y1-y2)**2) > 0.5")
```

>> 1.86 ms ± 112 µs per loop (mean ± std. dev. of 10 runs, 100 loops each)

This kind of filtering operation appears all the time in a data science/machine learning pipeline, and you can imagine how much compute time can be saved by strategically replacing NumPy evaluations with Numexpr expressions.

## Complex Numbers

You can make the jump from the real to the imaginary domain pretty easily. Numexpr works equally well with complex numbers, which are natively supported by Python and NumPy. Here is an example, which also illustrates the use of a transcendental math operation, a logarithm:

```
a = np.random.random(1000000)
b = np.random.random(1000000)
cplx = a + b*1j

%%timeit -n100 -r10
c = np.log10(cplx)
```

>> 55.9 ms ± 159 µs per loop (mean ± std. dev. of 10 runs, 100 loops each)

```
%%timeit -n100 -r10
c = ne.evaluate("log10(cplx)")
```

>> 9.9 ms ± 117 µs per loop (mean ± std. dev. of 10 runs, 100 loops each)

## Impact of the Array Size

Next, let's examine the impact of the size of the NumPy array over the speed improvement. For this, let's choose a simple conditional expression with two arrays like 2*a+3*b < 3.5 and plot the relative execution times (after averaging over 10 runs) for a wide range of sizes. The code is in the accompanying Jupyter notebook, and the final result is shown in Figure 7-12.

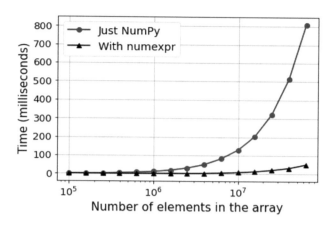

***Figure 7-12.*** *Impact of the size of the array on speed improvement*

# The pandas eval Method

It turns out that pandas has an eval method where you can select to use a Numexpr engine to speed up the operation of evaluating a Python symbolic expression (as a string). Figure 7-13 shows a snapshot of the method from the official pandas documentation.

engine : {*'python', 'numexpr'}, default 'numexpr'*

> The engine used to evaluate the expression. Supported engines are
>
> - None : tries to use numexpr, falls back to python
> - 'numexpr': **This default engine evaluates pandas objects using**
>
>     numexpr for large speed ups in complex expressions with large frames.
>
> - 'python': **Performs operations as if you had** eval**'d in top**
>
>     level python. This engine is generally not that useful.
>
> More backends may be available in the future.

***Figure 7-13.*** *Partial snapshot of the Pandas eval method with the numexpr engine*

The following code demonstrates an example where you construct four DataFrames with 50,000 rows and 100 columns each (filled with uniform random numbers) and evaluate a nonlinear transformation involving those DataFrames, in one case with a native pandas expression and in other case using the pd.eval() method:

```
nrows, ncols = 50000, 100
df1,df2,df3,df4 = [pd.DataFrame(np.random.randn(nrows, ncols)) for _ in
range(4)]
```

```
%%timeit -n20 -r10
c=2*df1 - (df2/2) + (df3/df4)
```

>> 55.8 ms ± 1.8 ms per loop (mean ± std. dev. of 10 runs, 20 loops each)

```
%%timeit -n20 -r10
pd.eval('2*df1 - (df2/2) + (df3/df4)')
```

>> 17.3 ms ± 539 µs per loop (mean ± std. dev. of 10 runs, 20 loops each)

Note how you use a string with symbolic expressions for the DataFrames in the second case: pd.eval('2*df1 - (df2/2) + (df3/df4)')

You do a similar analysis of the impact of the size (number of rows, while keeping the number of columns fixed at 100) of the DataFrame on the speed improvement. The result is shown in Figure 7-14.

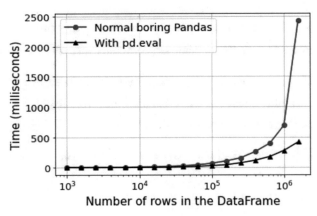

***Figure 7-14.*** *Impact of the size of the DataFrame on the speed improvement*

# How It Works, Supported Operators

The details of the mechanism that makes Numexpr work are somewhat complex and involve the optimal use of the underlying compute architecture. I won't cover that in this book. Basically, the expression is compiled using a Python compile function, variables are extracted, and a parse tree structure is built. This tree is then compiled into a Bytecode program, which describes the element-wise operation flow using something called *vector registers* (each 4096 elements wide). The key to speed enhancement is Numexpr's ability to **handle chunks of elements at a time**.

It skips NumPy's practice of using temporary arrays, which wastes memory and cannot even fit into cache memory for large arrays. Also, the virtual machine is written entirely in C, which makes it faster than native Python. It is also multi-threaded, allowing faster parallelization of the operations on suitable hardware. A simplified illustration is shown in Figure 7-15.

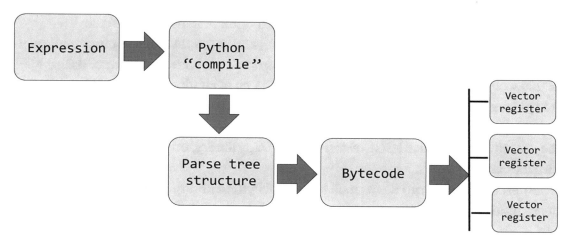

***Figure 7-15.*** *Simplified illustration of the inner workings of Numexpr*

Numexpr supports a wide array of mathematical operators for use in the expression but not conditional operators like if or else. The full list of operators can be found at https://numexpr.readthedocs.io/projects/NumExpr3/en/latest/user_guide. html#supported-operators.

You can also control the number of threads that you want to spawn for parallel operations with large arrays by setting the environment variable NUMEXPR_MAX_THREAD. Currently, the maximum possible number of threads is 64 but there is no real benefit of going higher than the number of virtual cores available on the underlying CPU node.

So, in this section, you saw how to take advantage of the special virtual machine-based expression evaluation paradigm for speeding up mathematical calculations in NumPy and pandas. Although this method may not be applicable for all possible tasks, a large fraction of data science, data wrangling, and statistical modeling pipelines can take advantage of this with minimal change in the code.

# Discover Best-Fitting Distributions Quickly

Imagine that you have some numeric data points and you want to find out which statistical distribution they might have come from. This is a classic statistical inference problem.

There are, of course, rigorous statistical methods to accomplish this goal. But maybe you are a busy data scientist. Or a busier software engineer who happens to be given this dataset to quickly write an application endpoint so that another ML app can use some synthetic data generated based on the best distribution that matches the data.

In short, you don't have a lot of time on hand and you want to find a quick method to discover the best-matching distribution that the data could have come from. Basically, in this scenario, you want to run an automated batch of goodness-of-fit (GOF) tests (https://en.wikipedia.org/wiki/Goodness_of_fit) on several distributions and summarize the results in a flash. You can, of course, write code from scratch to run the data through standard GOF tests using the Scipy library, one by one, for several distributions.

Alternatively, you can use a small but useful Python library called **distfit** to do the heavy lifting for you.

---

**What are GOF tests?**    The goodness of fit of a statistical model describes how well it fits a set of observations. Put simply, a measure of goodness of fit typically summarizes the discrepancy between the observed values and the values expected under the model in question. They find wide use in all kinds of statistical problems and hypothesis testing scenarios.

---

# Simple Fitting Example

You will generate some random synthetic data and try to find the best-matching distribution with only a few lines of code:

```
from distfit import distfit
import numpy as np

# Generate test data
data1 = np.random.normal(loc=5.0, scale=10, size=1000)
```

Then you initiate a model and fit the data to it:

```
# Initialize model
dist1 = distfit(bins=25,alpha=0.02,stats='ks')
# Fit the data
dist1.fit_transform(data1,verbose=1)
```

Note the similarity to the scikit-learn API; it has a `fit_transform` method, which you just used. Here, `alpha` denotes a confidence interval for fitting and `stats='ks'` denotes the scoring strategy standing for the Kolmogorov-Smirnov statistic (`https://en.wikipedia.org/wiki/Kolmogorov%E2%80%93Smirnov_test`). When you run this code in a Jupyter notebook, you get the (very) detailed output shown in Figure 7-16.

```
{'model': {'distr': <scipy.stats._continuous_distns.norm_gen at 0x2493c0c5370>,
  'stats': 'ks',
  'params': (5.168141032320424, 10.297680831713478),
  'name': 'norm',
  'model': <scipy.stats._distn_infrastructure.rv_frozen at 0x2493d248ca0>,
  'score': 1.1527914473738086e-07,
  'loc': 5.168141032320424,
  'scale': 10.297680831713478,
  'arg': (),
  'CII_min_alpha': -15.980709757845336,
  'CII_max_alpha': 26.31699182248618},
 'summary':                distr      score LLE                     loc          scale  \
 0          norm        0.0    NaN          5.168141        10.297681
 1             t        0.0    NaN          5.168624        10.297493
 2     genextreme       0.0    NaN          1.345935        10.208551
 3         gamma        0.0    NaN       -804.696532         0.130926
 4       lognorm        0.0    NaN       -442.600479       447.61915
 5          beta        0.0    NaN        -56.534935       129.443957
 6      loggamma        0.0    NaN      -2197.020027       320.587092
 7      dweibull   0.001945    NaN          5.968244         8.919706
 8         expon   1.108472    NaN        -25.240552        30.408693
 9        pareto   1.108472    NaN -710722358.209082  710722332.96853
 10      uniform   3.228419    NaN        -25.240552        64.035316
```

***Figure 7-16.*** *Detailed (partial) output of distribution fitting*

In fact, the fitting process creates and stores all kinds of information in that `dist1` object. Perhaps you are mostly interested in seeing some matching visualization and a summary of matching performance with various distributions.

## Plot and Summary

A simple `plot` command shows the best-fitted distribution and how it matches with your data points:

```
dist1.plot(verbose=1)
```

This results in the chart shown in Figure 7-17.

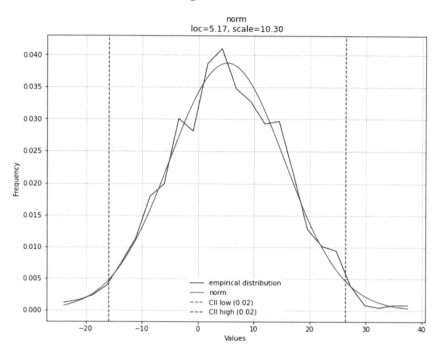

***Figure 7-17.*** *Best-matched distribution with the test data points*

A nice summary table is available with one line of code:

```
dist1.summary
```

It shows information about all the distributions that the `fit_transform` method went through under the hood. The score here is the metric that determines the best-matching distribution. It is like an error or distance metric, so the lower the score, better the match is. For this case, quite a few distributions match the data with nearly zero scores. After looking at the summary table in Figure 7-18, you can decide which one to pick, if needed.

| | distr | score | LLE | loc | scale | arg |
|---|---|---|---|---|---|---|
| 0 | norm | 0.0 | NaN | 5.168141 | 10.297681 | 0 |
| 1 | t | 0.0 | NaN | 5.168624 | 10.297493 | (5964061.469961431,) |
| 2 | genextreme | 0.0 | NaN | 1.345935 | 10.208551 | (0.24650762422035927,) |
| 3 | gamma | 0.0 | NaN | -804.696532 | 0.130926 | (6185.654208686727,) |
| 4 | lognorm | 0.0 | NaN | -442.600479 | 447.61915 | (0.02303400880174134,) |
| 5 | beta | 0.0 | NaN | -56.534935 | 129.443957 | (18.311101389857235, 20.103025094062506) |
| 6 | loggamma | 0.0 | NaN | -2197.020027 | 320.587092 | (962.7002556656262,) |
| 7 | dweibull | 0.001945 | NaN | 5.968244 | 8.919706 | (1.2805598141142776,) |
| 8 | expon | 1.108472 | NaN | -25.240552 | 30.408693 | 0 |
| 9 | pareto | 1.108472 | NaN | -710722358.209082 | 710722332.96853 | (21661180.97529108,) |
| 10 | uniform | 3.228419 | NaN | -25.240552 | 64.035316 | 0 |

***Figure 7-18.*** *Summary table of all the distributions the data was evaluated against*

Why are there only 11 distributions in this summary? Because, by default, it uses a list of the most popular distributions to scan through. If you want to search through a fixed list of distributions, you can specify the exact list as an argument to the `distfit` object while initializing it, with distribution names as common strings.

## Be Careful with Small Datasets

As with every other statistical learning model fitting process, this also works best with a large dataset. For small data, the fit may be ambiguous (multiple distributions showing similar match) or suboptimal (the wrong distribution is identified as the best fit).

For example, let's generate some data from the Beta distribution (https:// en.wikipedia.org/wiki/Beta_distribution) with parameters chosen such as they look almost like a Normal distribution. If you choose the parameters $\alpha$ and $\beta$ to be equal or close, you can accomplish this. Then, if you fit 1,000 data points, you may get the Normal distribution as the best-fitted distribution (Figure 7-19).

```
import numpy as np
data2 = np.random.beta(a=2.2,b=2.0,size=500)
dist2 = distfit(bins=50,alpha=0.02,stats='ks')
dist2.fit_transform(data2,verbose=1)
dist2.plot(title="Best-fitted with 500 data points",verbose=1)
```

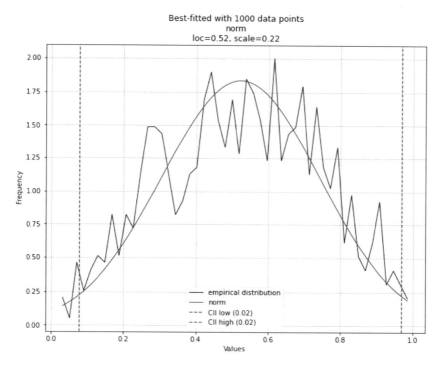

***Figure 7-19.*** *Data generated from the beta distribution fitted with 1,000 points*

However, if you extend the dataset size to 10,000 points, you will most likely get the correct answer (Figure 7-20).

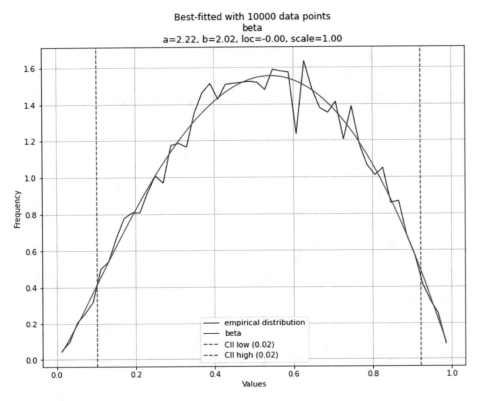

***Figure 7-20.*** *Data generated from the beta distribution fitted with 10,000 points*

## Other Things You Can Do

There are many things you can do with the `distfit` library:

You can choose which **statistical test** (RSS, Kolmogorov-Smirnov, etc.) to use for determining the best fit.

You can control the exact list of distributions you want to run through.

You can use the `distfit.predict` method to **predict** the probability of a response variable.

You can generate **synthetic** data using the `distfit.generate` method.

I have shown examples of continuous distribution fitting only. However, you can easily do fitting with **discrete** distributions.

# Summary

In this chapter, you explored lightweight Python packages that can speed up common data science tasks such as pipelining data wrangling and cleaning, numerical manipulation using NumPy and pandas, and finding the best-matched statistical distribution for numeric data points.

There are hundreds of such specialized libraries in the Python ecosystem that can lead to productive and efficient data science if you look for them. GitHub is a great place to start searching for them. Watch for the number of stars that a GitHub project has received to determine the quality of the package and determine whether it is mature/stable enough to include in your data science stack.

There are also excellent articles and blogs that specifically discusses new and exciting Python packages as alternatives to the established brands. Khyuen Tran's open-source book, Chapter 5 has compact (although code-heavy) discussions of many such useful libraries.

# CHAPTER 8

# Memory and Timing Profile

Data science tasks come with a wide variety of computational costs of both space and time. Data wrangling jobs may need the support of large storage, while advanced ML algorithms need high intensity computing speed. Some ML algorithms work better with the support of large local memory (RAM) and cannot perform well with data situated far from the CPU on a hard disk, while others are optimized to perform well with distributed data storage.

Furthermore, the nature of the data may change slowly or frequently depending on the application. Some models and data science code scale gracefully with the increasing size and complexity of the input data, some do not. When the scaling is not properly planned or baked into the code, the performance can suffer, even leading to possible catastrophic failure in time. In many of those situations, excessive memory usage by the code (or demand on the memory bandwidth) is at the root of the problem.

To plan for such situations or to design the data science code robustly, you must start with basics: measuring the efficiency of the code in terms of memory usage or profile. Obviously, this integrates tightly with the core philosophy of productive data science, which is the theme of this book. There are many tools and techniques for such measurements depending on the code and the underlying hardware. In Chapter 2, we talked about a basic timing measurement and a time decorator to measure the execution time of an ML function. In this chapter, my goal is to introduce you to some tools (with hands-on examples) that can be used to measure a memory usage profile of data science and ML code.

© Dr. Tirthajyoti Sarkar 2022
T. Sarkar, *Productive and Efficient Data Science with Python*, https://doi.org/10.1007/978-1-4842-8121-5_8

# Why Profile Memory Usage?

Memory usage measurement or profiling may seem an afterthought for most data science work. However, it is becoming more and more commonplace and critical to have. As a data scientist, if you can measure the memory profile of your code reliably and plan your larger codebase, you are sure to positively impact the robustness of your software platform.

## A Common Scenario

Suppose you have written a cool machine learning app or created a shiny neural network model. Now you want to deploy this model over some web service or REST API. Or, you might have developed a model based on data streams coming from industrial sensors in a manufacturing plant and now you must deploy the model on one of the industrial control PCs to serve decisions based on continuously incoming data.

As a data scientist, an extremely common question that you may expect from the engineering/platform team is "***what memory footprint*** does your model/code have?" or "***what's the peak memory usage by your code*** when running with some given data load?" This is quite natural to wonder about because hardware resources may be limited and a single ML module should not hog all of the memory of the system. This is particularly true for edge computing scenarios such as where the ML app may be running on the very edge such as inside a virtualized container on an industrial PC (and with no cloud-supported auto-scaling of memory or dynamic allocation).

Also, your model may be just one of hundreds of models running on that piece of hardware. Therefore, you must have some idea about the peak memory usage of the model because if a multiple models peak in their memory usage at the same time, which can crash the whole system. All these models do not necessarily come from the same data scientist either. Various teams might have developed them over time. It makes sense to have a common mechanism of measuring or gauging the memory usage (peak and average) of all those models (and data science code in general). The idea is illustrated in Figure 8-1.

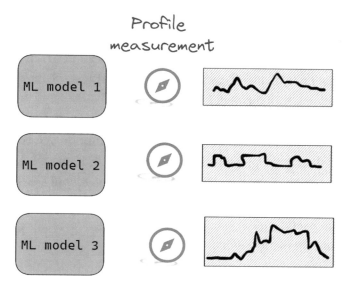

**Figure 8-1.** *Measuring (gauge) of memory and CPU (execution) profile of a multitude of ML models, all running on a single system*

# It's Not the Model Size (or Compression)

You may think that making a compact and less complex ML model may solve all of your problems. But that would be a mistaken assumption to make. When it comes to the question of peak memory usage, we are talking about the runtime memory profile (a dynamic quantity) of your entire code. This has very little to do with the size (or even the compression) of your ML model (which you may have saved as a special object on the disk, such as a scikit-learn `Joblib` dump, a simple Python pickle dump, or a TensorFlow HFD5).

Model compression and sizing is quite important, too. In many situations, you may be asked to pay special attention to it. You may have to restrict yourself from training a model with millions of parameters by choosing a simpler model architecture. You may have to try post-training model compression (e.g., intentionally reducing the floating-point accuracy of the numeric coefficients) to reduce the model size (on the disk). Often, these exercises lead to the reduction of active memory usage of the model while it is running. However, you still need to have active code and a mechanism in place to measure the memory usage profile in runtime.

# Scalene: A Neat Little Memory Profiler

Although there are many memory and CPU profilers, it is good to have a one-stop shop for getting a good view of the overall data science code. One such comprehensive utility is **Scalene**. Let's examine it in more detail.

As per its GitHub page, "Scalene is a high-performance CPU, GPU, and memory profiler for Python that does several things that other Python profilers do not and cannot do. It runs orders of magnitude faster than other profilers while delivering far more detailed information." It was developed at the University of Massachusetts. Check out the video at `www.youtube.com/watch?v=5iEf-_7mM1k&feature=youtu.be` for a comprehensive introduction.

So, Scalene promises the following:

- Profile for CPU, GPU, and memory

- Offer an order of magnitude faster execution than other profilers

- More detailed information than other similar tools

## Basic Usage

The install is by `pip`:

```
pip install scalene
```

One obvious limitation is that **currently, it works only for Linux OS**. If you run Windows or MacOS, you can use it by creating a virtual machine and running your scripts there.

The use of Scalene is extremely straightforward. You just type `scalene` in front of the name of your Python script:

```
scalene <MyApp.py>
```

Alternatively, you can use in inside a Jupyter notebook, first by executing this magic command:

```
%load_ext scalene
```

A typical output snapshot is shown in Figure 8-2. A more detailed explanation follows.

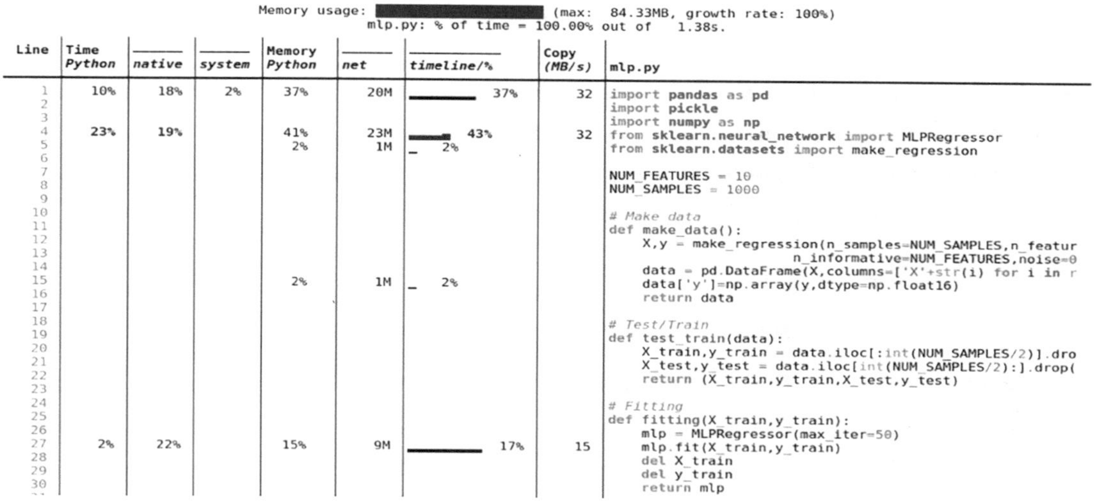

*Figure 8-2.* *A typical output snapshot from Scalene*

# Features

Here are some of the cool features of Scalene. Most of them are self-explanatory and can be gauged from Figure 8-2.

**Lines or functions**: Reports information both for entire functions and for every independent code line

**Threads**: Supports Python threads

**Multiprocessing**: Supports use of the multiprocessing library

**Python vs. C time**: Scalene breaks out time spent in Python vs. native code (e.g., libraries)

**System time**: It distinguishes system time (e.g., sleeping or performing I/O operations)

**GPU**: It can also report the time spent on an NVIDIA GPU (if present)

**Copy volume**: It reports MBs of data being copied per second

**Detects leaks**: Scalene can automatically pinpoint lines responsible for likely memory leaks!

# A Concrete Machine Learning Example

Let's get down to the business of putting Scalene to use for memory profiling standard machine learning code. You will look at two different types of ML models for reasons that will be clarified soon. You will use the scikit-learn library for all three models and utilize its synthetic data generation function to create your dataset:

- A multiple linear regression model

- A deep neural network model with the same dataset

The modeling code follows the exact same structure for these two models. External I/O ops are also indicated in Figure 8-3, as you will see that they may or may not dominate the memory profile depending on the type of model.

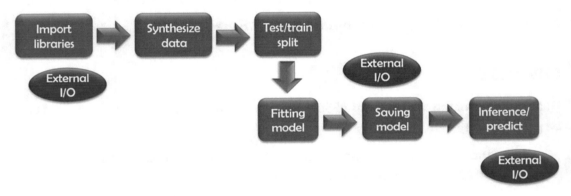

***Figure 8-3.*** *The common ML model code flow used for the Scalene demo example*

## Linear Regression Model

The complete code is in the accompanying Jupyter notebook. You use standard imports and two variables named NUM_FEATURES and NUM_SMPLES for doing some experiments later:

```
import pandas as pd
import pickle
import numpy as np
from sklearn.linear_model import LinearRegression
from sklearn.datasets import make_regression

NUM_FEATURES = 10
```

```
NUM_SAMPLES = 1000
```

For brevity, I won't show they data generation and model fitting code because it's standard. You save the fitted model as a pickled dump and load the pickled object along with a test CSV file for the inference:

```python
# Model saving function
def save(lm):
    """
    Saves a sklearn linear model as a pickled object
    """
    with open('LinearModel.sav',mode='wb') as f:
        pickle.dump(lm,f)

# Model run function
def model_run(model,testfile):
    """
    Loads and runs a sklearn linear model from pickled object
    """
    lm = pickle.load(open(model, 'rb'))
    X_test = pd.read_csv(testfile)
    _ = lm.predict(X_test)
    return None
```

You run everything under a main loop for clarity with Scalene execution and reporting (you will understand shortly):

```python
if __name__ == '__main__':
    data = make_data()
    X_train,y_train,X_test,y_test = test_train(data)

    lm = fitting(X_train,y_train)
    save(lm)
    model_run('LinearModel.sav','Test.csv')
```

You run the command

```
$ scalene linearmodel.py --html >> linearmodel-scalene.html
```

You get the results in Figure 8-4 as output. Note that you use the `--html` flag and the pipe operator (`>>`) to channel the output to an HTML file for easy reporting.

```
                          Memory usage: ████████████  (max:  79.98MB, growth rate: 100%)
                                    linearmodel.py: % of time = 100.00% out of    1.28s.

Line │ Time                     │ Memory                                │ Copy  │
     │ Python │ native │ system │ Python │ net  │ timeline/%            │ (MB/s)│ linearmodel.py
─────┼────────┼────────┼────────┼────────┼──────┼───────────────────────┼───────┼──────────────────────────────────────────────
  1  │  13%   │  22%   │   1%   │  42%   │ 20M  │ ████      42%         │  34   │ import pandas as pd
  2  │        │        │        │        │      │                       │       │ import pickle
  3  │        │        │        │        │      │                       │       │ import numpy as np
  4  │  20%   │  32%   │        │  50%   │ 25M  │ █████     52%         │  34   │ from sklearn.linear_model import LinearRegression
  5  │   1%   │        │        │   4%   │  2M  │ ██         4%         │   2   │ from sklearn.datasets import make_regression
  6  │        │        │        │        │      │                       │       │
  7  │        │        │        │        │      │                       │       │ NUM_FEATURES = 10
  8  │        │        │        │        │      │                       │       │ NUM_SAMPLES = 1000
  9  │        │        │        │        │      │                       │       │
 10  │        │        │        │        │      │                       │       │ # Make data
 11  │        │        │        │        │      │                       │       │ def make_data():
 12  │        │        │        │        │      │                       │       │     X,y = make_regression(n_samples=NUM_SAMPLES,n_featur
 13  │        │        │        │        │      │                       │       │                           n_informative=NUM_FEATURES,noise=0
 14  │        │        │        │        │      │                       │       │     data = pd.DataFrame(X,columns=['X'+str(i) for i in r
 15  │        │        │        │        │      │                       │       │     data['y']=np.array(y,dtype=np.float16)
 16  │        │        │        │        │      │                       │       │     return data
 17  │        │        │        │        │      │                       │       │
 18  │        │        │        │        │      │                       │       │ # Test/Train
 19  │        │        │        │        │      │                       │       │ def test_train(data):
 20  │        │   2%   │        │        │      │                       │       │     X_train,y_train = data.iloc[:int(NUM_SAMPLES/2)].dro
 21  │        │        │        │        │      │                       │       │     X_test,y_test = data.iloc[int(NUM_SAMPLES/2):].drop(
 22  │        │        │        │        │      │                       │       │     return (X_train,y_train,X_test,y_test)
 23  │        │        │        │        │      │                       │       │
 24  │        │        │        │        │      │                       │       │ # Fitting
 25  │        │        │        │        │      │                       │       │ def fitting(X_train,y_train):
 26  │        │        │        │        │      │                       │       │     lm = LinearRegression(n_jobs=1)
 27  │        │        │        │        │      │                       │       │     lm.fit(X_train,y_train)
 28  │        │        │        │        │      │                       │       │     del X_train
 29  │        │        │        │        │      │                       │       │     del y_train
 30  │        │        │        │        │      │                       │       │     return lm
 31  │        │        │        │        │      │                       │       │
 32  │        │        │        │        │      │                       │       │ # Saving model
 33  │        │        │        │        │      │                       │       │ def save(lm):
 34  │        │   2%   │        │        │      │                       │       │     with open('LinearModel.sav',mode='wb') as f:
 35  │        │        │        │        │      │                       │       │         pickle.dump(lm,f)
 36  │        │        │        │        │      │                       │       │
 37  │        │        │        │        │      │                       │       │ # Running model/inference
 38  │        │        │        │        │      │                       │       │ def model_run(model,testfile):
 39  │        │        │        │        │      │                       │       │     """
 40  │        │        │        │        │      │                       │       │     Loads and runs a sklearn linear model
 41  │        │        │        │        │      │                       │       │     """
 42  │        │        │        │        │      │                       │       │     lm = pickle.load(open(model, 'rb'))
 43  │        │        │        │        │      │                       │       │     X_test = pd.read_csv(testfile)
 44  │        │        │        │        │      │                       │       │     _ = lm.predict(X_test)
 45  │        │        │        │        │      │                       │       │     return None
 46  │        │        │        │        │      │                       │       │
 47  │        │        │        │        │      │                       │       │ if __name__ == '__main__':
 48  │        │        │        │        │      │                       │       │     data = make_data()
 49  │        │        │        │        │      │                       │       │     X_train,y_train,X_test,y_test = test_train(data)
 50  │        │   2%   │        │   3%   │  1M  │ █          3%         │   2   │     X_test.to_csv("Test.csv",index=False)
 51  │        │        │        │        │      │                       │       │     lm = fitting(X_train,y_train)
 52  │        │        │        │        │      │                       │       │     save(lm)
 53  │        │        │        │        │      │                       │       │     model_run('LinearModel.sav','Test.csv')
─────┼────────┼────────┼────────┼────────┼──────┼───────────────────────┼───────┼──────────────────────────────────────────────
     │        │        │        │        │      │                       │       │ function summary for linearmodel.py
 19  │        │   2%   │        │        │      │                       │       │ test_train
 33  │        │   2%   │        │        │      │                       │       │ save

Top net memory consumption, by line:
(1)     4:    25 MB
(2)     1:    20 MB
(3)     5:     2 MB
(4)    50:     1 MB
```

***Figure 8-4.*** *Scalene output after the linear regression model code was run through it*

The most important observation from this profile is that the **memory footprint is almost entirely dominated by the external I/O** such as pandas and scikit-learn estimator loading. A tiny amount of memory usage goes to writing the test data to a CSV file on the disk.

*The actual ML modeling, NumPy or pandas operations, and inference do not impact the memory at all.* This is a somewhat unexpected and non-obvious fact. Clearly, without a proper memory profiler like `scalene`, you could not have discovered this.

## What Happens as the Model and Data Scale?

You can scale the dataset size (number of rows) and the model complexity (number of features) and run the same memory profiling to document how the various operations behave in terms of memory consumption.

The result is shown in Figure 8-5. The X-axis represents the number of features/ number of data points as a pair. Note that this plot depicts percentage and not the absolute values to showcase the relative importance of the various types of operations.

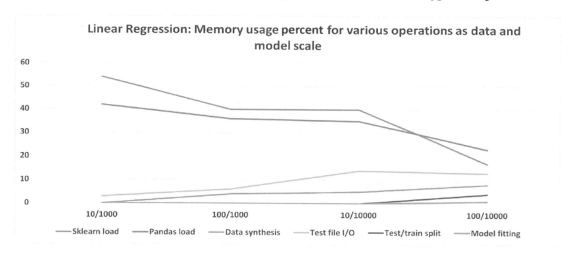

***Figure 8-5.*** *Impact of data and model (number of parameters) scaling for the linear model*

From these experiments, you can conclude that a **scikit-learn linear regression estimator** is quite efficient and **does not consume much memory for actual model fitting or inference**. It does, however, have a fixed memory footprint in terms of the code and consumes that much while getting loaded. However, the percentage of that code footprint goes down as the data size and model complexity increase.

Therefore, if you are working with a small to moderate linear model (e.g., thousands of data points but only tens of parameters), you may want to focus on data file I/O to optimize the data loading, storage, modeling, and inference code for better memory utilization. For example, you can use a different file storage option than plain CSV (e.g., Parquet or similar modern data format optimized for in-memory analytics; go to `https://medium.com/productive-data-science/why-you-should-use-parquet-files-with-pandas-b0ca8cb14d71` for more information).

## Deep Learning Model

If you run similar experiments with a two-hidden-layer neural network (with 50 neurons in each hidden layer), the result looks like Figure 8-6. It uses the `MLPRegressor` estimator from the `sklearn.neural_network` module. The code is in the accompanying Python script.

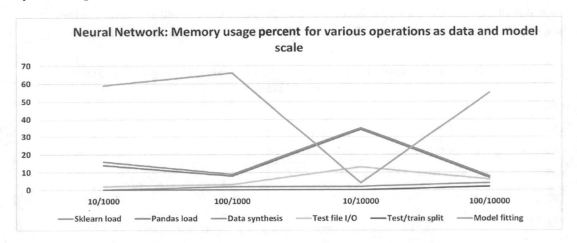

**Figure 8-6.**  *Impact of data and model (number of parameters) scaling for neural network model*

Clearly, the neural network model consumes a lot of memory at the training/fitting step, unlike the linear regression model. However, for a small number of features and large data size, the fitting takes a low amount of memory. You can also experiment with various architectures and hyperparameters and document the memory usage to arrive at the setting that works for a specific data science task.

## Key Approaches and Advice

If you repeat the experiments with the same code files, the results will vary widely depending on your hardware (disk/CPU/GPU/memory type). The purpose of the results shown above is not to focus on the actual values or even on the trends. I want you to learn to do memory profiling experiments for your own code.

# Key Advice

Some key advice, in this regard, is the following:

Preferably write small functions focused on one single task in your code.

Keep some free variables like the number of features and number of data points so that you can run the same code file with minimal changes to check the memory profile when the data/model scales.

If you are comparing one ML algorithm to another, try to keep the structure and flow of the overall code as identical as possible to reduce confusion. Preferably, just change the estimator class and compare the memory profiles.

Data and model I/O (import statements, model persistence on the disk) can be surprisingly dominating in terms of memory footprint depending on your modeling scenario. Never ignore them while doing optimization.

For the reason above, consider comparing the memory profiles of the same algorithm from multiple implementation/packages (e.g., Keras vs. PyTorch vs. scikit-learn). If memory optimization is your primary goal, you may have to look for the implementation that has a minimal memory footprint yet can do the job satisfactorily even if it is not the absolute best in terms of features or performance.

If the data I/O becomes a bottleneck, explore faster options or other storage types such as replacing pandas CSV with a Parquet file and Apache Arrow storage.

## Other Things You Can Do with Scalene

In this section, I discussed the bare minimum memory profiling with a focus on a canonical ML modeling code. Scalene CLI has other options you can take advantage of:

- Profiling CPU time only and no memory profile
- Reduced profiling with non-zero memory footprint only
- Specifying CPU and memory allocation minimum thresholds
- Setting the CPU sampling rate
- Multithreading and checking the difference

## Final Validation Is Sometimes Necessary

In many cases, ML models are run on edge devices where hardware resources are limited, especially on the memory (RAM) side. For such low-resource situations, it's a good idea to host a validation environment/server that will accept a given modeling code (after it is developed and tested but before it is deployed) and run it through a memory profiler to create runtime statistics. If it passes the predetermined criteria of the memory footprint, then it can be accepted for further deployment. The idea is illustrated in Figure 8-7.

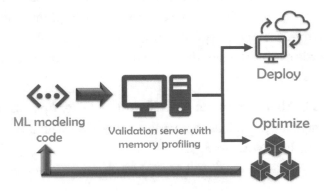

*Figure 8-7.* *Validation check with memory profile before deployment of a ML model*

Frameworks like Scalene can be very useful in these situations. By setting up such a validation gateway, data scientists can make the overall platform much more stable and robust against accidental memory overshoot and system crash.

# Timing Profile with cProfile

You have already seen some basic tricks and techniques to measure execution time of simple code blocks or a function with a timing decorator. In this section, I will discuss a built-in Python library named cProfile that can give you a detailed timing profile about the various parts of your data science code with a simple command. The advantage is that you don't have to insert code snippets like time.time() in various places (as shown in Chapter 2) and track them manually.

## Basic Usage

The cProfile library comes with the default Python installation, so there is nothing to install. Here's the basic usage with simple code where you add two NumPy arrays:

```
import numpy as np
import cProfile

SIZE = 10_000_000
a = np.arange(SIZE)
b = np.random.normal(size=SIZE)

cProfile.run('a+b')
```

The main thing to notice is that you must wrap the code within a string and pass it on to the cProfile.run function. Here the code is simply 'a+b'. The output may look something like Figure 8-8. Note that the exact time will vary, of course, depending on the underlying hardware.

```
        3 function calls in 0.064 seconds

Ordered by: standard name

ncalls  tottime  percall  cumtime  percall filename:lineno(function)
     1    0.064    0.064    0.064    0.064 <string>:1(<module>)
     1    0.000    0.000    0.064    0.064 {built-in method builtins.exec}
     1    0.000    0.000    0.000    0.000 {method 'disable' of '_lsprof.Profiler' objects}
```

***Figure 8-8.*** *Output snapshot of cProfile run with a simple Numpy array addition*

The interesting thing to remember is that the only piece of code that was measured for timing is the snippet a+b. The array creation is not being measured here, only the addition.

If you want to measure the timing profile of all the steps, you could write

```
code = """SIZE = 10_000_000
a = np.arange(SIZE)
b = np.random.normal(size=SIZE)
a+b"""

cProfile.run(code)
```

Here you put all the code inside the string variable code and then pass that on to the cProfile.run function. The output looks different (Figure 8-9), as expected.

```
        5 function calls in 0.528 seconds

   Ordered by: standard name

   ncalls  tottime  percall  cumtime  percall filename:lineno(function)
        1    0.071    0.071    0.528    0.528 <string>:1(<module>)
        1    0.000    0.000    0.528    0.528 {built-in method builtins.exec}
        1    0.029    0.029    0.029    0.029 {built-in method numpy.arange}
        1    0.000    0.000    0.000    0.000 {method 'disable' of '_lsprof.Profiler' objects}
        1    0.428    0.428    0.428    0.428 {method 'normal' of 'numpy.random.mtrand.RandomState' objects}
```

***Figure 8-9.***  *Output snapshot of cProfile run with array creation and addition*

Note that the extra array creation operations resulted in a total of five function calls, as opposed to three for the basic addition code.

# With a Function as an Argument

You could, of course, create a standalone function and pass the name of that object to cProfile.run function for the same task:

```
def add():
    SIZE = 10_000_000
    a = np.arange(SIZE)
    b = np.random.normal(size=SIZE)
    c=a+b

cProfile.run('add()')
```

The output (Figure 8-10) is similar to the output in Figure 8-9, but an additional function call is registered that comes from the construction of the add function itself.

```
      6 function calls in 0.688 seconds

   Ordered by: standard name

   ncalls  tottime  percall  cumtime  percall filename:lineno(function)
        1    0.067    0.067    0.666    0.666 1735574101.py:1(add)
        1    0.022    0.022    0.688    0.688 <string>:1(<module>)
        1    0.000    0.000    0.688    0.688 {built-in method builtins.exec}
        1    0.035    0.035    0.035    0.035 {built-in method numpy.arange}
        1    0.000    0.000    0.000    0.000 {method 'disable' of '_lsprof.Profiler' objects}
        1    0.565    0.565    0.565    0.565 {method 'normal' of 'numpy.random.mtrand.RandomState' objects}
```

***Figure 8-10.*** *Output snapshot of cProfile run with a standalone function (same NumPy ops)*

The function that is passed on to cProfile can have any argument as well. In many cases, you can change the arguments and see the impact on the profile results. This is one of the most obvious use-cases of the library. Let's rewrite the add function to accept a size argument:

```
def add(size):
    a = np.arange(size)
    b = np.random.normal(size=size)
    c = a+b
```

Then you can use it to profile the array operations with 10 million elements (Figure 8-11):

```
SIZE = 10_000_000
cProfile.run('add(SIZE)')
```

```
                    SIZE = 10_000_000
                    cProfile.run('add(SIZE)')
                    6 function calls in 0.593 seconds
```

***Figure 8-11.*** *Running cProfile and passing in an argument to the function of 10 million elements*

When you change the number of elements to 20 million, it reflects immediately (Figure 8-12):

```
SIZE = 20_000_000
cProfile.run('add(SIZE)')
```

```
SIZE = 20_000_000
cProfile.run('add(SIZE)')
```

            6 function calls in 1.141 seconds

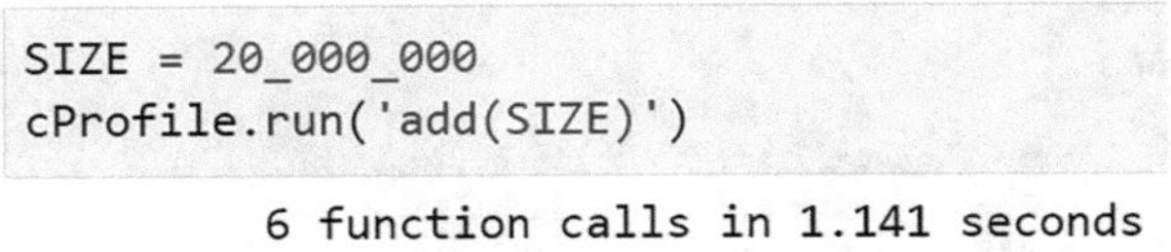

***Figure 8-12.*** *Running cProfile and passing in an argument to the function for 20 million elements*

## Using the Profiler Class

cProfile has a special Profiler class that stores all the important information, and it can be enabled/disabled programmatically. You can also use the pstats library and pass this Profiler object to it for printing and extracting data. Here is the code to measure and print the total execution time:

```
import cProfile, pstats

profiler = cProfile.Profile()
# Enable profiler
profiler.enable()
# Function execution
add(SIZE)
# Disable profiler
profiler.disable()
# pstats
stats = pstats.Stats(profiler)
# Print the total time and number of calls
print("Total function calls:", stats.total_calls)
print("Total time (seconds):", stats.total_tt)
```

The result looks like the following:

```
>> Total function calls: 48
>> Total time (seconds): 1.1527893999999999
```

Here you get the execution time from the `total_tt` attribute of the `stats` object and the number of calls from the `total_calls` attribute.

Consequently, this opens up the possibility to programmatically control the profiling and storing of information as needed. For example, you can profile the execution of the same add function over a range of arrays sizes:

```
size = [int(i*1e6) for i in range(5,26,5)]
total_tt = []
for s in size:
    profiler = cProfile.Profile()
    profiler.enable()
    add(s)
    profiler.disable()
    stats = pstats.Stats(profiler)
    total_tt.append(round(stats.total_tt,3))
```

The timings are stored in the `total_tt` array. When plotted, it shows the expected pattern (Figure 8-13).

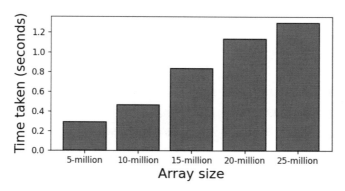

***Figure 8-13.*** *Computation time extracted using cProfile for various array sizes*

# Data Science Workflow Profiling

While measuring the execution time of these small standalone functions serves as a basic demonstration of the usage of these profilers, the real utility is realized when they are used in a large-scale data science workflow. Such a workflow has a variety of modules and functions, and you can set up profiling for all of them if necessary. The output may be logged into a database or even be fed into a monitoring system that will track the performance of the modules over time and act if needed (e.g., if a function performs poorly by taking too much time in a certain run or for a certain input data). The idea is illustrated in Figure 8-14.

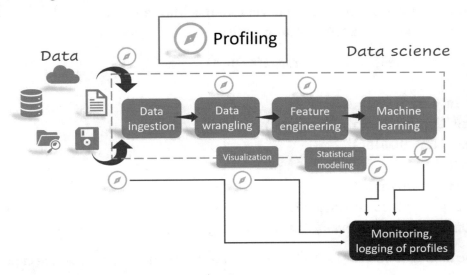

***Figure 8-14.*** *Time and memory profiling at various data science workflow stages*

## Summary

In this chapter, you examined the importance of memory profiling your ML code for smooth and easy interfacing with the platform/engineering team that will deploy the code on a service/machine. Profiling memory can also show you surprising ways to optimize the code based on the combination of specific datasets and algorithms you are dealing with. You saw a typical ML modeling code example being profiled with a powerful yet lightweight Python library. You saw representative results with linear regression and neural network models and received some general advice.

Next, you saw the basic usage of the built-in Python timing profiler cProfile and how it can be used with raw code or function modules. You learned how to extract the total execution time or number of function calls using this library for NumPy operations. This idea can be extended to any data science workflow that consists of many stages and modules.

Every data science team or organization has its own style for measuring code and module efficiency and memory footprint. The motivation for this chapter was to introduce you to the importance of these measurements and show some hands-on examples so that you can explore further and be ready for such implementation.

# CHAPTER 9

# Scalable Data Science

Data science tasks may encounter a wide variety of dataset sizes, ranging from kilobytes to petabytes. Some business spreadsheets will only have a few hundred rows while a whole factory may send a deluge of sensor data to a single dataset, resulting in billions of rows per day or even per hour. Some datasets can have many rows and a small number of columns, while others may consist of a few rows but millions of columns as feature dimensions. Even within the same organization or a data science team there can be multiple pipelines dealing with different types of input, and they may be facing a wide variation in the dataset size and complexity.

It is often a natural practice for data scientists to build a scaled prototype of a data science job (such as combining data wrangling, ML algorithms, and some prediction functions). They build such a prototype, test it with a typical dataset that is expected to hit the pipeline, evaluate the result or measure some performance metric with a few ML algorithms, tune them, and finally make a choice. This is an experimental mentality, and it serves the spirit of *doing science with data* very well. However, to support this quick analysis and prototyping, a data scientist must be able to quickly scale across a wide variety of dataset sizes and complexity as the need arises. They should not run into issues like being out of memory while prototyping on their laptop.

This chapter talks about the common problems and limitations that arise while scaling out to larger datasets and what tools are out there to address these issues. Specifically, you will visit some of the limitations that arise while doing analysis with large datasets using the most common data analysis library, Python pandas, and explore two alternative libraries or add-ons that can be used to overcome these limitations.

In fact, scalability is closely related to the ability to do parallel processing of large data. Therefore, this theme will be continued in the next chapter where you will explore Python libraries that support parallel processing natively for data science tasks.

© Dr. Tirthajyoti Sarkar 2022
T. Sarkar, *Productive and Efficient Data Science with Python*, https://doi.org/10.1007/978-1-4842-8121-5_9

# Common Problems for Scalability

Python is a great language for data science. Libraries like pandas open myriad possibilities for data scientists to slice and dice the data any way they like and create meaningful insights and high-impact analytics reports with a relatively small amount of programming. However, they have some serious limitations when it comes to dealing with large datasets even one as simple as a CSV file with a billion rows.

Two of the most common issues that a data scientist may encounter as the scale of the data grows are out-of-core failures and inefficiencies related to the Python single-threading characteristic.

*Out-of-core* really means the inability to load the full data properly in the working memory (RAM) of the machine. Single threading is related to the fundamental Python design feature of the Global Interpreter Lock (GIL) (`https://realpython.com/python-gil/`) that allows a single thread to put a lock on the interpreter so that other threads cannot get a hold of it. Together, they can make doing efficient data analysis on large datasets (anything larger than a few gigabytes) with limited hardware quite tricky.

## Out-of-Core (a.k.a. Out of Memory)

pandas is the most popular data analysis library in Python, and it is at the front end of any standard data science pipeline. However, if you have ever tried to work with data files larger than a few GB, you may have seen the memory error that is thrown by pandas (Figure 9-1).

```
.py", line 1872, in form_blocks
    float_blocks = _multi_blockify(float_items, items)
  File "C:\Program Files\Python\Anaconda\lib\site-packages\pandas\core\internals
.py", line 1930, in _multi_blockify
    block_items, values = _stack_arrays(list(tup_block), ref_items, dtype)
  File "C:\Program Files\Python\Anaconda\lib\site-packages\pandas\core\internals
.py", line 1962, in _stack_arrays
    stacked = np.empty(shape, dtype=dtype)
MemoryError
Press any key to continue . . .
```

***Figure 9-1.***  *A memory error thrown by pandas*

Of course, this error depends on the exact state of the system memory such as how many other processes are running alongside the pandas code and what type of memory they are blocking. Nonetheless, it is a well-known fact that pandas cannot handle multi-GB datasets (no matter how simple in structure they may be) efficiently.

Furthermore, this inefficiency and limitation can rear its ugly head even with a large dataset that could be somehow loaded in the memory without any memory error at the beginning. Due to the way pandas handles in-memory objects and calculations, it is quite easy to run into the same memory error in your data science code. This can be exacerbated by code that produces many large in-memory DataFrames in quick succession with intermediate calculations.

For example, imagine what the following code can do. Let's assume that the Large-file.csv has 10 million rows and 20 columns.

```
df1 = pd.read_csv("Large-file.csv") # Successful
df2 = df1.dropna()
df3 = df2[df2['col1'] > 10 and df2['col2'] < 20]

def complex_calc(x):
    # Some complex math

df3['new-col'] = df3['col3'].apply(complex_calc)

def some_transformation(df):
    # Transformation code
    return transformed_df

df4 = some_transformation(df3)
...
```

This is a generic code snippet, but you get the idea that this code is inefficient, particularly when dealing with large pandas DataFrame objects. It produces multiple intermediate DataFrames and does not purge them from memory when their job is done. At the end, it may use only the final DataFrame for a machine learning modeling, but the system memory is already clogged with so many useless objects that it will result in a memory error and the whole pipeline will crash. This is illustrated in Figure 9-2.

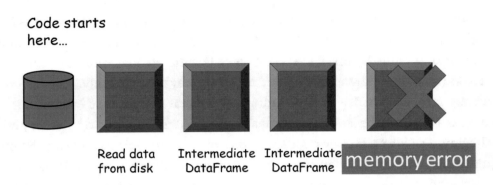

**Figure 9-2.** *A memory error produced by too many intermediate DataFrames (bad coding practice) even when a large file could be read from the disk*

Of course, one way to get around this issue is to rigorously maintain a good coding habit where unused objects are tracked and purged regularly. However, while doing prototyping on their Jupyter notebooks, data scientists are bound to write quick and dirty code without following this practice, and this will hinder their scalability options with large datasets.

# Python Single Threading

The GIL was one of the earlier design choices in the Python language and it solved quite a few important problems related to memory leaks and racing conditions. Put simply, it is a locking mechanism that allows only one thread to hold the control of the Python interpreter. This means that only one thread can be in a state of execution at any given point in time.

Generally, its impact isn't visible to programmers executing single-threaded programs. In fact, many data science tasks can run just fine without worrying about GIL as they execute a series of tasks one after another and do not employ many parallel processing tricks. However, it can become a performance bottleneck in CPU-bound and multi-threaded code.

For larger datasets, sometimes it makes sense to divide the data into multiple chunks and utilize a parallel processing execution pipeline. The idea is to send the chunked data to each core of the CPU and execute the analysis as much in parallel as possible. When the executions are done, the results can be combined to get back a transformed dataset. While this does not necessarily help to fit a larger dataset in memory, it can make analysis of the same dataset faster by the parallel execution.

The beauty here is that this approach can speed up data science exploration and prototyping tasks even without paying for large CPU clusters on the cloud. It is really a matter of taking advantage of the 8 or 16 cores that routinely come with the single modern-day CPU inside a data scientist's laptop. However, you must make sure that the data science code and libraries are not getting in the way, and that you are using libraries that can take full advantage of the multi-core hardware platform.

# What Options Are Out There?

To solve the memory issue (while loading and transforming large datasets) there are many possible solutions depending on the situation you are in. Some are related to your choice of hardware and some have to do with your data loading strategy. Let's talk about them in a systematic manner.

## Cloud Instances

For larger and larger datasets, there is always a brute-force solution of renting out a cloud instance with a large RAM attached. As an example, these days you can rent out an AWS (Amazon Web Service) Elastic Compute (EC2) instance with 128GB of RAM for less than a dollar per hour. Figure 9-3 shows the pricing for a **r6g.4xlarge** instance (a so-called memory optimized EC2 instance, www.amazonaws.cn/en/ec2/instance-types/#Memory_Optimized_Instances).

| Instance name ▲ | On-Demand hourly rate ▽ | vCPU ▽ | Memory ▽ | Storage ▽ | Network performance |
|---|---|---|---|---|---|
| r6g.4xlarge | $0.8064 | 16 | 128 GiB | EBS Only | Up to 10 Gigabit |

*Figure 9-3.* *A memory-optimized EC2 (AWS) instance pricing*

Once set up, you can install all your favorite Python libraries, read large data files stored locally (e.g., to a mapped SSD) or from an AWS S3 folder, and do pandas data transformation without worrying about memory errors. While it may still seem expensive to a causal user, organizations or teams who need that much memory to process pandas DataFrames regularly probably won't mind paying ~$0.8 an hour for a smooth and error-free data science task flow.

233

However, remember that pandas will still be limited to use only one CPU core at a time and, by default, it will exhibit slowness while loading and dealing with large files. Just running run-of-the-mill pandas code on a large-memory cloud instance may stop some frequent memory error situations, but it **may not fundamentally make the data science pipeline productive or efficient** *at scale*.

---

**What is a memory-optimized EC2 instance?**    A cloud service like AWS must cater to a wide variety of users with various needs. Someone may need fast processing with a CPU cluster, someone else may need a high network bandwidth, and someone else may require large on-board memory (RAM). Memory-optimized instances are just that: they provide a large amount of RAM at an optimized cost. They do not necessarily have the best-in-class CPUs or network bandwidth, but they work best for jobs that demand large slices of physical memory during execution. Within these instances, there are multiple choices depending on cost and available CPU types. The r6g.4xlarge is really the starting point of this lineup that goes up to a 768GB memory option with a reasonable hourly cost.

AWS is not the only cloud service to offer this. Every major player—Google Cloud or Microsoft Azure, for example—offers similar high-memory instances as Infrastructure-as-a-Service (IaaS) that can address the problem of insufficient memory while executing a data science task (on a local machine).

---

# Google Colab

Google Colaboratory (or Colab, as it is known popularly; `https://research.google.com/colaboratory/faq.html`) is also a cloud service at its core. Basically, it runs a Jupyter notebook service that is hosted on Google cloud servers. You can use a CPU, GPU, or even a TPU (if you are lucky) for free just by having a Google account.

**The greatest advantage of Colab, as compared to AWS or GCP, is its ease of use and low barrier of entry**. If you have your data science Python code in a Jupyter notebook, Colab can help get you started on this cloud instance instantly (as soon as you upload your notebook to the instance). Unlike AWS or GCP barebone instances, there is no setup or installation needed. You can directly access Colab notebooks through your browser and start running your code in a matter of minutes.

---

**What is a Tensor Processing Unit?**    Tensor Processing Units (TPUs) are Google's custom-developed application-specific integrated circuits (ASICs) used to accelerate machine learning workloads. These ASICs are designed from the ground up with the sole aim of optimizing the speed and power of computation tasks that appear in deep learning such as matrix multiplication and addition, special activations functions, other linear algebra routines like matrix inversion, and so on. Their internal architecture is quite different from traditional CPUs that are designed for general purpose computing tasks. Memory bandwidth memory transfer speed of a TPU is also enhanced as this factors critically in a deep learning training performance.

---

For some specific situations, this may indeed increase productivity and efficiency. For example, if the local laptop does not have a good enough CPU or a GPU card installed, or the RAM is under 8GB, then switching to Google Colab should enhance the productivity instantly.

The typical instance (free of cost) has ~12-13 GB of RAM and a CPU equivalent to an Intel Xeon processor. Getting a GPU instance is also quite easy, with the most common GPU being a Tesla K80 (compute 3.7, having 2496 CUDA cores and 12GB GDDR5 VRAM). While the CPU core count is nothing boast about, having a larger RAM and GPU memory may help data science exploration, especially if it involves GPU-intensive tasks like training a deep neural network or even vectorized computation involving NumPy arrays. If 12GB RAM seems too little, you can upgrade to Colab Pro (`https://colab.research.google.com/signup`), which offers double the RAM for only $10/month (a whole lot cheaper than paying for an equivalent EC2 instance with 24GB of RAM).

However, despite its attractive features, **Colab does have some serious limitations** for practicing data scientists who are trying to explore larger datasets and scale up their data science workflow. At the outset, it puts a time limit on the running time of the notebook, so if you leave it idle for a certain amount of time, the instance will die (along with any variables and internal states). Basically, you must plan your code execution carefully and be ever vigilant to take full advantage of Colab.

Also, file loading (whether uploading from local drive or reading from the Web) is painfully slow (most probably a deliberate choice to control the bandwidth usage over the Google Cloud infrastructure). Therefore, while you can do in-memory analytics and data transformations rather quickly, the initial loading can take an inordinate amount of time or may even crash your notebook. Upgrading to Colab Pro or Pro+ (from a completely free account) alleviates these issues to some extent but not fully.

## pandas-Specific Tricks

Since I started the scalability discussion by pointing out the out-of-core issues in pandas, it makes sense to loop back to ground zero and examine what suggestions the pandas developers have to address this issue.

There is a dedicated resource page on the pandas documentation portal about this topic: "Scaling to large datasets" (`https://pandas.pydata.org/pandas-docs/stable/user_guide/scale.html`). It starts like this:

> *Pandas provides data structures for in-memory analytics, which makes using pandas to analyze datasets that are larger than memory datasets somewhat tricky. Even datasets that are a sizable fraction of memory become unwieldy, as some pandas operations need to make intermediate copies.*

It goes on to point out some useful tricks and techniques for coping with memory issues. I discuss some of them below and add a few more.

### Load Only the Columns You Need

Often, a particular data transformation task requires only a small fraction of the columns that the complete dataset features. If you have a dataset with 10 million rows and 100 columns, and you need only the first 5, it makes absolute sense to load only those 5 columns and not even look at the rest. You avoid loading a whopping 950 million pieces of data into memory. The essential trick here is to include the necessary argument in your data loading function.

Write

```
df = pd.read_csv("Large-file.csv",
                 names = ['Col-1','Col-2','Col-3'])
```

instead of

```
df = pd.read_csv("Large-file.csv")
```

This little change can indeed make or break your data transformation pipeline.

## Column-Specific Functions (If Applicable)

Following the same idea as above, it is a good practice (wherever applicable) to write separate functions that deal with specific columns/features in the dataset as needed (Figure 9-4). For example, a dataset may have the following:

- **String data** corresponding to name and address. This can be handled by a specific function.

- **Datetime data** corresponding to some business transaction. This should be handled by another specific function that loads and process only these columns.

- **Pure numeric data**, which can be handled many ways, even read as a pure NumPy array and utilizing vectorizing tricks (as discussed elsewhere in this book) to speed up the data transformation process.

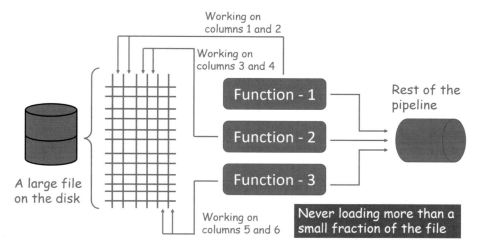

***Figure 9-4.*** *Functions to deal with specific columns of a large on-disk file, never loading more than a small fraction into memory*

## Explicitly Specify/Convert Data Types

The default data types in pandas are not designed to be the most memory efficient. This is especially true for text/string data columns with relatively few unique values (alternatively known as *low-cardinality data*). By using more efficient and targeted data types, you can significantly reduce the memory usage and process larger datasets.

There is a dataset called loan_data.csv on file (supplied with the book). Let's see how explicitly specifying the data type can reduce the memory usage while working with this dataset:

```
import pandas as pd
df = pd.read_csv("../loan_data.csv")
df.memory_usage(deep=True)
```

The function memory_usage() shows the true memory usage by the in-memory object. The output is shown in Figure 9-5. The output of df.info() is shown in the same figure, indicating that the default loading assigned the general-purpose object data type to that column while others were assigned data types like int64 or float.

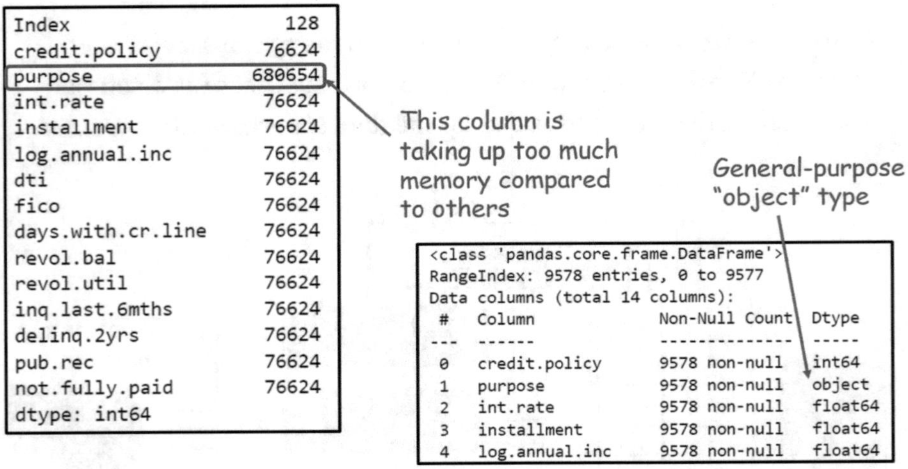

**Figure 9-5.** *Default data loading assigned a general-purpose data type to a text/ string column, causing it to take up too much memory*

You might also have noticed that the credit.policy is an unsigned integer taking on values 1 or 0. Why do you need a 64-bit integer data type to represent that? So, let's also type convert that column:

```
df['credit.policy'].unique()
>> array([1, 0], dtype=int64)
```

Here is the code for doing the data type conversions (explicit specifications):

```
df2 = df.copy()
df2['purpose'] = df2['purpose'].astype('category')
df2['credit.policy'] = df2['credit.policy'].astype('uint8')
del(df)
```

Here, first you do a copy on the existing DataFrame. Then, you use the astype function to assign the category data type to the purpose column and unit8 (8-bit unsigned integer) to the credit.policy column. Lastly, as a good practice, you delete the old DataFrame object from the memory since you no longer need it for your data science pipeline.

You can see the stark difference in Figure 9-6.

```
df2.memory_usage(deep=True)

Index                128
credit.policy       9578         These columns are now
purpose            10370         taking up the least
int.rate           76624        amount of memory
installment        76624        compared to the others.
log.annual.inc     76624
dti                76624
fico               76624
days.with.cr.line  76624
revol.bal          76624
revol.util         76624
inq.last.6mths     76624
delinq.2yrs        76624
pub.rec            76624
not.fully.paid     76624
dtype: int64
```

***Figure 9-6.*** *Loan dataset memory usage after explicit data type specification/ conversion*

This memory saving may seem trivial for this example, but small savings like this add up quickly for a long and data-intensive pipeline and can reduce the total overhead significantly.

# Libraries for Parallel Processing

Parallel computing is an extensive field of its own. It is not trivial to implement optimized code in Python that will execute parallel threads/processes flawlessly and with high performance. Fortunately, there are some fantastic Python frameworks for doing parallel processing with minimal learning curves.

I will discuss a couple of them, Dask and Ray, with hands-on examples in the next chapter, so I won't get into those details here.

## Libraries for Handling Out-of-Core Datasets

There are special libraries to handle out-of-core datasets. Vaex and Modin are two such frameworks. Let's discuss them in more detail with hands-on examples next.

## A Note About the Preferred OS

Although a many data scientists use Windows OS for their day-to-day tasks, it has been observed that (in general, and while doing the technical review of this book) advanced libraries like Vaex, Modin, Ray, and Dask may have trouble being set up or performing smoothly on Windows OS. Therefore, you are strongly encouraged to use a Linux-based OS for practicing with these libraries and running some of the Jupyter Notebooks that are provided. You can either

- Use a Linux-based OS (e.g., Ubuntu, Fedora, or Red Hat) on your local machine natively

- Run a virtual machine (VM) using tools like Oracle VirtualBox on your Windows-based machine, with a Linux-based OS on the VM

- Use a cloud instance with a Linux-based OS (including the Amazon Linux flavor that comes with any EC2 instance)

## Hands-On Example with Vaex

Vaex is a Python library designed for working with **lazy out-of-core DataFrames**. One of its central goals is to help visualize and explore big tabular datasets. Vaex is high-performant for large datasets. For example, it can help calculate statistics such as mean, sum, count, standard deviation, and more on an $N$-dimensional grid of up to a billion objects/rows per second.

In this section, you will see hands-on examples of such calculations and visualizations with the Vaex library.

# Features at a Glance

Here is a quick summarization of the key features of Vaex:

> **Performance**: It can work easily with huge tabular data. Its processing capability is in the order of billions rows/second.

> **Lazy/virtual columns**: The computation is done on the fly, without wasting precious RAM/virtual memory.

> **Memory efficient**: No memory copies when doing routine data slicing such as filtering/selections/subsets.

> **Visualization**: Natively and directly supported. Lots of functions to realize routine visualization from huge tabular datasets.

> **User friendly API**: The DataFrame object is the main API and it is all that a general user will ever need. The API feels very similar to pandas and therefore presents with minimal learning curve when replacing pandas code with Vaex for out-of-core data processing.

> **Lean and compartmentalized**: Vaex is separated into multiple subpackages and you can install any combination of them as per your specific needs. For example, `Vaex-astro` supports astronomy related transformations and FITS file reading. `Vaex-viz` support all visualizations. But if all you want is to calculate statistics and not visualize the data, you don't have to install it. For modern file types like Apache Arrow, it has a package named `Vaex-arrow`.

# Basic Usage Example

Start by using an example dataset provided with Vaex:

```
import vaex
df = vaex.example()
```

When you run this code first time, it will download the dataset from the Web, so an Internet connection is required while running this code first time. It will store the dataset (a .hdf5 file) in a folder called data.

You can examine the information about the file:

```
df.info()
```

You will see something like Figure 9-7.

## helmi-dezeeuw-2000-FeH-v2-10percent

**rows**: 330,000

## Columns:

| column | type | unit | description | expression |
|---|---|---|---|---|
| id | uint8 | | | |
| x | float32 | | | |
| y | float32 | | | |
| z | float32 | | | |
| vx | float32 | | | |
| vy | float32 | | | |
| vz | float32 | | | |
| E | float32 | | | |
| L | float32 | | | |
| Lz | float32 | | | |
| FeH | float32 | | | |

***Figure 9-7.***  *Vaex example dataset information*

The slicing and indexing of the data are just like pandas. For example, say you want to see only the x, y, vx, and vy columns for rows 3 to 7:

```
df[['x','y','vx','vy']][3:8]
```

It will give you the expected output (Figure 9-8).

| # | x | y | vx | vy |
|---|---|---|---|---|
| 0 | 4.71559 | 4.58525 | -232.421 | -294.851 |
| 1 | 7.21719 | 11.9947 | -1.68917 | 181.329 |
| 2 | -7.78437 | 5.98977 | 86.7009 | -238.778 |
| 3 | 8.08373 | -3.27348 | -57.4544 | 120.117 |
| 4 | -3.55719 | 5.41363 | -67.0511 | -145.933 |

***Figure 9-8.*** *Vaex example of indexing the dataset*

The calculation of statistics is fast. On my laptop, calculating the mean of 330,000 rows took under 20ms.

```
%%timeit
df.x.mean()

>> 19.6 ms ± 2.1 ms per loop (mean ± std. dev. of 7 runs, 10 loops each)
```

# No Unnecessary Memory Copying

The best thing about Vaex is that it does not create unnecessary copies of DataFrame objects while doing simple filtering operations or intermediate calculations. Even the base DataFrame has minimal memory impact. The computations are done in a lazy, on-the-fly (*when necessary*) manner.

Check the memory footprint with this code:

```
import sys
# Vaex dataframe
print("Size of Vaex DF:", sys.getsizeof(df))
# Convert to Pandas dataframe
df_pandas = df.to_pandas_df()
print("Size of Pandas DF:", sys.getsizeof(df_pandas))
```

The output is astonishing:

```
Size of Vaex DF: 48
Size of Pandas DF: 13530144
```

You can run all the necessary calculations on the Vaex dataframe object with much less worry about memory errors cropping up.

For example, you can filter the dataframe for only those rows that have negative x values and positive z values:

```
df_filtered = df[df.x < 0 and df.z > 0]
sys.getsizeof(df_filtered)
```

```
>> 48
```

As expected, the new `df_filtered` dataframe still has a low memory footprint, but it only has 164464 rows compared to original 330,000 rows.

```
df_filtered.shape
>> (164464, 11)
```

## Expressions and Virtual Columns

You can create custom expressions and assign them to virtual columns with no memory copying (again). Working with pure pandas code, every such operation runs a chance of creating memory overhead. Let's say you want to calculate the root of the sum of the squares of two columns from the example dataset:

```
import numpy as np
sqroot_exp = np.sqrt(df['x']**2+df['y']**2)
```

Now, if you examine this `sqroot_exp`, you will see that it is a special expression (not evaluated yet). It has not created any memory overhead.

```
type(sqroot_exp)
```

```
>> vaex.expression.Expression
```

If you do this in pandas, it will create a pandas series object:

```
sqroot_pandas = np.sqrt(df_pandas['x']**2+df_pandas['y']**2)
type(sqroot_pandas)
>> pandas.core.series.Series
```

Now, such Vaex expressions can be added to a DataFrame, creating a *virtual column*. These virtual columns are similar to normal DataFrame columns, except they do not waste any memory.

```
# Assignment of expression to a virtual column
df['sqroot'] = sqroot_exp
# Evaluation only when needed
df['sqroot'].mean()

>> array(8.38820497)
```

# Computation on a Multidimensional Grid

One of the most interesting features of Vaex is the ability to calculate statistics on user-selectable grids in a fast and efficient manner. This has many practical applications when you are interested in finding local minima or maxima or the distribution of numeric quantities over specific regions from a maze of numbers.

```
counts_x = df.count(binby=df.x, limits=[-5, 5], shape=32)
counts_x

>> array([4216, 4434, 4730, 4975, 5332, 5800, 6162, 6540, 6805, 7261,
7478,7642, 7839, 8336, 8736, 8279, 8269, 8824, 8217, 7978, 7541, 7383,7116,
6836, 6447, 6220, 5864, 5408, 4881, 4681, 4337, 4015], dtype=int64)
```

The result is nothing but a NumPy array with the number counts in 32 bins distributed between x = -5, and x = 5. The key thing to note here is the `binby` argument inside the function that works similar to `GroupBy` in SQL or even pandas. Here the data was grouped by the x column (`binby=df.x`).

So, with this single line of code, you

- Filtered/restricted the data within -5 and 5

- Counted the number of data points

- Binned the counts in 32 bins

Figure 9-9 shows the visualization.

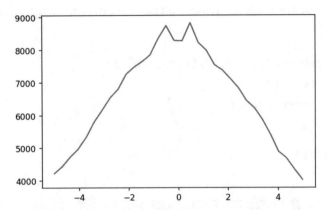

***Figure 9-9.*** *Counts of x column data for a specific range and bin count*

Want a more powerful example? You can calculate the root of the sum of the squares of velocities vx, vy, and vz to get the resultant velocity. However, you may want to do it for a certain range of x and y data and bin the result for easy visualization.

```
# Just an expression
velo = np.sqrt(df.vx**2 + df.vy**2 + df.vz**2)
# Pass the expression to the function
# Binned by x and y, over limits of -10 to 10
xy_mean_v = df.mean(velo, binby=[df.x, df.y],
                    limits=[[-10, 10], [-10, 10]],
                    shape=(64, 64))
```

You can do a 2D plot of the resultant velocity over the same xy range:

```
plt.figure(dpi=120,figsize=(3,3))
plt.imshow(xy_mean_v.T,
           origin='lower',
           extent=[-10, 10, -10, 10])
plt.show()
```

Figure 9-10 shows the result.

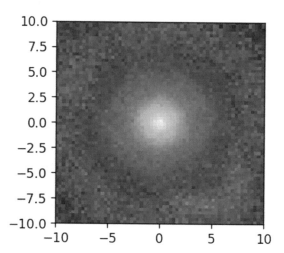

***Figure 9-10.*** *Resultant velocity calculated and visualized over specific ranges of x and y data*

## Dynamic Visualizations Using Widgets and Other Plotting Libraries

The N-dimensional grid-based computation is designed to be fast with Vaex. This allows you to extend the visualization to be dynamic using widgets and third-party libraries like bqplot. Unfortunately, these dynamic visualizations are not possible to render in the pages of a book. However, some code and results are shown in the Jupyter notebook.

For example, this simple code creates a plot widget in the Jupyter notebook where you can pan and zoom around and choose a few data transformations from the drop-down menu. (Figure 9-11 shows a static snapshot of the widget.)

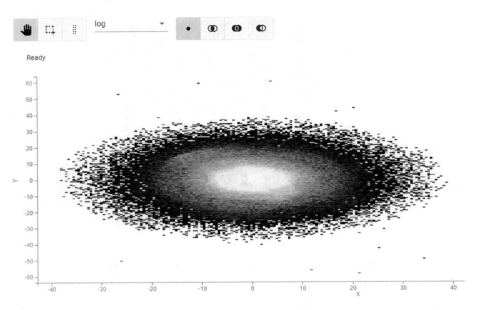

***Figure 9-11.*** *Snapshot of a dynamic visualization with a Vaex plot widget method*

The usefulness of such utility methods cannot be overemphasized for large-scale data analysis. You can plot complex transformations on large, out-of-core datasets (say 10GB or 20GB in size) with only a few lines of code to visualize the hidden patterns. This increases the productivity and efficiency of such a data analysis pipeline far beyond what would have been possible with only pandas and Matplotlib code.

## Vaex Preferred HDF5 Format

The magic in Vaex happens because of internal optimization and data representation. One of the design choices is to work with HDF5 file formats as much as possible. Therefore, the best way to work with Vaex is to load other types of data into this format before you start exploring. For convenience, Vaex provides many utility methods to convert other files or data structures to this format. You can convert from CSVs, Arrow tables, Python dictionaries, NumPy arrays, JSON, and more.

For example, this code converts a moderate-sized CSV file (close to a million rows and 15 columns) into a HDF5 file:

```
df2 = vaex.from_csv("Large-data.csv", convert=True)
```

When you run this code, another file named Large-data.csv.hdf5 gets created in the folder where the Large-data.csv file resides. You must not forget to set convert=True for this to happen.

After that, you can read/open this HDF5 much faster than what is possible with pandas CSV reading. Here is the complete code:

```
# Pandas reading CSV
t1 = time.time()
df2_pandas = pd.read_csv("Large-data.csv")
t2 = time.time()
print(f"Took {round(1000*(t2-t1),3)} milliseconds with Pandas")

# Vaex conversion from CSV
df2 = vaex.from_csv("Large-data.csv", convert=True)

# Vaex reading HDF5
t1 = time.time()
df2 = vaex.open("Large-data.csv.hdf5")
t2 = time.time()
print(f"Took {round(1000*(t2-t1),3)} milliseconds with Vaex")
```

The results speak for themselves:

```
Took 2354.523 milliseconds with Pandas
Took 14.057 milliseconds with Vaex
```

In today's world of data science, a dataset with a million rows is not a particularly large one. Even this modest sized file caused pandas to take over 2 seconds to read from the disk. With Vaex, after conversion to HDF5, it becomes so much faster. Therefore, for a data processing pipeline utilizing the power of libraries like Vaex, it makes sense to convert (in a systematic manner) all the text-based data files (CSV or even JSON if that makes sense) to HDF5 and read them as a Vaex DataFrame as much as possible, as illustrated in Figure 9-12.

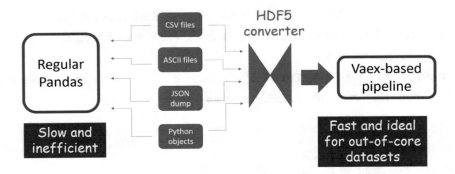

**_Figure 9-12._**  *Converting to HDF5 and working with Vaex results in a faster and more productive data science pipeline, particularly for out-of-core datasets*

# Hands-On Examples with Modin

Modin is a library whose actual utility falls into the realm of parallel processing or multi-core processing. It uses a **Ray** or **Dask** back end to provide an effortless way to speed up pandas notebooks, scripts, and libraries. The main attractiveness of Modin is its tight integration and identical API to that of pandas.

You will see the use of a Dask DataFrame and Ray in the next chapter. However, unlike these distributed DataFrame libraries, Modin provides seamless integration and compatibility with existing pandas code including DataFrame construction. Basically, you just need to change a single line of code to get started.

## Single CPU Core to Multi-Core

For most of the data science workload to use Modin, you just start like this:

```
import modin.pandas as pd
```

From a simple change in one line of code, the benefit that you get is enormous. This comes from the fact that despite all the great features and capabilities, **the core implementation of pandas is inherently single-threaded**. This means that only one of the multiple CPU cores can be utilized at any given time for executing normal pandas code. In a single CPU machine (e.g., a data scientist's laptop), it would look something like Figure 9-13.

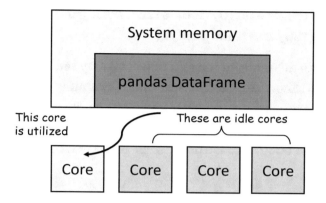

***Figure 9-13.*** *The pandas code utilizing only a single core of the system*

However, just wrapping the pandas code with Modin (a single line of code change), you can utilize all the cores (by setting up a Dask or Ray backend cluster/worker system), as shown in Figure 9-14.

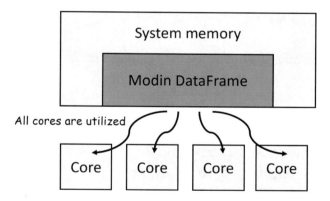

***Figure 9-14.*** *Modin code utilizing all the CPU cores*

# Out-of-Core Processing

Let's now demonstrate the out-of-core processing capability of Modin. Here, the phrase "core" does not refer to the CPU core but really to the system memory or RAM.

The following code creates a DataFrame with ~1 million ($2^{20}$ to be precise) rows and 256 columns with random integers. Note the use of modin.pandas here.

```
import modin.pandas as pd
import numpy as np
```

```
raw_data = np.random.randint(0, 100, size=(2**20, 2**8))
df = pd.DataFrame(raw_data).add_prefix("col")
```

When you execute this code for the first time, you may see some user warnings and message (Figure 9-15) about the Dask cluster setup (assuming that you are using the Dask back end for the parallel processing/ clustering). In the next chapter, you will see how to start and monitor a Dask cluster. The good thing with Modin is that all of this gets taken care of under the hood, and the user doesn't have to write the cluster setup code.

```
UserWarning: Dask execution environment not yet initialized. Initializing...
To remove this warning, run the following python code before doing dataframe operations:

    from distributed import Client

    client = Client()

UserWarning: Distributing <class 'numpy.ndarray'> object. This may take some time.
```

***Figure 9-15.*** *Warning message related to Dask cluster setup for Modin code execution (first time only)*

You can check the information about the DataFrame:

```
df.info()
```

It will show something like this:

```
<class 'pandas.core.frame.DataFrame'>
RangeIndex: 1048576 entries, 0 to 1048575
Columns: 256 entries, col0 to col255
dtypes: int32(256)
memory usage: 1.0 GB
```

So, under the hood, it uses the pandas.core.frame.DataFrame class but when you check the type of the DataFrame object, it is a Modin pandas object, not the regular pandas.

```
type(df)
>> modin.pandas.dataframe.DataFrame
```

Now you come to the key part of this demo. **The following code concatenates 20 such 1GB DataFrames into a single large DataFrame**. Check out the time it takes to do this and think what could have gone wrong if you tried this with normal pandas code (assuming your local machine has a 16GB RAM).

```
import time
t1 = time.time()
big_df = pd.concat([df for _ in range(20)])
t2 = time.time()
print(f"Took {round(1000*(t2-t1),3)} milliseconds")
```

It should be done under a second.

```
Took 236.584 milliseconds
```

If you want to see the shape of this large DataFrame big_df:

```
big_df.shape
>> (20971520, 256)
```

So, it does have over **20 million rows and 256 columns**. This would be almost impossible to handle as a persistent in-memory object with pure pandas.

If you check the memory usage explicitly:

```
big_df.memory_usage(deep=True)
>>
Index       167772160
col0         83886080
col1         83886080
col2         83886080
col3         83886080
            . . .
col251       83886080
col252       83886080
col253       83886080
col254       83886080
col255       83886080
Length: 257, dtype: int64
```

So, each column's memory usage is over 80MB. In total, for 256 columns (and one index), this represents over 20GB of memory usage. My laptop has only 16GB of RAM and surely the Jupyter notebook, where this code is being run, did not take up all the memory. This is the direct demonstration of out-of-core computing with Modin.

You can treat this large DataFrame as a regular pandas DataFrame for all purposes from now on. For example, calculating the mean on col0 is done under 2 seconds.

```
t1 = time.time()
big_df['col0'].mean()
t2 = time.time()
print(f"Took {round(1000*(t2-t1),3)} milliseconds for calculating mean
of col0")
```

>> Took 2677.044 milliseconds for calculating mean of col0

How about calculating the mean of the entire DataFrame? Instead of one column, now you are operating over all 256 columns of data.

```
t1 = time.time()
big_df.mean()
t2 = time.time()
print(f"Took {round(1000*(t2-t1),3)} milliseconds for calculating mean of
the entire DataFrame")
```

>> Took 37654.585 milliseconds for calculating mean of the entire DataFrame

So, the time goes from 2.7 seconds to 37.7 seconds. Not a 256X increase in the computing time, but much less. This is the fruit of parallel processing and allocating data chunks optimally to each worker that the Dask cluster has set up in the background.

## Other Features of Modin

Modin is a live, open-source project and new contributions get added all the time. It also has

- Distributed XGBoost support for fast machine learning

- Standard SQL connection support to execute SQL queries on databases

- Gradually maturing support for various input data ingestion APIs (reading all kinds of files and data formats). In this matter, if something is tricky to support, it defaults to the pandas reading API automatically for ingestion, and then processes the object as a Modin DataFrame.

For more details and updates, interested readers should definitely check out the official documentation at `https://modin.readthedocs.io/en/stable/index.html`.

# Summary

In this chapter, you started addressing the concept of scaling out a data science workload to multiple CPU cores and beyond the system memory. This is particularly important for dealing with increasingly larger datasets, going from the realm of megabytes to gigabytes to terabytes and more. The conventional Python data science ecosystem using NumPy, pandas, and Matplotlib is great at smaller datasets but starts becoming inefficient while dealing with large file sizes, particularly reading from the disk or performing aggregation and statistical computations. pandas may throw up memory errors for a lot of trivial situations involving multi-GB level datasets because it makes a lot of unnecessary memory copies while doing regular data wrangling.

You explored common tricks and techniques within pandas to address these issues such as selective data loading, explicit type setting, and more. Then, you followed hands-on examples of out-of-core computing and scalability with large file and dataset size with two powerful libraries, `Vaex` and `Modin`. Doing data transformation (or visualization) with such large datasets would have been slow and inefficient with pure pandas code.

Among these, `Modin` uses a `Ray` or `Dask` back end for distributing computing load to multiple CPU cores. In the next chapter, you will take this discussion of scalable data science further by exploring these parallel or distributed computing aspects.

# CHAPTER 10

# Parallelized Data Science

In the last chapter, I talked about how data science tasks may encounter a wide variety of dataset sizes, ranging from kilobytes to petabytes. There can be a range of scale either in the number of samples or the extent of feature dimensionality. To handle complex data analytics and machine learning, data scientists employ a dizzying array of models, and that ecosystem scales up quickly, too.

Handling data and models *at scale* is a special skill to be acquired. When a data scientist starts learning the tradecraft, they first focus on understanding the mathematical basis, data wrangling and formatting concepts, and how to source and scrape data from various sources. In the next stage, they focus mainly on various ML algorithms and statistical modeling techniques and how to apply them for various tasks. Model performance and hyperparameter tuning remains their sole focus.

However, in almost all real-life scenarios, the success of a data science pipeline (and its value addition to the overall business of the organization) may depend on how smoothly and flawlessly it can be deployed *at scale* (i.e., how easily it can handle large datasets, faster streaming data, rapid change in the sampling or dimensionality, etc.). In this era of Big Data, the principles of the five V's (or six) must be embraced by enterprise-scale data science systems.

Of course, a single data scientist will not oversee implementing this whole enterprise or the pipeline. However, knowledge about scaling up the data science workflow is fast becoming a prerequisite for even an entry-level job in this field. There are a few different dimensions to that knowledge: **cloud computing**, **Big Data technologies** like Hadoop and Spark, and **parallel computing** with data science focus, for example.

The topics of cloud computing and associated tools (think AWS, Google Cloud Service, or Azure ML) are squarely beyond the scope of this book. Additionally, there are excellent resources (both online courses and textbooks) for learning the essentials of distributed data processing with the Hadoop infrastructure and related technologies. This chapter focuses on the Python-based parallel computing aspects that can be used directly for data science tasks. Much like the last chapter, I will discuss some of the

© Dr. Tirthajyoti Sarkar 2022
T. Sarkar, *Productive and Efficient Data Science with Python*, https://doi.org/10.1007/978-1-4842-8121-5_10

limitations that arise while doing analysis with large and complex datasets using the most common data analysis and numerical computing libraries like pandas or NumPy and discuss alternative libraries to help with those tasks.

It is to be noted, however, that this is not going to be an exhaustive discussion about general parallel computing tricks and techniques with Python. In fact, I will avoid detailed treatment of the topics that often come up in a standard Python parallel computing tutorial or treatise, such as working with built-in modules like `multiprocessing`, `threading`, or `asynco`. The focus, like any other chapter in this book, is squarely on data science, and therefore, I will cover two libraries named **Dask** and **Ray** that truly add value to any data science pipeline where you want to mix the power of parallel computing.

# Parallel Computing for Data Science

You'll start with a simple code snippet to understand where you want to go. Assuming you have standard Python installed on your laptop, execute this code (on a CLI or inside a Jupyter notebook):

```
import multiprocessing as mp
print("Number of processors: ", mp.cpu_count())
```

You are highly likely to get a response like 4 or 6. This is because all modern CPUs consist of more than one core; they're parallel computing units, effectively. There are subtle differences between the actual *physical* cores (electronic units with those nanometer-scale transistors) and *logical* cores, but for all computing purposes, you can think of the logical cores as the fundamental units in your system.

For more detailed information on the CPU installed on your laptop, you may execute the following snippet:

```
import psutil

print("="*20, "CPU Info", "="*20)
# number of cores
print("Physical cores:", psutil.cpu_count(logical=False))
print("Total cores:", psutil.cpu_count(logical=True))
# CPU frequencies
cpufreq = psutil.cpu_freq()
```

```
print(f"Max Frequency: {cpufreq.max:.2f}Mhz")
print(f"Current Frequency: {cpufreq.current:.2f}Mhz")
# CPU usage
print("CPU Usage Per Core:")
for i, percentage in enumerate(psutil.cpu_percent(percpu=True,
interval=1)):
    print(f"Core {i}: {percentage}%")
print(f"Total CPU Usage: {psutil.cpu_percent()}%")
```

On my laptop, I get the following:

```
==================== CPU Info ====================
Physical cores: 2
Total cores: 4
Max Frequency: 2195.00Mhz
Current Frequency: 2195.00Mhz
CPU Usage Per Core:
Core 0: 64.7%
Core 1: 40.9%
Core 2: 58.5%
Core 3: 29.2%
Total CPU Usage: 55.6%
```

So, we have multiple cores, **and we should be able to take advantage of that hardware design in our data science tasks**. What might that look like?

# Single Core to Multi-Core CPUs

Although this is a book about data science, sometimes it is necessary (and nostalgic) to take a slight detour into the hardware realm and revisit the history of development on that side. For parallel computing, a lot of hardware development had to happen over a long period of time before the modern software stack started taking full-blown advantage of that development. It will be beneficial to get a brief glimpse of this history to put our discussion in context.

The earliest commercially available CPU was the **Intel 4004**, a 4-bit 750kHz processor released in 1971. Since then, processor performance improvements were mainly due to clock frequency increases and data/address bus width expansion. A watershed moment was the release of the Intel 8086 in 1979 with a max clock frequency of 10MHz and a 16-bit data width and 20-bit address width.

The first hint of parallelism came with the first **pipelined CPU** design for the Intel **i386 (80386)** which allowed running multiple instructions in parallel. Separating the instruction execution flow into distinct stages was the key innovation here. As one instruction was being executed in one stage, other instructions could be executed in the other stages and that led to some degree of parallelism.

At around the same time, superscalar **architecture** was introduced. In a sense, this can be thought of as the precursor to the multi-core design of the future. This architecture duplicated some instruction execution units, allowing the CPU to run multiple instructions at the same time if there were no dependencies in the instructions. The earliest commercial CPUs with this architecture included the Intel i960CA, AMD 29000 series, and Motorola MC88100.

The unstoppable march of Moore's Law (shrinking the transistor sizes and manufacturing cost at an exponential pace; `www.synopsys.com/glossary/what-is-moores-law.html`) helped fuel this whole revolution in microarchitecture with the necessary steam. Semiconductor process technology was improving and lithography was driving the transistor nodes to the realm of sub 100 nm ($1/1000^{th}$ of the width of a typical human hair), supporting circuitry, motherboards, and memory technology (taking advantage of the same manufacturing process advancements).

The **war for clock frequency** heated up and AMD released the **Athlon CPU**, hitting the 1GHz speed for the first time, at the turn of the century in 1999. This war was eventually won by Intel, who released a dizzying array of high-frequency single-core CPUs in the early 2000s, culminating in the **Pentium-4** with a base frequency around 3.8GHz - 4GHz.

But fundamental physics struck back. High clock frequencies and nanoscale transistor sizes resulted in faster circuit operations, but the **power consumption** shot up as well. The direct relationship between frequency and power dissipation posed an insurmountable problem for scaling up. Effectively, this power dissipation resulted in so-called higher *leakage current* that destabilized the entire CPU and system operation when the transistor count was also going up into billions (imagine billions of tiny and unpredictable current leakages happening inside your CPU).

To solve this issue, **multi-CPU** designs were tried that housed two physical CPUs sharing a bus and a common memory pool on a motherboard. The fundamental idea is to stop increasing the frequency of operations and go parallel by distributing the computing tasks over many equally powerful computation units (and then accumulate the result somehow). But due to communication latencies from sharing external (outside the package) bus and memory, they were not meant to be truly scalable designs.

Fortunately, **true multi-core** designs followed soon after where multiple CPU cores were designed from the ground up **within the same package**, with special consideration for parallel memory and bus access. They also featured **shared caches** that are separate from the individual CPU caches (L1/L2/L3) to improve inter-core communication by decreasing latency significantly. In 2001, IBM released **Power4**, which can be considered the first multi-core CPU, although the real pace of innovation and release cycle picked up after Intel's 2005 release of the Core-2 Duo and AMD's Athlon X2 series.

Many architectural innovations and design optimizations are still ongoing in this race. Enhancing core counts per generation has been the mainstay for both industry heavyweights, Intel and AMD. While today's desktop workstation/laptops regularly use 4 or 6 core CPUs, high-end systems (enterprise data center machines or somewhat expensive cloud instances) may feature 12 or 16 cores per CPU.

For the data science revolution and progress, it makes sense to follow this journey closely and reap the benefits of all the innovations that hardware design can offer. But it is easier said than done. Parallelizing everyday data science tasks is a non-trivial task and needs special attention and investment.

# What Is Parallel in Data Science?

For data science jobs, both data and models are important artifacts. Therefore, one of the first considerations to be made for any parallel computing effort is to the focal point of parallelizing: data or model.

Why do you need to think this through? Because some artifacts are easier to be imagined to be parallelized than the others. For example, assume you have 100 datasets to run some statistical testing on and 4 CPU cores in your laptop. It is not hard to imagine that it would be great if somehow you could distribute the datasets evenly across all the cores and execute the same code in parallel (Figure 10-1). This should reduce the overall time to execute the statistical testing code significantly, even if the scheme involves some upfront overhead for dividing and distributing data, and some end-of-the-cycle aggregation or accumulation of the processed data.

Although this is not hard to imagine, the actual implementation is not that straightforward for a traditional Python-based data science stack using pandas or SciPy. As discussed in the last chapter, Python is inherently single-threaded and doing parallel processing with Python code needs some prior setup and clever manipulation. When a data scientist is using high-level analytics libraries like pandas, it is even more important to know the limitations for parallel processing (if any).

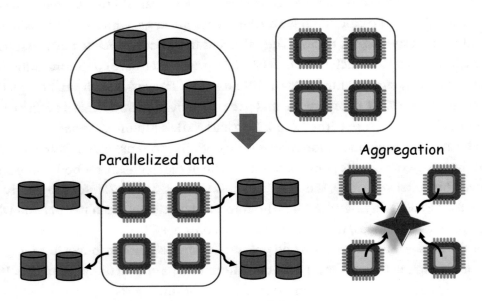

**Figure 10-1.** *Distributing datasets across multiple computing cores*

Moreover, data science is not limited to model exploration and statistical analysis on a single person's laptop (or a single cloud-based compute node) anymore. From a single machine (however powerful it might be), the advantages are apparent for large-scale data analytics when one connects to a cluster architecture consisting of multiple computers banded together with high-speed network. In the limiting case, such a cluster aims to become a single entity of computing for all intents and purposes: *a single brain arising out of parallel combination and communication among many smaller brains.*

Naturally, data scientists start imagining all kinds of possibilities that can be tried and tested with this *collective brain*. Alongside splitting a large collection of datasets, they can think of splitting models (or even modeling subtasks) into chunks and executing them in a parallel fashion. Datasets can be sliced and diced in multiple ways and all those dimensions might be parallelized, depending on the problem at hand. Some tasks may benefit from splitting data samples in rows; others may benefit from column-wise splitting.

Even many optimization tasks can be parallelized with sufficient effort and thrown to multiple compute nodes. One example could be running parallel local area searches for finding the best cost function of a global problem. All these ideas are captured in Figure 10-2.

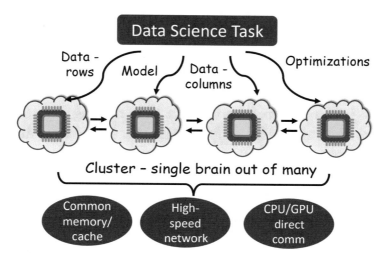

***Figure 10-2.*** *Cluster of computing nodes for parallelizing data science tasks in various dimensions: data, model, optimizations, and so on*

# Parallel Data Science with Dask

Dask is a feature-rich, easy-to-use, flexible library for parallelized and scalable computing in the Python ecosystem. While there are quite a few choices and approaches for such parallel computing with Python, the great thing about Dask is that it is specifically optimized and designed for data science and analytics workloads. In that way, it really separates itself from other major players such as Apache Spark.

In a typical application scenario, Dask comes to the rescue when a data scientist is dealing with large datasets that would have been tricky (if not downright impossible) to handle with the standard Python data science workflow of NumPy/ pandas/scikit-learn/TensorFlow. Although these Python libraries are the workhorses of any modern data science pipeline, it is not straightforward how to take advantage of large parallel computing infrastructure or clusters with these libraries.

At the minimum, one must spend quite a bit of manual effort and set up customized code or preprocessing steps to optimally distribute a large dataset or split a model that can be executed on the parallel computing infrastructure. Moreover, this limitation is not only for cloud-based clusters but applies to a single machine scenario as well. It is not apparent how to take advantage of all the logical cores or threads of a powerful workstation (with a single standalone CPU) when doing a pandas data analysis task or using SciPy for a statistical hypothesis testing. Some of the design features of these libraries may even fundamentally prevent us from using multiple CPU cores at once.

Fortunately, Dask takes away the pain of planning and writing customized code for turning most types of data science tasks into parallel computing jobs and abstracts away the hidden complexity as much as possible. It also offers a DataFrame API that looks and feels much like the pandas DataFrame so that standard data analytics and data wrangling code can be ported over with minimal change and debugging. It also has a dedicated ML library (APIs similar to that of scikit-learn). Let's explore how Dask works and more features in the next sections.

---

**Is Dask the same as Spark?**   This article (`https://coiled.io/is-spark-still-relevant-dask-vs-spark-vs-rapids/`) lays out the similarities and differences nicely. In brief, Dask is more "friendly and familiar" to data scientists working with Python codebase and solving problems that do not always restrict themselves to SQL-type data queries.

---

# How Dask Works Under the Hood

At its core, Dask operates by using efficient data structures (arrays and DataFrames) and a cleverly designed graph. Basically, it uses a **client-scheduler-worker** cluster architecture (Figure 10-3) to optimally distribute subtasks, collect them together, and calculate the outcome/prediction. The intricacies of parallel computing are abstracted away from regular Python programmers or data scientists, so working with large datasets is made easy and accessible. Figure 10-3 shows a schematic illustration.

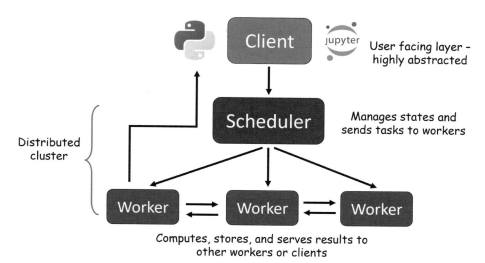

*Figure 10-3.* *Dask client-scheduler-worker operations under the hood*

The most useful fundamental building blocks of Dask are the following:

- Dask array

- Dask DataFrame

- Dask bag

- Dask task graph

## Dask Array

This is an implementation of a subset of the NumPy *n*-dimensional array (or ndarray) interface using blocked algorithms that effectively cut up a large array into many small arrays/chunks. This facilitates computation on out-of-core (larger than memory) arrays using all the cores in a computer in a parallel fashion. These blocked algorithms are coordinated using Dask task graphs. For more details on Dask arrays, go to the official documentation at https://docs.dask.org/en/latest/array.html.

## Dask DataFrame

Essentially, a Dask DataFrame is a large-scale parallelized DataFrame composed of many smaller pandas DataFrames, split along the index. Depending on the size and situation, the pandas DataFrames may exist on the disk for out-of-core computing on a single machine, or they may live on many different computing nodes in a cluster. A single Dask DataFrame operation triggers many operations down the chain (i.e., on the constituent pandas DataFrames in a parallel manner).

Efficiency and ease of use are main goals of the Dask project. Therefore, Dask DataFrames are partitioned row-wise, grouping rows by index value for efficiency. At the same time, they can expose the same API and methods as those coming from the pandas stable. A data scientist won't feel the difference or need to change existing code but can utilize the parallelism just by working with the Dask DataFrame API. In fact, the pandas official documentation suggests using Dask for scaling out to large datasets (Figure 10-4).

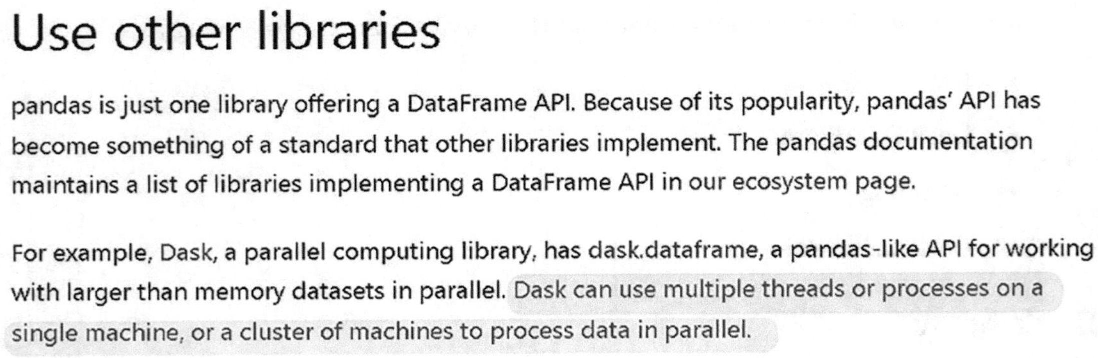

# Use other libraries

pandas is just one library offering a DataFrame API. Because of its popularity, pandas' API has become something of a standard that other libraries implement. The pandas documentation maintains a list of libraries implementing a DataFrame API in our ecosystem page.

For example, Dask, a parallel computing library, has dask.dataframe, a pandas-like API for working with larger than memory datasets in parallel. Dask can use multiple threads or processes on a single machine, or a cluster of machines to process data in parallel.

***Figure 10-4.*** *The pandas official documentation suggests using Dask for large datasets*

## Dask Bag

This is a data structure that implements operations like map, filter, fold, and groupby on collections of generic Python objects like lists or tuples. It uses a small memory footprint using Python iterators and is inherently parallelized.

Apache Spark has its famous Resilient Distributed Dataset (RDD; https://databricks.com/glossary/what-is-rdd). A Dask Bag is a Pythonic version of that RDD, suitable for operations inherently popular with users of the Hadoop file system. They are mostly used to parallelize simple computations on unstructured or semi-structured data such as text data, JSON records, log files, or customized user-defined Python objects.

# Dask Task Graph

Dask uses the common approach to parallel execution in user-space: *task scheduling*. With this approach, it breaks the main high-level program/code into many medium-sized tasks or units of computation (e.g., a single function calls on a non-trivial amount of data). These tasks are represented as nodes in a graph. Edges run between nodes if one task is dependent on the data produced by another. A task scheduler is called upon to execute this whole graph in a way that respects all the inter-node data dependencies and leverages parallelism wherever possible, thereby speeding up the overall computation.

There are many techniques for scheduling: *Embarrassingly Parallel, MapReduce, Full Task Scheduling*, etc. Often task scheduling logic hides within other larger frameworks like Luigi, Storm, Spark, and IPython Parallel. Dask encodes full task scheduling (Figure 10-5) with minimal incidental complexity using common Python artifacts (i.e., dictionaries, tuples, and callables). Dask can even use Python-native schedulers such as Threaded and Multiprocessing.

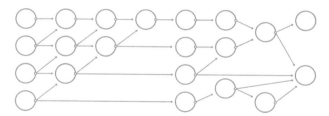

***Figure 10-5.*** *Dask uses a full task scheduling approach for its task graph*

Taking the fundamental data structures and schedulers, we can illustrate the flexibility of Dask as shown in Figure 10-6.

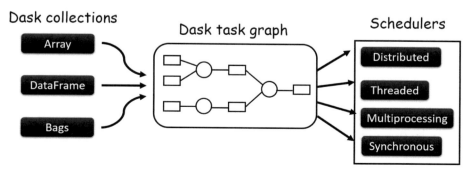

***Figure 10-6.*** *Dask collections, task graph, and schedulers*

## Works on Many Types of Clusters

One of the great features of Dask is that tasks and code can be deployed over many types of clusters:

- Hadoop/Spark clusters running YARN

- HPC clusters running job managers like SLURM, SGE, PBS, LSF, or others

- common in academic and scientific labs

- Kubernetes clusters

This makes Dask a truly powerful engine for parallel computing no matter the underlying distributed data processing infrastructure choice. Naturally, Dask code and pipelines can be easily ported from one organization to another or shared among the teams of a large data science organization.

# Basic Usage Examples

Here is how you can define and examine some of the data structures you just learned about. Let's start with arrays and then go on to show some examples with DataFrames and Bags.

---

**A note about Dask and Ray code examples /**   Almost all the code snippets in this chapter are for illustration and conceptualization purpose only. They are not fully executable, working code. The reason for this is brevity. The book focuses on concepts and learning and does not intend to act as a code manual. Working code examples are provided in the accompanying Jupyter notebooks (or GitHub links).

---

## Array

Define a Numpy array of 100,000 elements (Gaussian random numbers) and create a Dask array from that using the da.from_array() method:

```
import numpy as np
import pandas as pd
```

```
import dask.dataframe as dd
import dask.array as da
import dask.bag as db

arr = np.random.normal(size=100_000).reshape(500,200)
dask_arr = da.from_array(arr,chunks=(100,100))
```

Note that for creating the Dask array, you have chosen a chunk size of (100, 100). In a Jupyter notebook, if you just examine this dask_arr object, it is even visualized nicely (Figure 10-7).

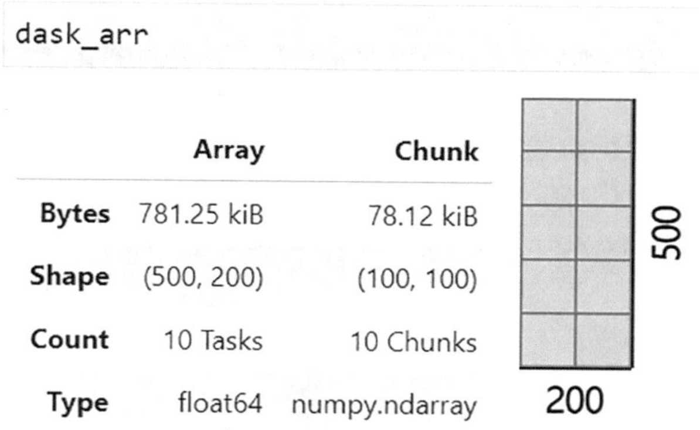

| dask_arr | | |
|---|---|---|
| | **Array** | **Chunk** |
| **Bytes** | 781.25 kiB | 78.12 kiB |
| **Shape** | (500, 200) | (100, 100) |
| **Count** | 10 Tasks | 10 Chunks |
| **Type** | float64 | numpy.ndarray |

***Figure 10-7.*** *A 2D Dask array created from a NumPy array of random numbers*

All the chunks have the same size of 78.12 kiB whereas the total dataset is 781.25 kiB. These chunks can effectively be distributed over cores or machines for parallel computing. You can go ahead and define a 3D array in a similar fashion:

```
arr = np.random.normal(size=100_000).reshape(50,200,10)
dask_arr = da.from_array(arr,chunks=(50,20,10))
```

Now the Dask array looks like a stack of bricks with a 3D shape (Figure 10-8).

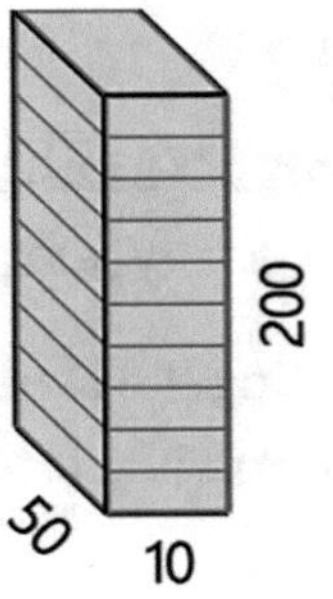

**Figure 10-8.** *A 3D Dask array created from a NumPy array of random numbers*

Dask operates on the principle of lazy valuation where final values are not computed unless explicitly asked to do so. You can define a summation operation on the 3D array like this where you are also counting the time for the operation:

```
import time
t1 = time.time()
task1 = dask_arr.sum(axis=2)
t2 = time.time()
print("Time (milliseocnds):", round((t2-t1)*1000,3))
task1
```

In the Jupyter notebook, this will show a visualization. Note the time taken for this operation is ~4 milliseconds (Figure 10-9). Nothing has been computed; just a task graph has been built, and the expected output array shape has been determined.

CHAPTER 10    PARALLELIZED DATA SCIENCE

```
t1 = time.time()
task1 = dask_arr.sum(axis=2)
t2 = time.time()
print("Time (milliseconds):", round((t2-t1)*1000,3))
task1
```

```
Time (milliseconds): 3.999
```

|  | Array | Chunk |
|---|---|---|
| **Bytes** | 78.12 kiB | 7.81 kiB |
| **Shape** | (50, 200) | (50, 20) |
| **Count** | 30 Tasks | 10 Chunks |
| **Type** | float64 | numpy.ndarray |

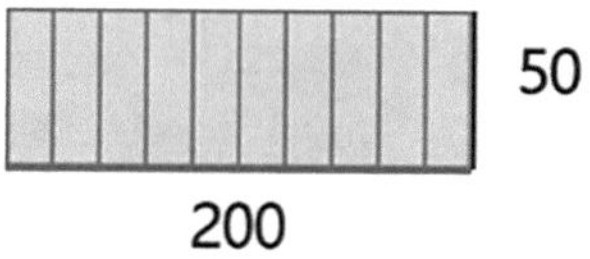

*Figure 10-9.* *A simple summation operation leads to a new array and task graph*

Similarly, you can add another operation to this chain, determining the max value out of those summed values along the columns (i.e., axis=1):

```
t1 = time.time()
task2=task1.max(axis=1)
t2 = time.time()
print("Time (milliseocnds):", round((t2-t1)*1000,3))
task2
```

Again, the task2 is shown as an array with a shape of (50,), and it took ~6 milliseconds for this to be built (Figure 10-10).

```
t1 = time.time()
task2=task1.max(axis=1)
t2 = time.time()
print("Time (milliseconds):", round((t2-t1)*1000,3))
task2
```

Time (milliseconds): 5.999

|  | Array | Chunk |
|---|---|---|
| **Bytes** | 400 B | 400 B |
| **Shape** | (50,) | (50,) |
| **Count** | 44 Tasks | 1 Chunks |
| **Type** | float64 | numpy.ndarray |

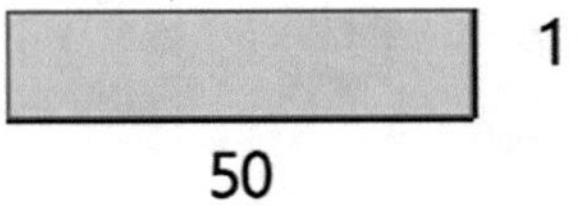

1

50

***Figure 10-10.*** *Determining the max out of the summed values along columns*

Finally, you need to call a special computation method to evaluate the result – result = task2.compute(). The computation time is much higher here (~24 milliseconds) and you get the one-dimensional array of max values as expected (Figure 10-11). This is where all the tasks in the task graph are executed over multiple cores in a parallel fashion.

```
t1 = time.time()
result=task2.compute()
t2 = time.time()
print("Time (milliseocnds):", round((t2-t1)*1000,3))
print("="*40)
print("Result:\n")
print(result)
```

```
Time (milliseocnds): 23.985
========================================
Result:

[ 8.20376347   6.81514322 10.71014311   9.56123543   9.87424841   8.1678258
   9.25362142   6.88081303   7.58215514   9.96070282   8.06762946   9.90991664
   8.45045481   7.42665067   9.77733545   8.0062088    8.09773538   8.47654512
  10.02758927   9.02053207   8.21597788   7.68340507   9.28841218 10.2206227
  10.33909096   6.78129201 10.12508648   8.24886617   9.49483907   6.59391729
   9.33334661   7.69205114   8.36703685   7.31321315   7.00957787   7.91146618
  10.43512876   8.12108536   9.86026751   7.80963788   9.79952717 11.29513906
   7.40358535   9.66389599   6.61055314   6.09541635   8.05787834 10.64292572
   7.77117279   9.5708752 ]
```

**Figure 10-11.**  *Final computation for the 3D array*

In fact, you can check the details of the task graph just by examining the dask attribute of any array such as task2 (Figure 10-12).

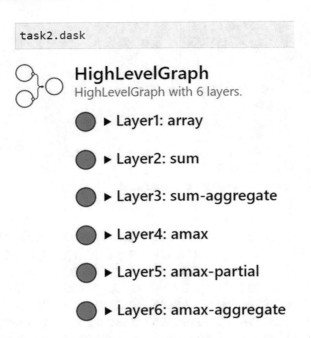

*Figure 10-12.* *A high-level task graph for the sum-max operations*

In the Jupyter notebook, each of these layers can be expanded to see more details. You are encouraged to check out the accompanying notebook.

## DataFrames

Dask DataFrames are equally easy to use if you are already familiar with pandas. You can create a DataFrame with timeseries data using Dask's built-in `datasets` module:

```
from dask import datasets

df = datasets.timeseries(
    start='2022-01-01',
    end='2022-01-31',
    freq='1min',
    partition_freq='1d',)
```

Now, if you just type `df` in a Jupyter notebook cell, it won't show the data snapshot that you are used to seeing in a pandas DataFrame. This is because Dask operates on lazy evaluation and just typing `df` does not demand any actual computation. Instead, it will show the schema (i.e., datatypes) and the general structure information (Figure 10-13). Note that it has 30 partitions because you chose the `partition_freq = '1d'` in the code and the start and end dates fall on the 1st and 31st of the month.

**Dask DataFrame Structure:**

| | id | name | x | y |
|---|---|---|---|---|
| **npartitions=30** | | | | |
| **2022-01-01** | int32 | object | float64 | float64 |
| **2022-01-02** | ... | ... | ... | ... |
| **...** | ... | ... | ... | ... |
| **2022-01-30** | ... | ... | ... | ... |
| **2022-01-31** | ... | ... | ... | ... |

Dask Name: make-timeseries, 30 tasks

***Figure 10-13.*** *A time series DataFrame in Dask showing the data schema*

If you want to see the first few entries, the familiar head method will serve that purpose and, by default, the computation will be done (i.e., the actual data will be shown) as in Figure 10-14.

```
df.head(n=3)
```

| | id | name | x | y |
|---|---|---|---|---|
| **timestamp** | | | | |
| **2022-01-01 00:00:00** | 1040 | Norbert | 0.769071 | 0.202093 |
| **2022-01-01 00:01:00** | 984 | Kevin | 0.985783 | 0.361957 |
| **2022-01-01 00:02:00** | 939 | Laura | -0.721564 | -0.644398 |

***Figure 10-14.*** *A Dask DataFrame showing the first few entries*

Most pandas-type operations are supported. For example, to know how many unique names there are, you write the following code:

```
df['name'].nunique().compute()
>> 26
```

Now, to group by those names and compare their variances of x and y data side by side, you can write

```
df.groupby(by='name').var().compute()[['x','y']]
>>
             x             y
name
Alice     0.331361      0.318624
Bob       0.328595      0.336009
Charlie   0.324984      0.334246
Dan       0.329188      0.333593
Edith     0.324070      0.332390
Frank     0.340098      0.335124
<truncated output>
```

Direct plotting is also supported like pandas. Using a special `resample` method (because the data is a time series), you can plot the mean data like this (Figure 10-15):

```
df[['x', 'y']].resample('24h').mean().compute().plot()
```

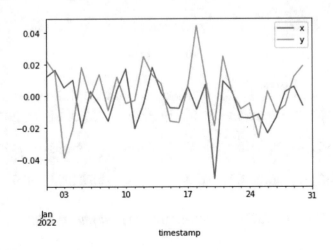

***Figure 10-15.*** *Time series resampled data mean*

Randomly accessing a partition's data is fast but still needs to be computed to see the actual data. For example, to see all the time for the 25th of January partition (Figure 10-16), you can write this:

```
df.loc['2022-01-25'].compute()
```

| timestamp | id | name | x | y |
|---|---|---|---|---|
| 2022-01-25 00:00:00 | 999 | Tim | 0.082126 | 0.059601 |
| 2022-01-25 00:01:00 | 1050 | Yvonne | 0.405951 | 0.927564 |
| 2022-01-25 00:02:00 | 1014 | Oliver | -0.943153 | 0.877603 |
| 2022-01-25 00:03:00 | 994 | Bob | -0.839904 | -0.669831 |
| 2022-01-25 00:04:00 | 1021 | Norbert | -0.525939 | 0.132539 |
| ... | ... | ... | ... | ... |
| 2022-01-25 23:55:00 | 1012 | Kevin | 0.425903 | -0.521117 |
| 2022-01-25 23:56:00 | 998 | Norbert | 0.572189 | 0.565643 |
| 2022-01-25 23:57:00 | 1004 | Edith | -0.144321 | -0.133911 |
| 2022-01-25 23:58:00 | 1070 | Sarah | 0.521525 | -0.237634 |
| 2022-01-25 23:59:00 | 987 | Charlie | 0.145602 | -0.959385 |

1440 rows × 4 columns

***Figure 10-16.*** *Accesing and computing the data for a particular day/partition*

## Dask Bags

Here's a Dask Bag example that contains some JSON records. This could be randomly generated information and the code for generating such JSON data is given in the accompanying notebook/source code. You can have five JSON records (about five people) in a folder called data. You read them in a Dask Bag structure via following code (note the use of map and json.loads functions):

```
import dask.bag as db
import json

bag = db.read_text('data/*.json').map(json.loads)
```

Again, due to lazy evaluation, you cannot see inside the Bag unless you explicitly ask for that. You can use either take method for that:

```
bag.take(2)
```

This should show something like Figure 10-17. The records contain information about people's name, occupation, phone number, and address. The record is multi-level. For example the address field has another level of data fields: address and city.

```
({'age': 63,
  'name': ['Stuart', 'Berry'],
  'occupation': 'Mineralologist',
  'telephone': '290-142-4549',
  'address': {'address': '474 Valdez Bypass', 'city': 'Stockton'},
  'credit-card': {'number': '3481 460420 21743', 'expiration-date': '08/24'}},
 {'age': 61,
  'name': ['Jacob', 'Frank'],
  'occupation': 'Minicab Driver',
  'telephone': '+1-(746)-566-5338',
  'address': {'address': '572 Rex Alley', 'city': 'Florence'},
  'credit-card': {'number': '2421 4440 8569 8618',
   'expiration-date': '10/17'}})
```

***Figure 10-17.*** *Dask bag containing JSON records (the first two records are shown here)*

Now you can do operations like map, filter, and aggregation on this records data. For example, you may want to filter only those people whose age is over 50 and whose credit-card expiration date year is beyond 2022. You write a simple filtering function and pass it to the Bag object's filter method. Note that you must use take or compute to get the actual computation done.

```
def filter_func(record):
    cond1 = record['age'] > 50
    cond2 = int(record['credit-card']['expiration-date'].split('/')
[-1]) > 22
    return cond1 and cond2

bag.filter(filter_func).take(2)
```

This may return something like Figure 10-18.

```
({'age': 63,
  'name': ['Stuart', 'Berry'],
  'occupation': 'Mineralologist',
  'telephone': '290-142-4549',
  'address': {'address': '474 Valdez Bypass', 'city': 'Stockton'},
  'credit-card': {'number': '3481 460420 21743', 'expiration-date': '08/24'}},
 {'age': 61,
  'name': ['Faustino', 'Frye'],
  'occupation': 'Au Pair',
  'telephone': '+1-(136)-978-2565',
  'address': {'address': '378 Blair Freeway', 'city': 'Carlsbad'},
  'credit-card': {'number': '3736 813403 82353', 'expiration-date': '12/24'}})
```

*Figure 10-18. Filtering operation done on the records contained in the Dask Bag*

There are many powerful usages for Dask Bags with semi-structured datasets that would have been difficult to accomplish just with an array or DataFrames.

# Dask Distributed Client

All the usage examples in the earlier sections feature the formalism and lazy evaluation nature of Dask APIs (arrays, DataFrames, and Bags), but they don't showcase the distributed/parallelized nature of computation in an obvious manner. For that, you must select and use the distributed scheduler from the Dask repertoire. It is actually a separate module or lightweight library called Dask.distributed that extends both the concurrent.futures and Dask APIs to moderate sized clusters.

Some of the core features of this module are as follows:

**Low overhead and latency**: There is only about 1ms of overhead for each task. A small computation and network roundtrip can be completed in less than 10ms.

**Data sharing between peers**: Worker nodes (e.g., logical cores on a local machine or cheap computing nodes in a cluster) communicate with each other to share data.

**Locality of the data**: Computations happen where the data lives. Scheduling algorithms distribute and schedule tasks following this principle. This also minimizes network traffic and improves the overall efficiency.

**Complex task scheduling**: This is probably the most attractive feature. The scheduler supports complex workflows and is not restricted to standard map/filter/reduce operations that are the primary feature of other distributed data processing frameworks like Hadoop-based systems. This is absolutely necessary for sophisticated data science tasks involving $n$-dimensional arrays, machine learning, image or high-dimensional data processing, and statistical modeling.

The flexibility and power of the scheduler also stems from the fact that it is **asynchronous** and **event driven**. This means it can simultaneously respond to computation requests from multiple clients and track the progress of a multitude of workers that have been given tasks already. It is also capable of concurrently handling a variety of workloads coming from multiple users while also managing a dynamic worker population with possible failures and new additions.

The best thing for the user, a data scientist, is that they can use all these features and powers with pure Python code and a minimal learning curve. Cluster management or distributed scheduling is not a trivial matter to accomplish programmatically. A data scientist using Dask does not have to bother about those complexities as they are abstracted away. That's where the theme of *productive data science* gets its support from libraries like Dask.

In fact, with just two lines of code, you can start a local cluster (utilizing the CPU cores of a local machine):

```
from dask.distributed import Client
client = Client()
```

Now, if you type client in the Jupyter notebook cell, you will see a description like Figure 10-19. Note that it shows a hyperlink to a dashboard, which you will see in action soon.

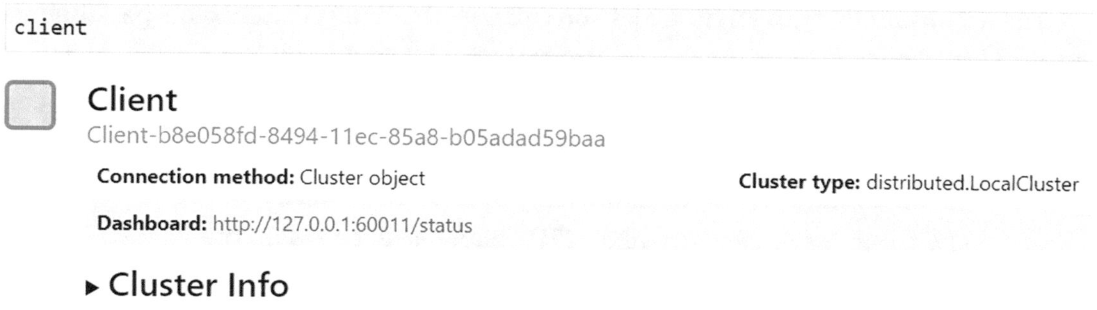

```
client
```

☐ **Client**
Client-b8e058fd-8494-11ec-85a8-b05adad59baa

> **Connection method:** Cluster object                **Cluster type:** distributed.LocalCluster
>
> **Dashboard:** http://127.0.0.1:60011/status

▸ **Cluster Info**

***Figure 10-19.*** *Starting up a Dask-distributed cluster/scheduler (on a local machine)*

If you keep expanding the Cluster Info drop-down, you may see something like Figure 10-20. Note how it shows the threads/workers of the local machine and the available system memory.

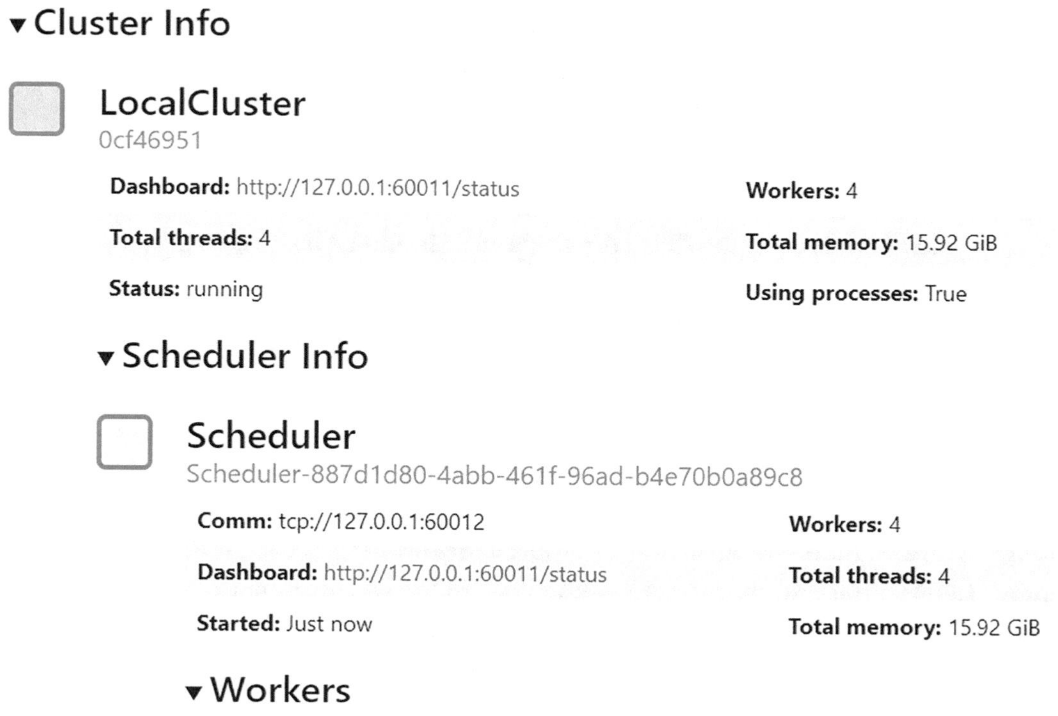

▼ **Cluster Info**

☐ **LocalCluster**
0cf46951

> **Dashboard:** http://127.0.0.1:60011/status         **Workers:** 4
>
> **Total threads:** 4                                 **Total memory:** 15.92 GiB
>
> **Status:** running                                  **Using processes:** True

   ▼ **Scheduler Info**

   ☐ **Scheduler**
   Scheduler-887d1d80-4abb-461f-96ad-b4e70b0a89c8

   > **Comm:** tcp://127.0.0.1:60012                    **Workers:** 4
   >
   > **Dashboard:** http://127.0.0.1:60011/status       **Total threads:** 4
   >
   > **Started:** Just now                              **Total memory:** 15.92 GiB

   ▼ **Workers**

***Figure 10-20.*** *Cluster and scheduler info for Dask distributed client setup*

The important thing to know is that you can pass on many customizable parameters to the `Client` constructor when you create your scheduler/cluster. Some of the most prominent ones are

> `address`: IP address (with port) of a real cloud-based, remote cluster or the local host machine. If you can afford to rent a high-end cloud instance with a high CPU count (as discussed in the previous chapter), the Dask scheduler can directly connect to it and start utilizing the resources. When not specified, only the local host machine is taken up as the computing node.

> `n_workers`: Explicitly specifying the number of CPU cores that the cluster will be able to use. This could be important for resource constrained situations or if there are many Dask tasks to be distributed among a finite number of CPU cores.

> `threads_per_worker`: Just like specifying number of CPU cores, this dictates the number of threads per core. Generally, this number is 1 or 2.

> `memory_limit`: This is another useful keyword to use for optimally managing the total system memory for the distributed client. This limit is on a per-CPU core basis and should be a string (e.g., '2 GiB').

Once the scheduler is started up, it manages the distributed computing aspects by itself. However, there is a certain way to submit jobs to the scheduler using `map` and `submit` methods. Here is a (somewhat contrived) example.

Suppose you have a few datasets of random variables (generated from a specific statistical distribution) and you want to measure the differences between their max and median, and then take an average of those measurements. Each dataset may contain 1,000 values and there are 21 such datasets. Taken together, this could be a measure of some sort of outliers in the data (i.e., how much the max value is higher than the median values for a certain batch of data). You have the data generation code in the accompanying notebook. The distributions (of individual datasets) are shown in Figure 10-21.

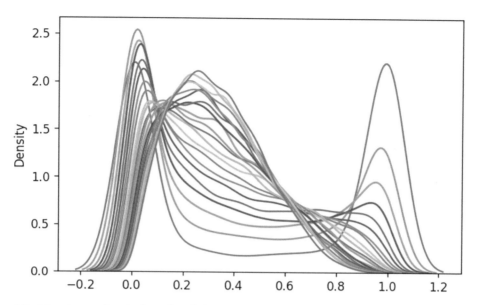

***Figure 10-21.*** *A synthetic batch of data for which a distributed processing needs to be run*

So, this involves the following computations:

- 21 max computation (from 1,000 data points each time)

- 21 median computation (from 1,000 data points each time)

- Two arithmetic mean computations (of 21 max/median values each time)

- A final difference calculation

You write the Dask code as follows (assuming that the datasets are contained in a Python list called dists). The code for generating such randomized numbers in a list is given in the accompanying source code/notebook.

```
# Mapping statistical computations to data distributions
A = client.map(np.max, dists)
B = client.map(np.median, dists)

# Submitting averaging jobs
mean_max = client.submit(np.mean, A)
mean_min = client.submit(np.mean, B)
```

At this point, if you examine the mean_max object, you will see it is something called a Dask Future (a sort of promise that will be calculated or acted upon in future, similar to a concept in JavaScript):

```
mean_max
```

```
>> Future: mean status: finished, type: numpy.float64, key: mean-2e5b19a3
2f99725e1cf4f6f5ba8e295a
```

The entire distributed task is just planned at this point and no actual computation has happened. You must call result to execute the actual computations:

```
final = mean_max.result() - mean_min.result()
final
>> 0.6780617253952232
```

However, more interesting things can be observed simply by looking at the dynamic dashboard that Dask provides. You can simply click on the hyperlink shown in Figure 10-20 and see something like Figure 10-22.

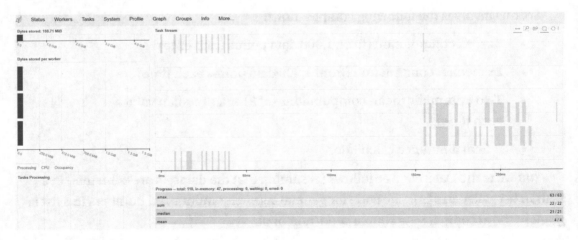

***Figure 10-22.***  *Task status view of the dynamic Dask dashboard*

This is a static snapshot of the task status tab of the dashboard. When the parallel processes execute (distributed over multiple CPU cores), the graph changes and updates dynamically as all the data chunks are split and shared among workers. A good visual demonstration of this dynamic process can be seen in an article that I published at `https://medium.com/productive-data-science/out-of-core-larger-than-ram-machine-learning-with-dask-9d2e5f29d733` with a hands-on example involving the Dask Machine Learning library. You are encouraged to check out this article.

There are many other tabs in this dashboard. The information tab about workers is one among them (Figure 10-23). Again, here the view is static and after the processing was finished. Therefore, you see minimal usage of memory and CPU. But for a dynamic state, those numbers will be high and constantly changing.

CPU Use (%)

Memory Use (%)

| name | address | nthreads | cpu | memory | limit | memory % | managed | unmanage | unmanage | spilled |
|---|---|---|---|---|---|---|---|---|---|---|
| Total (3) | | 6 | 3 % | 188.2 MiB | 4.5 GiB | 4.1 % | 1.5 KiB | 187.8 MiB | 476.0 KiB | 0.0 |
| 0 | tcp://127.0 | 2 | 3 % | 62.4 MiB | 1.5 GiB | 4.1 % | 32.0 B | 62.2 MiB | 220.0 KiB | 0.0 |
| 1 | tcp://127.0 | 2 | 3 % | 64.4 MiB | 1.5 GiB | 4.2 % | 768.0 B | 64.1 MiB | 248.0 KiB | 0.0 |
| 2 | tcp://127.0 | 2 | 3 % | 61.4 MiB | 1.5 GiB | 4.0 % | 704.0 B | 61.4 MiB | 8.0 KiB | 0.0 |

***Figure 10-23.*** *Workers information view of the dynamic Dask dashboard*

# Dask Machine Learning Module

While Dask provides an amazing suite of parallel and out-of-core computing facilities and a straightforward set of APIs (Arrays, DataFrames, Bags, etc.,), the utility does not stop there. Going beyond the data wrangling and transformation stage, when data scientists arrive at the machine learning phase, they can still leverage Dask for doing the modeling and preprocessing tasks with the power of parallel computing. All of this can be achieved with a minimal change in their existing codebase and in pure Pythonic manner.

For ML algorithms and APIs, Dask has a separately installable module called `dask-ml`. Full treatment of that module is beyond the scope of this book. You are again encouraged to check out the above-mentioned article to get a feel about the API. Here, I will briefly discuss some key aspects of `dask-ml`.

# What Problems Does It Address?

Fundamentally, libraries like dask-ml addresses the dual problems of *data scaling* and *model scaling*.

**The data scaling challenge** comes about with the Big Data domain, for example, when the computing hardware starts having trouble containing training data in the working memory. So, this is essentially a **memory-bound** problem. Dask solves this problem by spilling data out-of-core onto drive storage and providing incremental meta-learning estimators that can learn from batches of data rather than having to load entire dataset in the memory.

**The model scaling challenge**, on the other hand, raises its ugly head when the parametric space of ML model becomes too large and the operations become **compute-bound**. To address these challenges, you can continue to use the efficient collections Dask offers (arrays, DataFrames, bags) and use a Dask Cluster to parallelize the workload on an array of machines. Even the task of parallelization has choices. It can occur through one of the built-in integrations (e.g., Dask's joblib back end to parallelize scikit-Learn directly) or one of dask-ml estimators (e.g., a hyper-parameter optimizer or a parallelized Random Forest estimator).

# Tight Integration with scikit-learn

Following through the principle of simplicity of use, dask-ml maintains a high degree of integration and the drop-in replacement philosophy with the most popular Python ML library, scikit-learn. Dask-ml provides data preprocessing, model selection, training, and even data generating functions just like scikit-learn does while supporting Dask collections as native objects to use with those APIs.

Generic code could go like this (not an actual working code):

```
import dask.dataframe as ddf
from dask_ml.model_selection import train_test_split
from dask_ml.preprocessing import MinMaxScaler
from dask_ml.xgboost import XGBRegressor

# Reading efficient parquet file format
data = ddf.read_parquet('Parquet file' engine='pyarrow'),
X = data[Feature_columns]
y = data[Label_column]
```

```
# Test/train split
train, train_labels, test, test_labels = train_test_split(X,y,
test_size=0.2,...)

# Scale/pre-process
train = MinMaxScaler.fit_transform(train)
test = MinMaxScaler.fit_transform(test)

# Parallelized estimator
est = XGBRegressor(...)
est.fit(train, train_labels)
est.score(test)
```

It is easy to spot the almost line-by-line similarity between this code and a standard scikit-learn pipeline. This is called the drop-in replacement ability of dask-ml. You may also notice the use of the Parquet file format for reading a large dataset efficiently (into a Dask DataFrame) from a disk drive or network storage. You may check out my article on this topic (https://medium.com/productive-data-science/out-of-core-larger-than-ram-machine-learning-with-dask-9d2e5f29d733). When executed, this code combines the advantage of out-of-core data handling of a Dask DataFrame with the parallelized estimator API and delivers a scalable machine learning experience for the data scientist, thereby boosting their productivity.

The dask-ml library also offers some meta-estimators/ wrappers to help parallelize and scale out certain tasks that would not have been possible with scikit-learn itself. For example, ParallelPostFit can be used to parallelize the predict, predict_proba, and transform methods, enabling them to work on large (possibly larger-than-memory) datasets. This is highly suited for real-life production deployments, as the live data can be pretty large even when the training was done with a smaller dataset. For smooth and stable performance of a prediction service, these post-fitting methods should scale gracefully whatever the dataset size may be and dask-ml helps accomplish this without a lot of code change. A generic code snippet for such a task may look like the following:

```
from sklearn.ensemble import GradientBoostingClassifier
from dask_ml.wrappers import ParallelPostFit

# Wrapping the sklearn estimator with Dask wrapper
clf = ParallelPostFit(estimator=GradientBoostingClassifier())
clf.fit(X, y)
```

```
# Big dataset for prediction
X_big, _ = make_classification(n_samples=100000, chunks=10000,)

# Probability of first 10 data points
clf.predict_proba(X_big).compute()[:10]
```

In the code above, note that the main estimator comes from scikit-learn itself. The Dask part is only a wrapper that utilizes the underlying estimator to work on a Dask collection like a DataFrame for lazy evaluation and out-of-core computing.

# Parallel Computing with Ray

Parallel computing in pure Python has recently been revolutionized by the rapid rise of a few great open-source frameworks, Ray being one of them. It was created by two graduate students in the UC Berkley RISElab (https://rise.cs.berkeley.edu/), Robert Nishihara and Philipp Moritz, as a development and runtime framework for simplifying distributed computing. Under the guidance of Professors Michael Jordan and Ion Stoica, it rapidly progressed from being a research project to a full-featured computing platform with many subcomponents built atop it for different AI and ML focused tasks (hyperparameter tuning, reinforcement learning, data science jobs, and even ML model deployment).

Currently, Ray is maintained and continuously enhanced by Anyscale (www.anyscale.com/), a commercial entity (startup company) formed by the creators of Ray. It is a fully managed Ray offering that accelerates building, scaling, and deploying AI applications on Ray by eliminating the need to build and manage complex infrastructure.

## Features and Ecosystem of Ray

Some of the core features of Ray are as follows:

> Ray achieves scalability and fault tolerance by abstracting the control state of the system in a **global control store** and keeping all other components stateless.

It uses a **shared-memory distributed object store** to efficiently handle large data through shared memory, and it uses a bottom-up hierarchical scheduling architecture to achieve low-latency and high-throughput scheduling.

Ray presents a lightweight API based on **dynamic task graphs** and **actors** to express a wide range of data science and general-purpose applications in a flexible manner.

Utilizing these features, a great many distributed computing tools and frameworks are being built that are powered by the engine of Ray. For an excellent reference article to get an overview of these tools, go to https://gradientflow.com/understanding-the-ray-ecosystem-and-community/. Figure 10-24 shows a visual illustration.

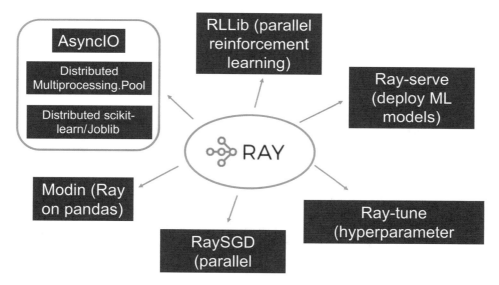

***Figure 10-24.***  *Distributed data science/ML ecosystem built atop Ray*

In this section, I will show only a couple of examples of running parallel data science workloads using Ray. You are highly encouraged to check out the official documentation (www.ray.io/docs) and try out all the great features that this library provides.

# Simple Parallelization Example

Before I show the hands-on examples, I want to mention that Ray is currently built and tested for Linux and Mac OS, and the Windows version is experimental and not guaranteed to be stable. Therefore, you are encouraged to **practice Ray examples in a Linux environment or create a virtual machine (VM)** on your Windows platform, install Ray, and continue.

For example, the following examples are run inside an Ubuntu Linux 20.04 environment that runs within a VM managed by Oracle Virtual Box software (installed on a Windows 11 laptop). The VM has also been assigned four logical CPU cores by the creator/user (Figure 10-25). This is important to note as the default starting number for the CPU cores may be only one and that will not demonstrate the expected speed-up for parallel processing tasks. A detailed guide on how to create such a VM is given in this article (https://brb.nci.nih.gov/seqtools/installUbuntu.html). If you are working on native Linux or Mac OS machine, then this step is unnecessary.

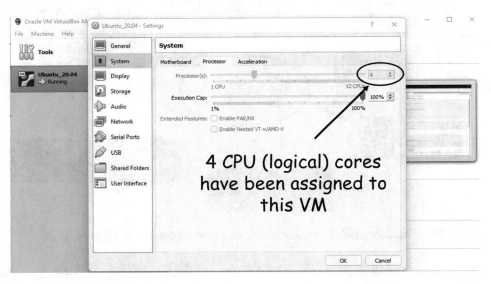

***Figure 10-25.*** *Multiple logical CPU cores assigned to a VM that is used to run Ray*

You can start Ray by the `ray.init()` method:

```
import ray
ray.init()
```

You may see something like the following upon running this code:

```
{'node_ip_address': '10.0.2.15',
 'raylet_ip_address': '10.0.2.15',
 'redis_address': '10.0.2.15:6379',
 'object_store_address': '/tmp/ray/
 session_2022-02-08_21-00-00_998495_21742/sockets/plasma_store',
 'raylet_socket_name': '/tmp/ray/session_2022-02-08_21-00-00_998495_21742/
 sockets/raylet',
 'webui_url': '127.0.0.1:8265',
 'session_dir': '/tmp/ray/session_2022-02-08_21-00-00_998495_21742',
 'metrics_export_port': 62074,
 'gcs_address': '10.0.2.15:43155',
 'node_id': '922916ef0c5dcf02dc25fea428b930df40ccf2450fa974bb307826fe'}
```

Note that the initiation of Ray starts things like Redis, object store, and Dashboard. In fact, you will notice a message printed at the top with the URL of the dashboard:

```
View the Ray dashboard at http://127.0.0.1:8265
```

If you click this hyperlink, you will see the Ray dashboard with workers and their status, as shown in Figure 10-26 (quite like the Dask dashboard discussed earlier).

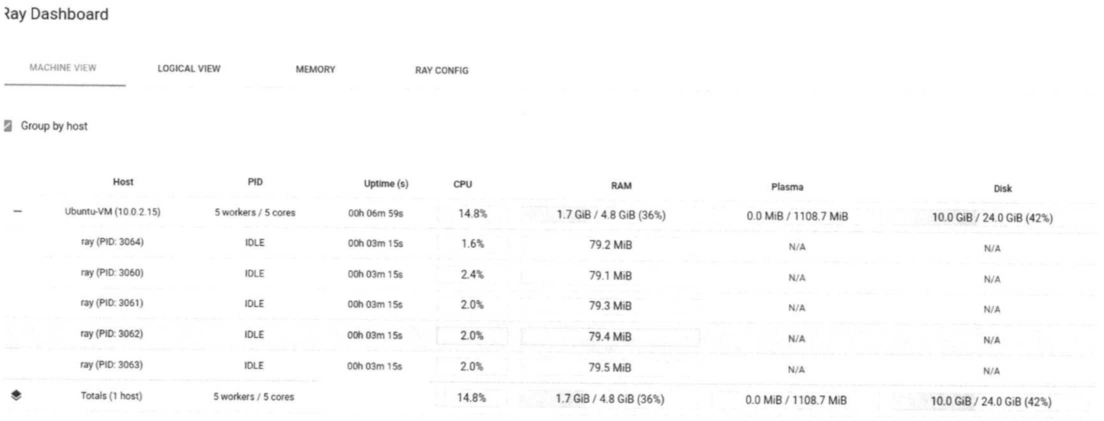

Ray Dashboard

MACHINE VIEW | LOGICAL VIEW | MEMORY | RAY CONFIG

Group by host

| | Host | PID | Uptime (s) | CPU | RAM | Plasma | Disk |
|---|---|---|---|---|---|---|---|
| – | Ubuntu-VM (10.0.2.15) | 5 workers / 5 cores | 00h 06m 59s | 14.8% | 1.7 GiB / 4.8 GiB (36%) | 0.0 MiB / 1108.7 MiB | 10.0 GiB / 24.0 GiB (42%) |
| | ray (PID: 3064) | IDLE | 00h 03m 15s | 1.6% | 79.2 MiB | N/A | N/A |
| | ray (PID: 3060) | IDLE | 00h 03m 15s | 2.4% | 79.1 MiB | N/A | N/A |
| | ray (PID: 3061) | IDLE | 00h 03m 15s | 2.0% | 79.3 MiB | N/A | N/A |
| | ray (PID: 3062) | IDLE | 00h 03m 15s | 2.0% | 79.4 MiB | N/A | N/A |
| | ray (PID: 3063) | IDLE | 00h 03m 15s | 2.0% | 79.5 MiB | N/A | N/A |
| | Totals (1 host) | 5 workers / 5 cores | | 14.8% | 1.7 GiB / 4.8 GiB (36%) | 0.0 MiB / 1108.7 MiB | 10.0 GiB / 24.0 GiB (42%) |

***Figure 10-26.*** *Snapshot of a Ray dashboard (with five CPU assignments)*

You can check the assigned resources to this Ray cluster with

```
ray.available_resources()
```

```
>> {'memory': 2325037056.0,
```

```
'node:10.0.2.15': 1.0,
'object_store_memory': 1162518528.0,
'CPU': 5.0}
```

Now, let's construct a few large DataFrames and calculate their statistics using pandas and Rays to show the parallel computing benefit:

```
NUM_ROWS = 100_000
NUM_COLS = 20
data_dict = {}
# Pandas DataFrames
for i in range(4):
    data = np.random.normal(size=(NUM_ROWS, NUM_COLS))
    data_dict['df'+str(i)] = pd.DataFrame(data,
                                    columns=['Col-'+str(i) for i in
                                    range(NUM_COLS)])
```

For pandas, you write a function that simply returns the statistics:

```
def build_stats(df):
    return df.describe().T
```

You measure the time to run this function over multiple DataFrames (here, four):

```
t1 = time.time()
results = [build_stats(data_dict['df'+str(i)]) for i in range(4)]
t2 = time.time()
print("Total time (milliseconds): ", round((t2-t1)*1000,2))
```

```
>> Total time (milliseconds):  1130.66
```

The trick to do the same thing with Ray and take advantage of the parallel computing is to use the decorator @ray.remote with the same function and use the ray.get() method to collect the result after it has been submitted for parallel execution. Here is the decorated function:

```
@ray.remote
def build_stats_ray(df):
    return df.describe().T
```

You can now write similar code for measuring the time:

```
t1 = time.time()
results = ray.get([build_stats_ray.remote(data_dict['df'+str(i)]) for i in
range(4)])
t2 = time.time()
print("Total time (milliseconds): ", round((t2-t1)*1000,2))
```

You will get a lower number for total execution time (this will vary on many factors like hardware, number of CPUs, Ray build, OS, etc.):

```
>> Total time (milliseconds):  575.77
```

Note how you call the build_stats_ray function with a .remote() method and how you wrap that with the ray.get() method to run everything in parallel. The takeaway is that although Ray offers a great many features, you must learn how to properly take advantage of them and how to submit a parallelizable task to the Ray cluster by pipelining the sub-components in correct order. Figure 10-27 shows the idea.

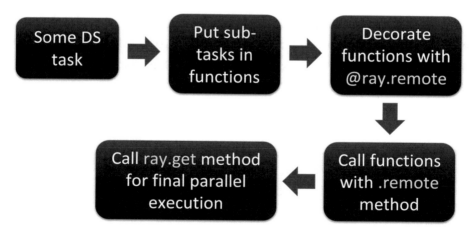

***Figure 10-27.***  *Pipeling sub-components in the correct order*

# Ray Dataset for Distributed Loading and Compute

Ray Datasets (https://docs.ray.io/en/latest/data/dataset.html) are the standard (and recommended) way to load and exchange data in the Ray ecosystem. These objects provide basic distributed data transformations such as map, filter, and repartition, and play well with a wide variety of file formats, data sources, and distributed frameworks for easy loading and conversion. They are also specifically designed to load and preprocess data with high performance for distributed ML training pipelines built with Ray such as Ray-Train. (`https://docs.ray.io/en/latest/train/train.html#train-docs`).

---

**Ray Datasets are a relatively new feature** and are available as Beta from Ray 1.8+ version onwards. If you are using an older version of Ray, you need to upgrade to take advantage of them. Also, make sure that the PyArrow library is installed.

---

Ray Datasets are a good candidate for the last-mile data processing blocks (before data is fed into a parallelized ML task flow) where the initial data sources are traditional RDBMS, output of ETL pipeline, or even Spark DataFrames.

Previously, I talked about Apache Arrow and how these modern data storage formats are revolutionizing the data science world. Ray Datasets, at their core, implement distributed Arrow. Each Dataset is essentially a list of Ray object references to blocks that hold Arrow tables (or Python lists in some cases). The presence of such block-level structure allows the parallelism and compatibility with distributed ML training. In this manner, Ray Datasets are similar to what you saw with Dask. Moreover, since Datasets are just lists of Ray object references, they can be **freely (almost no memory operation overhead) exchanged between Ray tasks, actors, and libraries.** This lets you have tremendous flexibility with their usage and integration, and it improves the system performance.

As mentioned, Ray Datasets work with almost every kind of data sources that you use in your everyday work. Figure 10-28 shows a partial snapshot of their input compatibility.

# Datasource Compatibility Matrices

| Input Type | Read API | Status |
| --- | --- | --- |
| CSV File Format | ray.data.read_csv() | ✅ |
| JSON File Format | ray.data.read_json() | ✅ |
| Parquet File Format | ray.data.read_parquet() | ✅ |
| Numpy File Format | ray.data.read_numpy() | ✅ |
| Text Files | ray.data.read_text() | ✅ |
| Binary Files | ray.data.read_binary_files() | ✅ |
| Python Objects | ray.data.from_items() | ✅ |
| Spark Dataframe | ray.data.from_spark() | ✅ |
| Dask Dataframe | ray.data.from_dask() | ✅ |
| Modin Dataframe | ray.data.from_modin() | ✅ |

*Figure 10-28.*  *Snapshot of Ray Datasets' input compatibility*

As an example, you can create a Ray Dataset with the range function:

```
ds = ray.data.range(100000)
```

If you examine it by typing ds in a Jupyter notebook cell, you will see

```
Dataset(num_blocks=200, num_rows=100000, schema=<class 'int'>)
```

So, by default, it has created 200 blocks of object reference and also assigned a schema of integer to the data. This parallelism and data type integration inherently makes the Dataset more efficient than traditional data sources like pandas DataFrame.

You can apply a mapping function to the Dataset just like others:

```
op_ds = ds.map(lambda x: np.sin(x)+np.cos(x))
```

The op_ds is itself a Ray Dataset now but its schema has changed due to the operation.

```
op_ds
>> Dataset(num_blocks=200, num_rows=100000, schema=<class 'numpy.float64'>)
```

Because the schema has changed, many NumPy methods are directly available now.

```
op_ds.std()
>> 1.0000051823664913
```

One cool thing is that you can read batches of the data (which are originally integers) as a Python list or pandas DataFrames and do calculations on those batches. This is very useful for distributed ML training on this kind of data. The following code reads batches of size 25,000 at a time as pandas DataFrame and prints out their statistics:

```
i = 1
for batch in ds.iter_batches(batch_size=25000,
                             batch_format='pandas'):
    print("Batch number: ",i)
    print("="*40)
    print(batch.describe(percentiles=[0.5]))
    print("="*40)
    i+=1
```

The result looks like Figure 10-29.

```
Batch number:  1
==========================================
                 0
count   25000.000000
mean    12499.500000
std      7217.022701
min         0.000000
50%     12499.500000
max     24999.000000
==========================================
Batch number:  2
==========================================
                 0
count   25000.000000
mean    37499.500000
std      7217.022701
min     25000.000000
50%     37499.500000
max     49999.000000
==========================================
Batch number:  3
==========================================
```

***Figure 10-29.*** *Partial result of batch iteration of a Ray Dataset as chunks of a pandas DataFrame*

The Dataset makes it possible to run **parallel data transformation tasks on blocks of data** as pandas. Here is a pseudo-code example:

```
# A Pandas DataFrame UDF
def transform_batch(df: pd.DataFrame):
    # Drop nulls.
    df = df.dropna(...)
    # Add new column.
    df["new_col"] = (...)
    # Transform existing column.
    df["feature_1"] = (...)
    # Drop column.
    df.drop(...)
    # One-hot encoding.
    categories = ["cat_1", "cat_2", "cat_3"]
    for category in categories:
        (...)
    return df
```

```
# batch_format="pandas" tells Datasets to provide the transformer
with blocks
# represented as Pandas DataFrames.
ds = ds.map_batches(transform_batch,
                    batch_format="pandas")
```

# Summary

In this chapter, I continued the discussion about making data science scalable across large datasets and models with parallel (and distributed) computing tools. I discussed that both raw data and large models can be processed with these parallel processing techniques. With the advent of modern multi-core CPUs and the easy availability of large computing clusters at a reasonable cost (from cloud vendors), the prospects of parallelized data science look bright.

I focused particularly on two Python frameworks, Dask and Ray. I covered, in detail, various core data structures and internal representations that Dask provides to make parallel computing easy and fun. I also discussed the Dask distributed client in detail with hands-on examples. For Ray, I covered the basic Ray parallelism with special decorators and methods and the distributed data loading functionalities.

In the next chapter, I will go beyond the realm of the CPU and venture into a different kind of scalability: how to port and take advantage of GPU-based systems for data science tasks.

# CHAPTER 11

# GPU-Based Data Science for High Productivity

In the last two chapters, you learned about various tools and frameworks for doing out-of-core and distributed/parallelized data science. The central goal has always been the same: enhancing the productivity of the data science pipeline. Productivity is often directly related to the speed of execution of various DS tasks including numerical processing, data wrangling, and feature engineering. When it goes to the advanced machine learning stage, depending on the modeling complexity, the matter of speed and performance assumes even a critical role.

It is now well established that the unprecedented success of modern ML systems has been critically dependent on their ability to process massive amounts of raw data in a parallel fashion using task-optimized hardware. The history of machine learning has clearly demonstrated that the use of specialized hardware like the graphics processing unit (GPU) played a significant role in the early success of ML.

For example, in 2012, Alex Krizhevsky (`https://qz.com/1307091/the-inside-story-of-how-ai-got-good-enough-to-dominate-silicon-valley/`), in collaboration with Ilya Sutskever and Geoffrey Hinton (`www.cs.toronto.edu/~hinton/`), designed a neural network eventually known as AlexNet (`https://proceedings.neurips.cc/paper/2012/file/c399862d3b9d6b76c8436e924a68c45b-Paper.pdf`) that won the famous ImageNet Large Scale Visual Recognition Challenge (`https://en.wikipedia.org/wiki/ImageNet_Large_Scale_Visual_Recognition_Challenge`). Among many novel features, it was one of the early neural nets to be trained on parallel GPU combinations that went on to beat classical ML algorithms in the ImageNet competition by a large margin. Consequently, the whole idea of deep neural networks got a huge boost and so did the essential role that GPU-based training hardware played in that success. Since then, a lot of emphasis has been given to building highly optimized

© Dr. Tirthajyoti Sarkar 2022
T. Sarkar, *Productive and Efficient Data Science with Python*, https://doi.org/10.1007/978-1-4842-8121-5_11

software tools and customized mathematical processing engines (both hardware and software) to leverage the power and architecture of GPUs and parallel computing for artificial intelligence and machine learning.

While the use of GPUs and distributed computing is widely discussed in academic and business circles for core AI/ML tasks (e.g., running a deep neural network of 100+ layers for image classification or billion-parameter BERT language synthesis model (`https://towardsdatascience.com/bert-explained-state-of-the-art-language-model-for-nlp-f8b21a9b6270`)), they get less coverage when it comes to their utility for regular data science and data engineering tasks. These data-related tasks are the essential precursor to any ML workload in an AI pipeline and they often constitute a majority percentage of the time and intellectual effort spent by a data scientist or even an ML engineer.

In fact, the famous AI pioneer Andrew Ng recently talked about moving from a model-centric to a data-centric approach (`https://spectrum.ieee.org/andrew-ng-data-centric-ai`) to AI tools development. The central idea there is to **not use large datasets but smaller datasets of higher quality**. This means spending much more time with the raw data and preprocessing it before an actual AI workload executes on your pipeline. Watch Andrew's interview at `www.youtube.com/watch?v=06-AZXmwHjo` (note this is a YouTube video link). This also means that if we can put the power of the GPU into such pre-ML data processing tasks, then the overall pipeline will benefit immediately.

However, the important question remains: **can we leverage the power of GPUs for regular data science jobs (e.g., data wrangling, descriptive statistics) too?** The answer is not trivial and needs some special consideration and knowledge sharing (Figure 11-1). In this chapter, I will focus on a specialized suite of tools called RAPIDS that helps any data scientist take advantage of GPU-based hardware for a wide variety of data science tasks (not necessarily deep learning or advanced ML). We expect that by utilizing the inherent parallel processing power of GPUs we can enhance the productivity of such common data science tasks significantly.

---

**What is ImageNet?**    It is an ongoing research effort to provide researchers around the world an easily accessible image database. This project is inspired by a growing sentiment in the image and vision research field: the need for more data. **The project has been instrumental in advancing computer vision and deep learning research**. The data is available for free to researchers for non-commercial use. The latest deep learning architectures are pitted against each other in an annual competition that centers around this data repository, and the performance of the algorithms/architectures/techniques are measured based on how they performed on images from this source.

**Figure 11-1.** *"Can we leverage the power of GPUs for regular data science jobs"?*

# The RAPIDS Ecosystem

The RAPIDS suite of open-source software libraries and APIs provides the ability to execute end-to-end data science and analytics pipelines entirely on GPUs. Nvidia incubated this project and built tools to take advantage of CUDA primitives for low-level compute optimization. It specifically focuses on exposing GPU parallelism and high-bandwidth memory speed features through the friendly Python language so popular with data scientists and analytics professionals.

Common data preparation and wrangling tasks are highly valued in the RAPIDS ecosystem as they take up a significant amount of time in a typical data science pipeline. A familiar dataframe-like API has been developed with a lot of optimization and robustness built in. It has also been customized to integrate with a variety of ML algorithms for end-to-end pipeline accelerations with incurring serialization costs.

RAPIDS also includes a significant amount of internal support for multi-node, multi-GPU deployment and distributed processing. It integrates with other libraries that make out-of-memory (i.e., dataset sizes larger than the individual computer RAM) data processing easy and accessible for individual data scientists.

The following subsections describe, in brief, the most prominent libraries in this ecosystem that data scientists will find quite useful.

---

**What is CUDA?**   CUDA is a parallel computing platform and programming model created by NVIDIA. First introduced in 2006, it has grown to become the most common choice for enabling GPU-accelerated computing with support for multiple programming languages (e.g., C, C++, Fortran, Python, and MATLAB) and APIs.

A noteworthy point is that CUDA by itself is neither a programming language, nor an API. It is a platform for building third-party libraries, SDKs, and profiling and optimization tools. It mainly supplies extensions or primitives to add to an existing programming language, and these extensions essentially connect the computation (performed by the high-level language or API) directly to the underlying GPU hardware.

The CUDA Toolkit (`https://developer.nvidia.com/cuda-toolkit`) includes GPU-accelerated libraries, a compiler, development tools, and the CUDA runtime. To boost performance across multiple application domains from AI to HPC, developers can harness NVIDIA CUDA-X—a collection of libraries, tools and technologies built on top of CUDA (`www.nvidia.com/en-us/technologies/cuda-x/`).

---

# CuPy

CuPy is a CUDA-powered array library that looks and feels like NumPy, the foundation of all numerical computing and ML with Python. Under the hood, it uses CUDA-based low-level libraries including cuBLAS, cuDNN, cuRand, cuSolver, cuSPARSE, cuFFT, and NCCL to make full use of the a given GPU architecture with the goal of providing GPU-accelerated computing with Python.

CuPy's interface is highly similar to that of NumPy and can be used as a simple drop-in replacement for most use cases. Here is the module-level detailed list of API compatibility between CuPy and NumPy: `https://docs.cupy.dev/en/stable/reference/comparison.html`. Notice that almost all common NumPy methods are duplicated in CuPy and the names are identical, too. For data science tasks, this essentially presents you with **GPU-powered speed-up without any significant learning curve**.

The **speed-up over NumPy can be significant** depending on the data type and use case. In the next section, I will show a hands-on example of a speedup comparison between CuPy and NumPy for two different array sizes and for various common numerical operations like slicing, statistical operations like sum and standard deviation over multi-dimensional array, matrix multiplication and inverse, Fast Fourier Transformation (FFT), and singular value decomposition (SVD).

# CuDF

Built on the Apache Arrow columnar memory format, CuDF is a GPU-accelerated data analysis library for loading, joining, aggregating, filtering, and manipulating tabular data in all manners imaginable. It is no surprise that it provides a **pandas-like API** that will be familiar to almost all data engineers and data scientists. The idea is that data scientists should be able to use CuDF to easily accelerate their workflows using powerful GPUs without delving deeply into the details of CUDA programming. Just like CuPy, the majority of the methods are just drop-in replacements from an existing pandas codebase.

Note, however, that **currently CuDF is supported only on Linux OS** and works with Python versions 3.7 and later. Other requirements for installing and using CuDF are

- CUDA 11.0+

- NVIDIA driver 450.80.02+

- Pascal architecture or better (compute capability >=6.0)

Therefore, you must undergo some environment setup and installation procedures before CuDF can be used. Here is a resource to quickly get started with this powerful library: `https://docs.rapids.ai/api/cudf/stable/10min.html`.

Combined, CuPy and CuDF present a wonderful opportunity to any data scientist, regardless of whether they are using deep learning or not, to enhance the productivity of their work using GPU-accelerated computing power.

# CuML

CuML is another library within RAPIDS that enables data scientists, analysts, and researchers to run traditional/classical ML algorithmic tasks with (mostly) tabular datasets on GPUs without knowing a lot of details of CUDA programming. In most cases, **CuML's Python API matches that of the popular Python library scikit-learn** to make the transition to GPU hardware fast and painless. Here is the GitHub page for the library for you to follow and dig deep into: `https://github.com/rapidsai/cuml`.

Along with CuPy and CuDF, in the next section you will also explore some hands-on examples of CuML functions and methods for common ML tasks and compare their execution speed and scalability with equivalent scikit-learn algorithms.

Going beyond the scenario of a *single GPU on a laptop*, CuML also integrates with Dask, wherever it can, to offer **multi-GPU** and **multi-node-GPU** support for an ever-increasing set of algorithms that take advantage of such distributed processing. Basically, instead of a single GPU, many modern high-end hardware platforms come equipped with four or even eight GPUs, sometimes interconnected by a special memory bus and data interfacing channels that completely bypass the CPU and traditional slow-speed motherboard communication bus for direct GPU-to-GPU connection.

# CuGraph

CuGraph is a collection of GPU-accelerated graph algorithms that processes data found in GPU DataFrames. The vision of CuGraph is to make graph analysis ubiquitous to the point that users just think in terms of analysis and not technologies or frameworks.

Data scientists will readily pick up how CuGraph integrates with the pandas-like API of CuDF. On the other hand, users familiar with NetworkX will quickly recognize the NetworkX-like API provided in CuGraph, with the goal of allowing existing code to be ported into RAPIDS with minimal effort. Currently, it supports a wide array of graph analytics algorithms:

- Centrality
- Community

- Link analysis

- Link prediction

- Traversal

Many scientific and business analytics tasks involve the use of extensive graph algorithms on large datasets. Libraries like CuGraph lend the assurance of higher productivity to those engineers when they invest in GPU-powered workstations.

# Hardware Story

The hardware side of this story cannot be emphasized enough. Driven by the grand success and wide adoption of AI and ML solutions, with particular emphasis on deep learning applications, there has been a plethora of investments and developments in the domain of customized hardware for running such workloads. For example, all major server and workstation suppliers (e.g., HP, IBM, Lenovo, Super Micro, etc.) that were solely focused on building computing infrastructure for cloud computing only now offer a dizzying array of GPU-optimized hardware options. Google's Tensor Processing Unit (TPU; https://en.wikipedia.org/wiki/Tensor_Processing_Unit), for instance, is an application-specific integrated circuit that is **designed from the ground up with the sole aim of speeding up computations unique to machine learning and deep learning workloads** such as linear algebra, matrix multiplication, special nonlinear transformation, and supporting multiple floating-point number formats. Nvidia, the leader in GPU research and development, is pioneering many such groundbreaking hardware platforms, too. In fact, a whole hardware ecosystem with specialized storage, shared memory architecture and chipsets, motherboard designs, and data communication channels and standards are being actively developed to cater to AI workloads (Figure 11-2).

Granted, the focus of such hardware development has always been specific types of AI workloads such as large-scale computer vision, powerful chatbots, or industrial-scale natural language processing. Nonetheless, with the help of frameworks such as RAPIDS, finally data scientists and analysts (i.e., those who do not necessarily use deep learning in any of their daily tasks) can rejoice and use these powerful AI-workstations to enhance their productivity.

***Figure 11-2.*** *Data scientists can rejoice and use AI-optimized hardware for their tasks*

## Choice of Environment and Setup

As noted, RAPIDS will work only on the Linux OS and with certain GPUs and above. Although CuPy works with earlier generation of GPUs, for CuDF and CuML, you must have a GPU with compute capability 6 or higher. NVIDIA provides a list of GPUs and their compute capability (`https://developer.nvidia.com/cuda-gpus#compute`) that you can check to make sure you have the right kind of GPU for taking advantage of the RAPIDS framework.

For laptops, if you have anything above GeForce 1050, RAPIDS will work. This, of course, includes the RTX line of GPUs. For workstations, a M6000 or K-series may not work but anything above P400 will work. For datacenter GPUs (when you may be renting a cloud instance, for example), it must be of the Pascal architecture or above, such as P4, P40, P100, V100, and A100.

Once you have the right GPU, you also need to make sure that CUDA 11.2 or above is installed. After that, a lot of custom setup and environment install needs to happen for RAPIDS to work properly. Therefore, two common ways to accomplish this are as follows:

- Use a hosted environment without getting into the details of the custom setup

- Use a NVIDIA docker image if you're using it on a bare-metal Linux OS (for example, on an EC2 instance)

For instance, the following examples were run using a free hosted setup on **Saturn Cloud**. This service is a **fully managed data science cloud service offering GPU-based infrastructure** and a transparent pricing. For the free tier, it has certain limitations on how many hours of free usage you get in a month. However, for basic learning, the free usage quota (30 hours of Jupyter Lab sessions in a month) should be enough. You are encouraged to sign up on their website and follow the examples in this book (and the associated Jupyter notebooks).

When you log in to the Saturn Cloud platform, you are presented with several choices for starting a Jupyter notebook. Each choice represents a managed service (e.g., a RAPIDS environment, TensorFlow, PyTorch, or a FastAPI instance). Figure 11-3 shows a typical snapshot of all the choices (note that it was taken in April 2022, and the offerings may change).

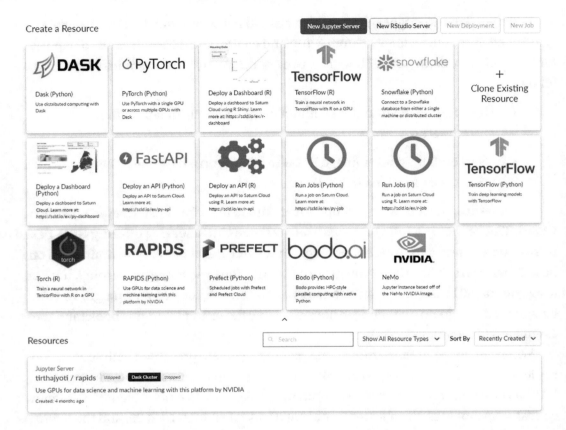

***Figure 11-3.*** *Saturn Cloud opening page with choices of various managed services*

At the bottom of Figure 11-3, you can see a RAPIDS Jupyter server already created by me. When you click on your version, the following screen (Figure 11-4) shows where you can start the Jupyter lab. Essentially, **Saturn Cloud deploys a docker container with Jupyter lab, RAPIDS, and other Python libraries preinstalled and properly configured on a GPU-based hardware/computing node**. It is to be noted that they also pair up a Dask cluster choice with this service so that you can take advantage of multi-GPU systems if you choose to do so. The free tier limits the type and number of GPUs that you can take advantage of; however, as mentioned, for basic learning, you don't need more than one GPU, and therefore you won't launch a Dask cluster.

***Figure 11-4.*** *Saturn Cloud's Jupyter server with RAPIDS*

Once the Jupyter lab starts up, you can verify that you have a compatible GPU for RAPIDS. Figure 11-5 shows the command and a typical output. Here, the GPU is a Tesla T4 (`www.nvidia.com/en-us/data-center/tesla-t4/`), the CUDA version is 11.4, and the NVIDIA driver version is 470.57.02.

```
!nvidia-smi
Last executed at 2022-02-15 00:57:37 in 875ms
Tue Feb 15 08:57:36 2022
+-----------------------------------------------------------------------------+
| NVIDIA-SMI 470.57.02    Driver Version: 470.57.02    CUDA Version: 11.4      |
|-------------------------------+----------------------+----------------------+
| GPU  Name        Persistence-M| Bus-Id        Disp.A | Volatile Uncorr. ECC |
| Fan  Temp  Perf  Pwr:Usage/Cap|         Memory-Usage | GPU-Util  Compute M. |
|                               |                      |               MIG M. |
|===============================+======================+======================|
|   0  Tesla T4            On   | 00000000:00:1E.0 Off |                    0 |
| N/A   38C    P0    33W /  70W |    342MiB / 15109MiB |      0%      Default |
|                               |                      |                  N/A |
+-------------------------------+----------------------+----------------------+

+-----------------------------------------------------------------------------+
| Processes:                                                                  |
|  GPU   GI   CI        PID   Type   Process name                  GPU Memory |
|        ID   ID                                                   Usage      |
|=============================================================================|
+-----------------------------------------------------------------------------+
```

***Figure 11-5.*** *A typical output for a Nvidia GPU status command*

# CuPy vs. NumPy

In this section, I will show some basic examples of CuPy usage and how it compares with the ubiquitous NumPy package. As NumPy finds wide and varying use in almost all data science and ML tasks, it is interesting to note that productivity of all those tasks can probably be increased significantly by switching to CuPy.

## Looks and Works Just Like NumPy

As mentioned, the CuPy API is designed to be drop-in replacement for NumPy code. Therefore, all the common methods are available for use. Start by importing both libraries (for comparison) and others:

```
import numpy as np, cupy as cp
import matplotlib.pyplot as plt
import time
```

You can define an array just like in NumPy:

```
a1 = cp.array([1,2,3])
a2 = cp.arange(1,11,2)
a3 = cp.random.normal(size=(3,3))
```

Only the type is different:

```
type(a3)
>> cupy._core.core.ndarray
```

You can have all the usual and useful NumPy operations such as broadcasting, transpose, inverse, and Boolean filtering.

```
a3.T
a3+1
a3.mean(axis=1)
a3*(a3>0)
```

The output of the last one is as follows:

```
>> array([[ 0.58731747, -0.        , -0.        ],
      [-0.        , -0.        ,  0.7699453 ],
      [ 1.80051069,  0.67680871,  1.3091392 ]])
```

# Much Faster Than NumPy

Although CuPy looks and feels same as NumPy, it is much faster for vectorized operations when supported by a high-performance GPU. Here is some code to show this conclusively:

```
SIZE = 200
%%timeit -n10 -r10
np.random.normal(size=(SIZE,SIZE))@np.random.normal(size=(SIZE,SIZE))
```

>> **3.67 ms ± 258 μs** per loop (mean ± std. dev. of 10 runs, 10 loops each)

This code measures the average time taken for a NumPy operation of matrix multiplication with (200 x 200) size.

Now, let's run the exact same code with a single change of replacing np by cp (i.e., using CuPy arrays and methods instead of NumPy):

```
%%timeit -n10 -r10
cp.random.normal(size=(SIZE,SIZE))@cp.random.normal(size=(SIZE,SIZE))
```

>> **127 μs ± 40.7 μs** per loop (mean ± std. dev. of 10 runs, 10 loops each)

Even a simple 200 x 200 matrix multiplication shows a more than 25X speedup (127 μs as compared to 3.67 ms). Imagine the extent of the performance improvement for large data science operations involving much larger numeric datasets.

# Data (Array) Size Matters

The performance improvement, demonstrated above, scales up quickly with the size of the array. Let's see this using a simple set of code. First, you write a timing measurement code using NumPy with np.linalg.solve() method (i.e., solving a set of simultaneous equations). Recall that this same method is used (under the hood) for solving a simple multiple linear regression algorithm.

```
import time, tqdm
size=[100*i for i in range(1,21)]

numpy_time = []
for s in tqdm(size):
    a = np.array([np.random.randint(-10,10,s).tolist() for i in range(s)])
```

```
b = np.array([np.random.randint(-100,100,s)]).T
t1 = time.time()
x = np.linalg.solve(a,b)
t2 = time.time()
delta_t = (t2-t1)*1000
numpy_time.append(delta_t)
```

You must repeat the same code for CuPy by replacing np with cp, as showed before. Finally, with a simple plotting code, you can see the comparison clearly (Figure 11-6). Observe that the performance improvement scales up with the array size and somewhat nonlinearly too. This means for even larger size arrays, the improvement will scale up even faster. **This kind of improvement, of course, can be achieved up to the point where the data (array) can be properly fit in the GPU memory.** This could be a limitation for datasets with tens of millions of rows or columns as the GPU memory can be smaller compared to a system memory (RAM). However, many batch operations or segmented operations can be designed to work around this limitation and still achieve significant speedup.

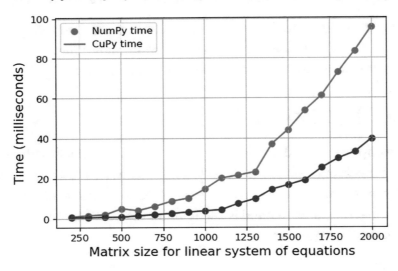

*Figure 11-6.* *CuPy and NumPy comparison with varying array sizes for a linear system solve*

Next, let's tackle the problem of singular value decomposition (SVD) using a randomly generated square matrix (drawn from a normal distribution) of varying sizes. I won't repeat the code block here but just show the result for brevity (Figure 11-7). Note that the CuPy algorithm does not show markedly superior performance to that of the NumPy algorithm in this problem class. Perhaps this is something to be taken up by the CuPy developers to improve upon.

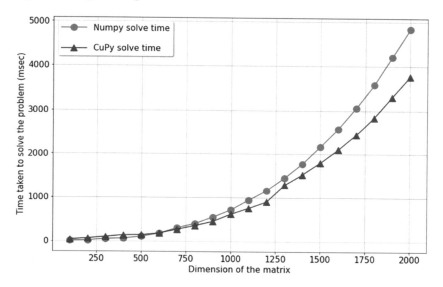

***Figure 11-7.*** *CuPy and NumPy comparison with varying matrix sizes for SVD*

Next, let's go back to the basics and consider the fundamental problem of matrix inversion (used in almost all machine learning algorithms). The result again shows a strongly favorable performance gain by the CuPy algorithm over that from the NumPy package (Figure 11-8).

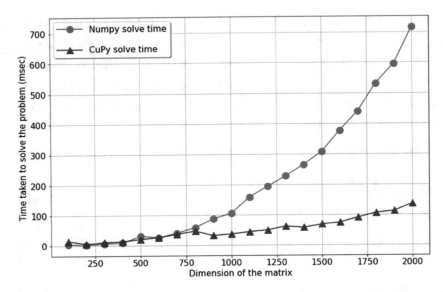

***Figure 11-8.*** *CuPy and NumPy comparison for matrix multiplication tasks*

# CuDF vs. pandas

Let's use the same Saturn Cloud instance and spin up a new Jupyter notebook for doing this exercise. The idea is to show some basic operations with CuDF and to demonstrate a simple computing speed comparison with pandas.

## Data Reading from an URL

Let's read a dataset from an URL hosted on my personal GitHub:

```
import numpy as np, cupy as cp, cudf
import pandas as pd
<more imports...>

url = "https://raw.githubusercontent.com/tirthajyoti/Machine-Learning-with-
Python/master/Datasets/College_Data"
content = requests.get(url).content.decode('utf-8')
cdf = cudf.read_csv(StringIO(content))
```

So you read a CSV file over the Internet and load it into a CuDF DataFrame. You can use the familiar `.head()` method to examine the first few entries:

```
cdf.head()
```

This produces the output shown in Figure 11-9.

| | Unnamed: 0 | Private | Apps | Accept | Enroll | Top10perc | Top25perc | F.Undergrad | P.Undergrad | Outstate | Room.Board | Books | Personal | PhD | Terminal | S.F.Ratio |
|---|---|---|---|---|---|---|---|---|---|---|---|---|---|---|---|---|
| 0 | Abilene Christian University | Yes | 1660 | 1232 | 721 | 23 | 52 | 2885 | 537 | 7440 | 3300 | 450 | 2200 | 70 | 78 | 18.1 |
| 1 | Adelphi University | Yes | 2186 | 1924 | 512 | 16 | 29 | 2683 | 1227 | 12280 | 6450 | 750 | 1500 | 29 | 30 | 12.2 |
| 2 | Adrian College | Yes | 1428 | 1097 | 336 | 22 | 50 | 1036 | 99 | 11250 | 3750 | 400 | 1165 | 53 | 66 | 12.9 |
| 3 | Agnes Scott College | Yes | 417 | 349 | 137 | 60 | 89 | 510 | 63 | 12960 | 5450 | 450 | 875 | 92 | 97 | 7.7 |
| 4 | Alaska Pacific University | Yes | 193 | 146 | 55 | 16 | 44 | 249 | 869 | 7560 | 4120 | 800 | 1500 | 76 | 72 | 11.9 |

***Figure 11-9.*** *CuDF DataFrame first few entries after loading the data from a URL*

## Indexing, Filtering, and Grouping

The indexing, column naming, and filtering works just like the pandas API. First, rename the Unnamed: 0 column to something more meaningful:

```
cdf.rename(columns={"Unnamed: 0": "College"}, inplace=True)
```

Then you can see a selective portion of the data:

```
cdf[['F.Undergrad','P.Undergrad']][2:4]
```

This produces the output in Figure 11-10.

```
cdf[['F.Undergrad','P.Undergrad']][2:4]
Last executed at 2022-02-19 14:19:11 in 14ms
```

| | F.Undergrad | P.Undergrad |
|---|---|---|
| 2 | 1036 | 99 |
| 3 | 510 | 63 |

***Figure 11-10.*** *CuDF DataFrame indexing selected columns and rows*

Now try a somewhat complicated filtering operation to extract and list colleges with a decent student-faculty ratio (under 10) but with low tuition expenditure (under $8000) as well:

```
filter_1 = cdf['S.F.Ratio']< 10
filter_2 = cdf['Expend'] < 8000

cdf[filter_1 & filter_2 ][['College','S.F.Ratio','Expend']]
```

The results are shown in Figure 11-11.

```
filter_1 = cdf['S.F.Ratio']< 10
filter_2 = cdf['Expend'] < 8000

cdf[filter_1 & filter_2 ][['College','S.F.Ratio','Expend']]
```
Last executed at 2022-02-19 14:50:46 in 20ms

|  | College | S.F.Ratio | Expend |
|---|---|---|---|
| 73 | Buena Vista College | 8.8 | 6333 |
| 109 | Chestnut Hill College | 8.3 | 7729 |
| 135 | College of St. Joseph | 9.5 | 6936 |
| 241 | Gwynedd Mercy College | 7.8 | 7483 |
| 341 | Marian College of Fond du Lac | 8.4 | 5352 |
| 580 | Tennessee Wesleyan College | 8.9 | 6286 |
| 608 | University of Charleston | 2.5 | 7683 |

***Figure 11-11.*** *Multiple filtering operation on the CuDF DataFrame*

A groupby operation, followed by an aggregation, works just like pandas too (Figure 11-12).

```
cdf.groupby('Private').mean()[['Accept','Grad.Rate']]
```
Last executed at 2022-02-19 14:54:10 in 29ms

|  | Accept | Grad.Rate |
| --- | --- | --- |
| **Private** | | |
| **No** | 3919.287736 | 56.042453 |
| **Yes** | 1305.702655 | 68.998230 |

*Figure 11-12.  Groupby and averaging operations on the CuDF DataFrame*

# NumPy Array Conversion

For many purposes, especially for plotting and visualization, you may need to convert the CuDF data fields to standard NumPy arrays. In these cases, just using the standard .values attribute will yield a CuPy array only. To get to the NumPy array, you need to use the .get() method on top of it.

Here is what you get with .values only:

```
phds=cdf['PhD'].values
type(phds)
>> cupy._core.core.ndarray
```

Using the .get method, you get the NumPy array and can plot a histogram of the number of PhDs (Figure 11-13).

```
phds=cdf['PhD'].values.get()
plt.title('Histogram of PhD',fontsize=15)
plt.hist(phds,edgecolor='k')
plt.show()
```

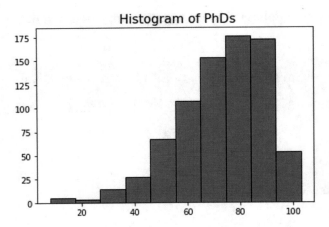

***Figure 11-13.*** *Histogram of PhDs from the CuDF DataFrame after NumPy array conversion*

## Simple Benchmarking of Speed

You can show the improvement in the computation performance (by using the T4 GPU, of course) with CuDF with a very simple benchmarking exercise.

Construct a NumPy array with 1 million rows and 100 columns with random numbers (drawing from a Gaussian distribution), and convert that to a pandas DataFrame first and a CuDF DataFrame next:

```
data = np.random.normal(size=(1000_000,100))
df = pd.DataFrame(data)
cdf = cudf.DataFrame.from_pandas(df)
```

Here, the `.from_pandas` method converts an existing pandas DataFrame to a CuDF DataFrame quickly and painlessly.

A simple mean calculation on the first column gives the following output for the pandas DataFrame:

```
%timeit -n10 -r10 df[0].mean()
>> 15 ms ± 1.16 ms per loop (mean ± std. dev. of 10 runs, 10 loops each)
```

The same exercise the CuDF DataFrame yields a much faster result:

```
%timeit -n10 -r10 cdf[0].mean()
>> 504 µs ± 52.7 µs per loop (mean ± std. dev. of 10 runs, 10 loops each)
```

Extending this exercise further, you run a loop by selecting an increasing number of columns each time and see how the computation time scales with the number of columns and how the benchmark comparison between pandas and CuDF looks:

```
for i in range(2,11):
    t1=time.time()
    df[[j for j in range(i)]].mean()
    t2=time.time()
    del_t = round(1000*(t2-t1),3)
    print(f"Calculation with {i} columns took {del_t} ms")
>>
Calculation with 2 columns took 3.333 ms
Calculation with 3 columns took 2.835 ms
Calculation with 4 columns took 2.878 ms
Calculation with 5 columns took 3.269 ms
Calculation with 6 columns took 3.589 ms
Calculation with 7 columns took 4.11 ms
Calculation with 8 columns took 4.606 ms
Calculation with 9 columns took 4.99 ms
Calculation with 10 columns took 5.478 ms
```

For the CuDF DataFrame, the calculation times are much shorter and it scales much slower:

```
Calculation with 2 columns took 3.333 ms
Calculation with 3 columns took 2.835 ms
Calculation with 4 columns took 2.878 ms
Calculation with 5 columns took 3.269 ms
Calculation with 6 columns took 3.589 ms
Calculation with 7 columns took 4.11 ms
Calculation with 8 columns took 4.606 ms
Calculation with 9 columns took 4.99 ms
Calculation with 10 columns took 5.478 ms
```

## Dask Integration, User-Defined Functions, and Other Features

CuDF plays nicely with a Dask cluster where the power of **multiple GPUs can be utilized for massively parallelized data processing**. It also natively supports **complex user-defined functions (UDFs**, as they are called) to be applied over selected axes or columns. These functions work block by block (pertaining to the internal representation of the data in the GPU memory) and exhibit a much faster computation speed than what would have been possible with a CPU-based pandas workflow. For the sake of brevity, I won't cover all these features, but you are encouraged to check out the excellent tutorials provided on the RAPIDS portal at `https://docs.rapids.ai/api/cudf/stable/user_guide/10min.html`.

# CuML vs. scikit-learn

After covering the basic usage of CuPy and CuDF and showing comparative benchmarks with NumPy and pandas, it makes sense to move up to the next stage of a data science pipeline and discuss about the GPU-powered equivalent of scikit-learn: CuML.

As most instances of conventional usage of GPU-powered hardware have been squarely in the machine learning domain, it is important to clarify what this comparative discussion is about. Here, we are focusing solely on the non-deep-learning aspects of the machine learning world (i.e., instances where a data scientist would apply out-of-the-box algorithms borrowing from the scikit-learn API). The point is that, in such circumstances, if the data scientist has access to a GPU-based system, they can improve the computing performance significantly without spending any time or effort on tweaking the code or learning about GPU programming. These are the situations where TensorFlow is not required, yet the power of GPU must be fully utilized.

## Classification with Random Forest

In this exercise, you will use a scikit-learn Random Forest classifier to train with a synthetic dataset and compare the performance and speed with a similar classifier from the CuML API. First, you create some synthetic data with 10,000 samples and 20 features:

```
NUM_ROWS = 10000
NUM_FEATURES = 20
```

```
from sklearn.datasets import make_classification

X,y = make_classification(n_samples=NUM_ROWS,
                          n_classes=2,
                          n_features=NUM_FEATURES,
                          n_informative=NUM_FEATURES,
                          n_redundant=0,
                          n_repeated=0)
```

You have imported the necessary functions and classes from the respective APIs. However, for such a comparative study, you need to be careful about the naming as the class and function names are largely identical between scikit-learn and CuML. Therefore, you can create your own versions while importing:

```
from sklearn.model_selection import train_test_split as sk_tts
from cuml.model_selection import train_test_split as cuml_tts
from sklearn.ensemble import RandomForestClassifier as SKRF
from cuml.ensemble import RandomForestClassifier as CURF
```

Note that you are importing not only the classifier but also the train/test splitting utility from CuML. As a general practice, **you should use every bit of the API that is offered by CuML when you are utilizing the power of a GPU**.

For proper comparison and data protection, you build two separate functions, one with a scikit-learn pipeline and another with the CuML API. Here is the scikit-learn version:

```
def sklearn_pipeline(X,y,n_estimators=100):
    """

    Executes Sklearn-based pipeline
    """

    t1 =time.time()
    X_train, X_test, y_train, y_test = sk_tts(X,y, test_size=0.3)
    model = SKRF(n_estimators=n_estimators)
    model.fit(X_train,y_train)
    t2 =time.time()
    del_t = round(1000*(t2-t1),3)
    score = round(model.score(X_test,y_test),3)

    return (score, del_t)
```

The code below is the CuML version. Note that to be compatible with certain GPU calculations, the data type is changed to np.float32 (i.e., 32-bit floating point precision for the CuML). Also, **CuML API works with CuPy arrays only**, and that's where the NumPy-to-CuPy conversion is required. Nonetheless, you measure the entire time taken by this pipeline, not just the training/fitting part. The function returns a tuple for the classification score (on the test set) and the time taken to execute.

```python
def cuml_pipeline(X,y,n_estimators=100):
    """
    Executes CuML-based pipeline
    """
    t1 =time.time()
    X = cupy.array(X,dtype=np.float32)
    y = cupy.array(y,dtype=np.float32)
    X_train, X_test, y_train, y_test = cuml_tts(X,y, test_size=0.3)
    model = CURF(n_estimators=n_estimators)
    model.fit(X_train,y_train)
    t2 =time.time()
    del_t = round(1000*(t2-t1),3)
    score = round(model.score(X_test,y_test),3)

    return (score, del_t)
```

Then you just run these pipelines one after another. For the scikit-learn case, here are the results:

```python
score_sk, t_sk = sklearn_pipeline(X,y)
print("Sklearn pipeline score: ",score_sk)
print("Sklearn pipeline time (ms): ",t_sk)
>>
Sklearn pipeline score:  0.937
Sklearn pipeline time (ms):  2132.17
```

For the CuML pipeline, here are the results:

```
score_cuml, t_cuml = cuml_pipeline(X,y)
print("CuML pipeline score: ",score_cuml)
print("CuML pipeline time (ms): ",t_cuml)
>>
CuML pipeline score:  0.936
CuML pipeline time (ms):  100.471
```

You can observe a massive speed-up for the CuML pipeline with the identical data input. The accuracy scores of both pipelines are almost identical, with the CuML score differing at the third decimal place, perhaps due to the 32-bit floating point precision conversion. But the speed improvement compensates for that miniscule accuracy change many times over.

---

Note that while running the code (or associated Jupyter notebook), the first time you may get a result that may show the scikit-learn pipeline is faster than the CuML pipeline. This is related to how the GPU memory is prefetched and cached with code and data, and it only happens for the very first run. This should be ignored. If you run the code again, you should get the same trend as shown in the results here.

---

Extending this further, let's investigate whether the model complexity factors into this relative improvement over scikit-learn when you use CuML. Fit the same data to the Random Forest models of increasing complexity (i.e., increasing number of root estimators/trees). The result shown in Figure 11-14 clearly demonstrates the fact that **CuML and its parallelized (GPU-powered) operation helps ensemble classifiers like Random Forest in a significant manner as the model complexity grows**. While the computing time goes up for both classifiers, the pace of growth is miniscule for CuML as compared to that of scikit-learn. There are some minor differences in the accuracy scores but the payoff in terms of the computation efficiency is much more significant.

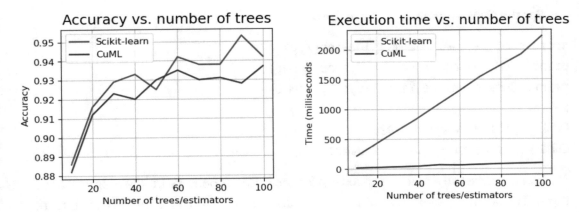

**Figure 11-14.** *Varying Random Forest classfier complexities with scikit-learn and CuML*

## K-Means Clustering

Next, consider an unsupervised learning problem of clustering using the all-too-familiar k-means algorithm. Here, you are again comparing a CuML function with an equivalent estimator from the Scikit-learn package. Just for reference, Figure 11-15 shows the API comparison between these two estimators. They look virtually identical, except the CuML uses something called "scalable-k-means++" as the initialization parameter. The CuML k-means estimator also accepts a `max_samples_per_batch` argument that allows controlled batch training.

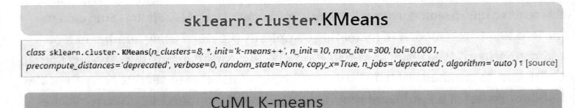

**Figure 11-15.** *API comparison between scikit-learn and CuML K-means estimators*

Figure 11-16 shows the result for a dataset with 10 features/dimensions.

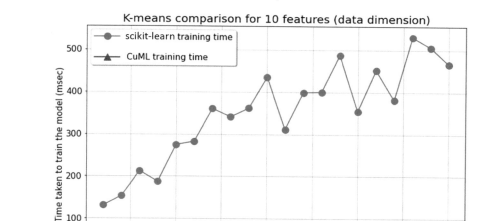

*Figure 11-16.*  *K-means clustering speed comparison for 10 features*

Figure 11-17 shows the result of another experiment with a 100-feature dataset. Clearly, both the sample size (number of rows) and dimensionality (number of columns) matter in how the GPU-based acceleration performed so well.

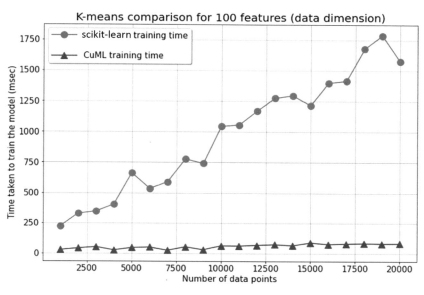

*Figure 11-17.*  *K-means clustering speed comparison for 100 features*

Further discussion and results on a linear regression problem can be found in this article by me: `https://medium.com/dataseries/gpu-powered-data-science-not-deep-learning-with-rapids-29f9ed8d51f3`. You are encouraged to check it out.

# Summary

This chapter focused on the usage and application of GPU-based hardware systems for data science tasks that do not necessarily involve deep learning models or inferencing, but still can benefit significantly from hardware-centric optimizations.

I introduced you to the fantastic ecosystem of RAPIDS, a GPU-centered data science framework with separate libraries for numerical computing, tabular data analytics, classical machine learning, graph analysis, and even signal processing. This framework is powered by CUDA-accelerated libraries and takes full advantage of NVIDIA GPUs (above a certain generation of GPU class and compute capability).

However, the best feature is that all of these modules try to mimic their non-GPU, pure-Python counterparts like NumPy, pandas, and scikit-learn. Therefore, for data scientists, the learning curve is short and (almost) drop-in code replacements can work most of the time. Following this principle, next you saw multiple hands-on examples of the basic usage of these libraries using a Tesla T4 GPU powered hosted runtime (on the cloud). I also showed benchmark comparisons of computation performance of equivalent operations and ML algorithms to clearly demonstrate the advantage of GPU-accelerated data science.

# CHAPTER 12

# Other Useful Skills to Master

As you progress towards the end of the grand journey of productive and efficient data science that you took in this book, I would like to dedicate one complete chapter to the set of various disparate useful skills that a data scientist should strive to master to enhance their productivity. Unlike the previous chapters, where you examined similarly grouped skills (e.g., memory profilers or distributed computing tools), the tools and skills you'll explore in this chapter may look somewhat disjointed from each other. It is true that they do not fall under one unifying class but taken as a whole, they truly aid any data scientist in performing their tasks with higher productivity.

I start with a discussion on the importance of learning basic web technologies such as HTML, CSS, and JavaScript. Building on the same concepts, next I discuss the utility of creating a simple web app for a data science project. I show a hands-on example with two Python libraries, Flask and PyWebIO. Thereafter, I talk about cloud technologies such as Amazon Web Service and show (with lined resources) the simple process of bringing the power of the cloud to a local data science workflow. Finally, I switch gears and discuss how, in many cases, using a so-called "low-code" framework can be useful and productive for a data science task. I demonstrate PyCaret, a popular low-code Python library in this regard.

As you can observe from this description, unlike previous chapters, this chapter is not focused on one (or a small number of) Python tools/libraries. While I may be discussing a few useful Python libraries in some sections, elsewhere I may be discussing general technology features without any reference to a specific Python tool. In those sections, I may have general suggestions for what topics to learn and how to go about that.

© Dr. Tirthajyoti Sarkar 2022
T. Sarkar, *Productive and Efficient Data Science with Python*, https://doi.org/10.1007/978-1-4842-8121-5_12

# Understanding the Basics of Web Technologies

You may be wondering why a data scientist needs to understand the nuts and bolts of web apps or general web technologies. The answer lies in the simple fact that a data scientist's responsibility should not just be limited to statistical analysis or building ML models. Above all, the job of a data scientist is to solve a business or scientific problem using data in a scientific manner. Communicating the result and presenting the modeling and analysis to the external world in an accessible (or even interactive) manner is a necessary goal of any reasonable data science job.

## A Consumer-Facing Layer

In other words, while analyzing datasets, finding hidden patterns, and building predictive models are rightfully considered the primary skills for a data scientist, it is equally important to communicate the key insights gleaned from those analyses and/or to build some sort of interactive layers on top of those models that works as the touch point for the external consumers. These aspects can be especially important if a data scientist is thinking about building a consumer-facing product or even starting their own business powered by data science methods.

**To build a functioning consumer-facing interactive layer on top of a data science core, creating a web app is an obvious choice**. In the early days of personal computing (until around the turn of the 21st century), building a standalone desktop app could have been sufficient. The technology and tools for such an app are quite different from the tools used in building a web app. However, in today's world, a web app is expected for any sort of computing or information technology product and data science is no exception in this regard. Therefore, it makes sense for a data scientist to understand the basics of building such an app. All the usual data science tools and technologies are still fully used, only to find a presentable outlet or user-interaction layer through a web app, as shown in Figure 12-1.

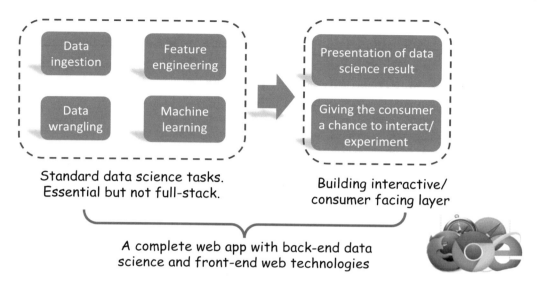

**Figure 12-1.** *A well-rounded data science project with a consumer-facing layer of a web application at the front end*

# All Useful Data Science Is Delivered Through Web Apps

Observing from the side of consumer, we realize that almost all *useful data science* is delivered to us through some web app or another. If we watch a suggested movie on Netflix or buy a product on Amazon, there is a recommendation engine and a sophisticated ML algorithm powdered by petabytes of data about ourselves and our buying/watching habits and choices behind that. But ultimately, the cumulative result of all that sophisticated data science work is presented through a simple web interface showing a movie or product link for us to click and enjoy.

Now, it is quite likely that in any reasonably sized organization, the web app developer is a person (or a team) who is separate from the data science team. However, it is extremely beneficial for the data scientists to know the details (to a reasonable degree) about the full technology stack that starts with the raw data (with their team) and ends with a nice, shiny web app developed by other software engineers using a different set of technologies. This kind of knowledge **facilitates conversations and brainstorming for solving existing problems (both on the data side and the web app side) and promotes innovative ideas**.

There are many dimensions to this kind of conversation, which facilitates problem solving and product innovation. Some typical examples are shown below. Let's assume a typical scenario of a data science pipeline running at the back end (along with some database integration) and a web app serving the results of that pipeline to users who may be logging on to a portal and even paying to use some of the services.

> Is the web app easy to scale with the existing data science/ processing pipeline? What are the challenges and how can the data science team help?

> What portion of visualization should be done on the data science (for example, using Python frameworks) back end vs. front-end JavaScript rendering? What JavaScript library works better with Python data objects? What are the caveats to watch for?

> Where are the exact touch points between the data science and the deployment layers? What about the interactive user inputs and their impact on the data science pipeline?

> How should the data science tasks be organized and managed to help the web app? How about containerization of various services? Will that help the app in terms of service quality and latency?

> What should be the strategies around data storage and databases that play equally well with the data science back end and web app front end?

> What (if any) other back-end services (e.g., user authorization, financial transactions) must play well with the data science service? What are the dependencies?

Clearly, to have meaningful impact on the overall business operations, the data science team must have a good grasp of the full stack of tools and technologies used (HTML, CSS, JavaScript, PHP, Ruby on Rails, Docker, Kubernetes, to name a few common ones). Other back-end services that operate very close to the data science services (using Python) and that may even consume the output of the data science pipeline somehow (before it is sent to the front end) may be written in languages like Go or Rust.

The point here is that a data scientist need not become an expert in all these tools and technologies. **But they must have the curiosity to know more about them and the inclination to see the complete technology stack as a holistic data-oriented enabler**. Python-based data science is a critically important piece of this enterprise, but it is the whole stack that delivers the final value to the customer and brings revenue to the organization.

# What Are Some Pathways to Learn?

Web apps (and full web-based services) development, and the associated tools and technologies, perhaps constitute the largest domain of knowledge in the universe of software engineering and information technology. There are dizzying number of choices and varieties, standards and protocols, languages and frameworks, and practices both good and bad. It is neither within the scope of this book nor within the expertise of the author to try to teach you about these technologies. However, I feel that some typical example-based suggestions can encourage you explore these areas along with your data science journey. They may include but are not limited to the following examples:

> Learning to build and **deploy a simple web application** based on a data analysis project, complete with exploratory visualizations and a simple predictive model

> Learning deeply about a Python-based web microframeworks such as **Flask** or **FastAPI** and how to serve a machine learning model using them

> Learning a front-end framework that is meant for visual analytics such as **D3.js**. Pursuing this kind of knowledge gives you a solid grasp of **fundamental JavaScript programming** while keeping you motivated by showing the power of visual data analysis on the Web

> Learning **markdown language** and acquiring **basic CSS skills** with the goal of creating attractive-looking Readme documents for GitHub repositories and open-source data science projects and packages that you have developed

> Learning about and implementing **database integration** with Python data science services with a live web application in mind

Learning about **container technologies** and how they enrich modern web applications and how they enable organizations to move away from the older-generation monolithic software building practice

It is clear from these suggestions that they are specifically **meant for data scientists who hail from a non-software or non-web-development background**. There are, in fact, many web developers who are extremely enthusiastic about data science and gradually transitioning into that kind of role. They, of course, are already deeply familiar with these tools. It is the other section of data science practitioners, coming from diverse backgrounds of physics, economics, statistics, and social sciences, that do a great service to themselves when they add web-related technologies to their repertoire. Having such well-rounded knowledge and a holistic view of the application will help them prosper in their jobs and prepare for newer challenges too.

# Building Simple Web Apps for Data Science

In this section, I demonstrate how to build a simple web app backed by a few data science tasks and services. First, I will showcase a ML model prediction example using one of the most popular Python web frameworks, Flask. This will require you to write a Python script and an HTML script that will be rendered on the web page. In the parlance of web app development, Python is the back end (that performs the data science tasks such as machine learning) whereas the HTML is the front-end technology for this app.

Next, I will showcase another Python library that abstracts away the front-end programming part even more and lets data scientists focus on the data science part while allowing them to build a useful web app with a minimal learning curve.

## Hands-On Example with Flask

Flask is a powerful yet lightweight web framework for Python that can be used to build fast-response web apps. It is particularly popular with the data science community as it presents a reasonably easy learning curve, while providing a lot of flexibility for building useful web apps for presenting their data science work (models or analysis). It effectively takes care of a lot of the environment and project setup involved in a web application. Consequently, the developer, a data scientist in this case, can focus on the real data science code and methods while Flask takes care of HTTP, routing, assets, and so on.

There are a lot of wonderful learning resources about Flask on the Internet that you are encouraged to find if you are interested in learning about this library. I will not get into those details here. Instead, I will present the code and the results directly for a small web app featuring predictions from an ML model.

There are two main files/scripts in a folder: a Python script (with Flask code) and a HTML file that is used as the front end for the app. Both files are supplied with the book. The Python script loads a pretrained ML model that is trained on the famous adult income dataset (`https://archive.ics.uci.edu/ml/datasets/adult`) for a classification task using a simple logistic regression model.

I will not go into the details of the HTML file as that is not the focus of this book. Instead, I will just show the output of the HTML, which is the page it produces (Figures 12-2 through 12-4). You can see textboxes that accept numerical input and drop-down boxes with category options. The ML model is trained to work with both input types. However, the Flask-based script must carefully convert and encode the input received from the HTML page for seamless processing with the ML model.

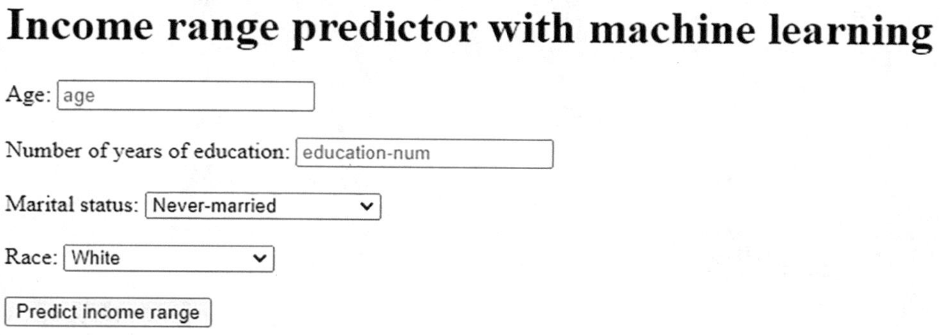

# Income range predictor with machine learning

Age: [age]

Number of years of education: [education-num]

Marital status: [Never-married ▾]

Race: [White ▾]

[Predict income range]

**Figure 12-2.** *Income range prediction model app page*

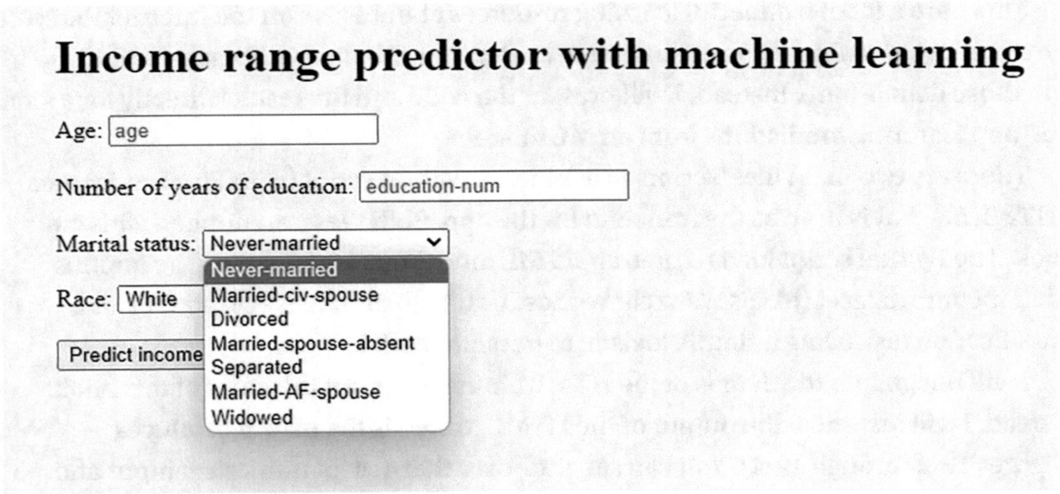

***Figure 12-3.*** *Marital status dropdown choices shown on the app*

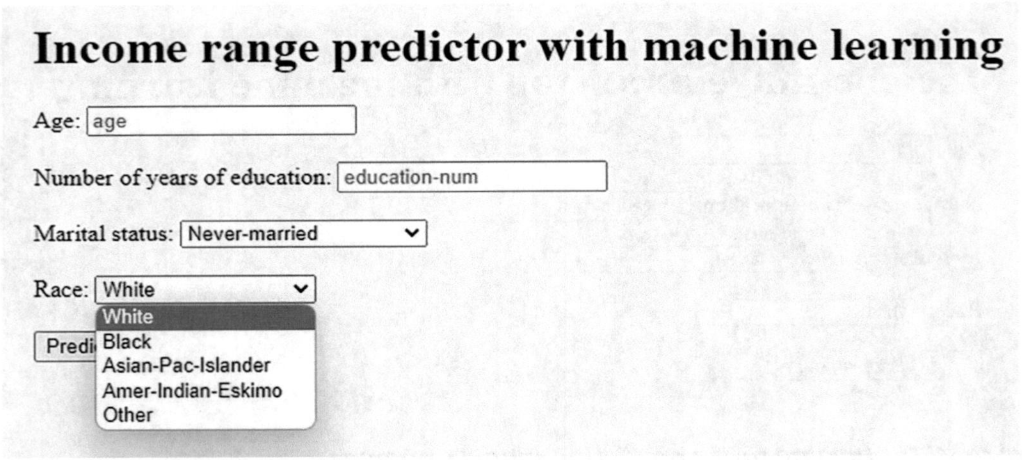

***Figure 12-4.*** *Race dropdown choices shown on the app*

Next, here's the Flask app code piece by piece:

```
from flask import Flask, render_template, request
import pickle
import numpy as np

app = Flask(__name__)
```

```
# Load model and scaler objects (from pickle dumps)
model = pickle.load(open('income_model.pkl','rb'))
scaler = pickle.load(open('income_model_scaler.pkl','rb'))
```

Here, you create the app object as a Flask class and load two objects from pickled dumps: the pretrained ML model called model and a scikit-learn scaling object called scaler. This scaler is an instance of the MinMaxScaler class used to scale the input data while training the model. For proper predictions, this needs to be saved and loaded into the app. The training of the model was done separately and is shown in a Jupyter notebook that is also supplied with this book.

The next piece of code just creates two routes (or endpoints) with the @app.route decorator. The noteworthy point here is the render_template function used in the home function definition where you pass in the name of the HTML file. This file must be stored under a folder called templates inside the same directory where the Flask app script is located. A typical arrangement of files/resources is shown in Figure 12-5.

The prediction route decorates the main prediction function predict, which is not shown in this snippet. In this route, you define the methods argument that basically lists the URL methods that are allowed for this route: GET and POST. These are operations that can be performed on this route by the browser (on the client side). These methods are basically the fundamental data exchange methods between the client (front end) and the server (back end) sides for any web application.

```
# Home page
@app.route("/")
def home():
    return render_template('ml1.html')
@app.route("/predict", methods=['GET','POST'])
# Prediction function
def predict():
```

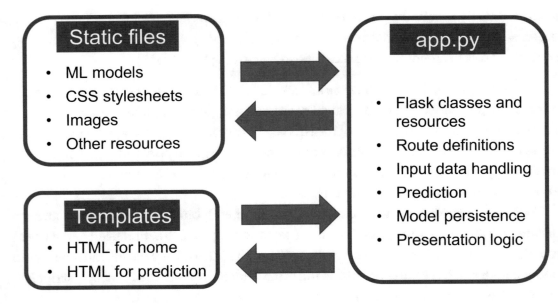

***Figure 12-5.*** *Typical Flask app files and resources arrangement*

Next, here's the prediction function in detail:

```
def predict():
    if request.method == 'POST':
        # Access the data from form
        age = int(request.form["age"])
        education_num = int(request.form["education-num"])
        marital_status = request.form["maritalstatus"]
        race = request.form["Race"]
        # Convert marital status and race to numbers
        marital_status = marital_encoder(marital_status)
        race = race_encoder(race)
        # Arrange input features in an array
        X = np.array([age, education_num,
                        marital_status, race])
        X = scaler.transform(X.reshape(1,-1))
        # Prediction
        prediction = model.predict(X)
        # Output formatting
```

```
output_fn = lambda x: 'below $50k' if x==0 else 'above $50k'
output = output_fn(int(prediction))

return render_template("ml1.html",
                        prediction_range='Your predicted annual
                        income is {}'.format(output))
```

Here, you are **receiving the data payload from the HTML form with the POST method and parsing it for extracting the individual input features** such as variables like age, education_num, marital_status, and race. A couple of these variables need to be converted/encoded into numerical features using helper functions (not shown in this code) as they are received in the payload as text strings from the HTML form. In fact, age and education_num are also read as text and converted to integer types using the int type conversion function.

Thereafter, you prepare the input feature vector, use the scaling transformer, and pass it on to the model object for prediction. The output prediction is also converted into a string object using a lambda function and that is what is printed as the final output. Also noteworthy is the use of the render_template function in the return statement. You basically return a formatted string that contains the output from the model and places it in the HTML element/tag with an id of prediction_range.

The placement of this prediction_range element in the HTML code is at the botttom of the page below the Submit button (that has an identifier of "Predict income range"). It has a H2 (header level 2) tag as well to make it prominent on the page.

```
<button type="submit" class="btn btn-primary btn-block btn-large">Predict
income range</button>
    </form>
    <br>
    <br>
    <h2>
    {{ prediction_range }}
```

The last part of the app code is for starting the web app using the app.run() method:

```
if __name__ == "__main__":
    app.run(debug=True)
```

You start this app by simply running the Python app on command line:

```
python app.py
```

This will start a web server and expose a particular port. You can simply go to the `localhost:5000` on the local browser and see the web app (i.e., the homepage rendered by the HTML file).

When you first load the web app, this won't be visible as it is coded as a `Jinja` template variable (with "{{ ... }}"). Jinja **is a helper Python library for** Flask **that takes care of all the HTML/CSS rendering** for Flask scripts with some predetermined encoding of variables and loop statements. Here, the {{ ... }} essentially holds a Python variable that comes from the Flask app script (through the `return` statement of the `predict` function).

Here is a recap of the whole process sequence. After a user clicks on the button `Predict income range` (shown in Figure 12-2), the input will be submitted through the HTML form (with textboxes and drop-down menu selections), the ML prediction will happen at the `app.py` level, and the result will be returned back to be rendered at the bottom of the page through this `Jinja` placeholder (Figure 12-6). Note the large font for the result string as it has the HTML H2 tag assoociated with it.

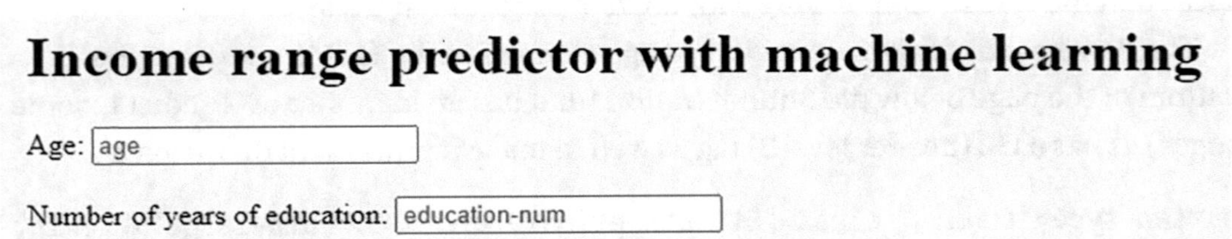

**Figure 12-6.**  *Rendering the final result for the Flask ML prediction app*

Although this example used a very simple data flow and a small ML model, **it showcased all the essential components of a Flask-based Python project** that are needed to build a powerful web application. For example, the data submission can be manual user input or reading from an online resource or a back-end database; the ML algorithm could be a simple logistic regression or a complex deep learning; there could be a large data wrangling and preprocessing pipeline before the features are extracted from the input layer; and the output could be a simple text rendering or a JavaScript-based fancy visualization. Whatever components the web app might feature, the core connection between them will follow the glue that is Flask and its resources.

# Hands-On Example with PyWebIO

PyWebIO is another helper library for building quick web apps without the need to know anything about HTML/CSS/JavaScript. PyWebIO provides a diverse set of imperative functions to obtain user input and output content on the browser, essentially turning the browser into a rich text terminal. Using PyWebIO, data scientists can build simple web applications just by writing Python scripts and inserting web-based GUI elements inside those scripts as they are required. Additionally, it supports file handling and image/plot generation natively to make the data scientists' life easier.

The full code for the app is supplied along with this book. Here, I just show the main function to highlight a few features (that are also different than what you saw in the Flask example):

```
def app():
    """

    Main app
    """

    put_markdown("""# A utility for analyzing a CSV file
## [Dr. Tirthajyoti Sarkar](https://www.linkedin.com/in/tirthajyoti-
sarkar-2127aa7/)
You can upload a data file (CSV) and,
- display histograms of the data coulmns
- download the summary statistics as a file.

    """)
```

```
data = input_group("Input data",[file_upload(label='Upload your CSV
file', accept='.csv',name='file'),
 radio('Display data?',['Yes','No'], name='display_data',value='No'),
 radio('Display plots?',['Yes','No'], name='display_plot',value='No'),
                            ])
file = data['file']
display_data = data['display_data']
display_plot = data['display_plot']

content = file['content'].decode('utf-8').splitlines()
df = content_to_pandas(content)

if display_data=='Yes':
    show_data(df)
if display_plot=='Yes':
    show_plots(df)
show_stats(df)
```

Note the use of the function put_markdown() that helps display simple markdown content on the web app. This largely eliminates the need of coding a lot of HTML/CSS content as templates or static files, as in the Flask example. Further, the input_group object and other elements like radio create corresponding radio button elements on the web app page, again eliminating the need to code them using HTML. Basically, **PyWebIO does not require a data scientist to do anything else other than work on a single Python script**, yet enables them to create a nice-looking web app.

I named this script csv-analysis.py as it accepts a CSV file (through a file uploading function) from the user, internally creates a pandas DataFrame representation, and shows some basic plots of the numeric variables. The app function, shown above, calls other helper functions like show_data() and show_stats() that accept the pandas DataFrame and display the raw data or descriptive statistics on the web page.

The last bit of code of the script looks quite similar to what you saw with the Flask example:

```
if __name__ == '__main__':
    start_server(app,port=9999,debug=True)
```

It basically starts a web server and exposes it through the port 9999. When you run this on a command line:

```
python csv-analysis.py
```

you see the following output on the command line:

```
Running on all addresses.
Use http://10.0.0.55:9999/ to access the application
```

So, you go to this address on the local browser (http://10.0.0.55:9999/) and see this neat little web app popping up (Figure 12-7). Note how the markdown content you coded in the Python script is rendered nicely on the web page with headers, hyperlinks, and bullets. The input data section is nicely grouped as well, complete with a file upload box and radio buttons for selecting the choice of data display or statistics display.

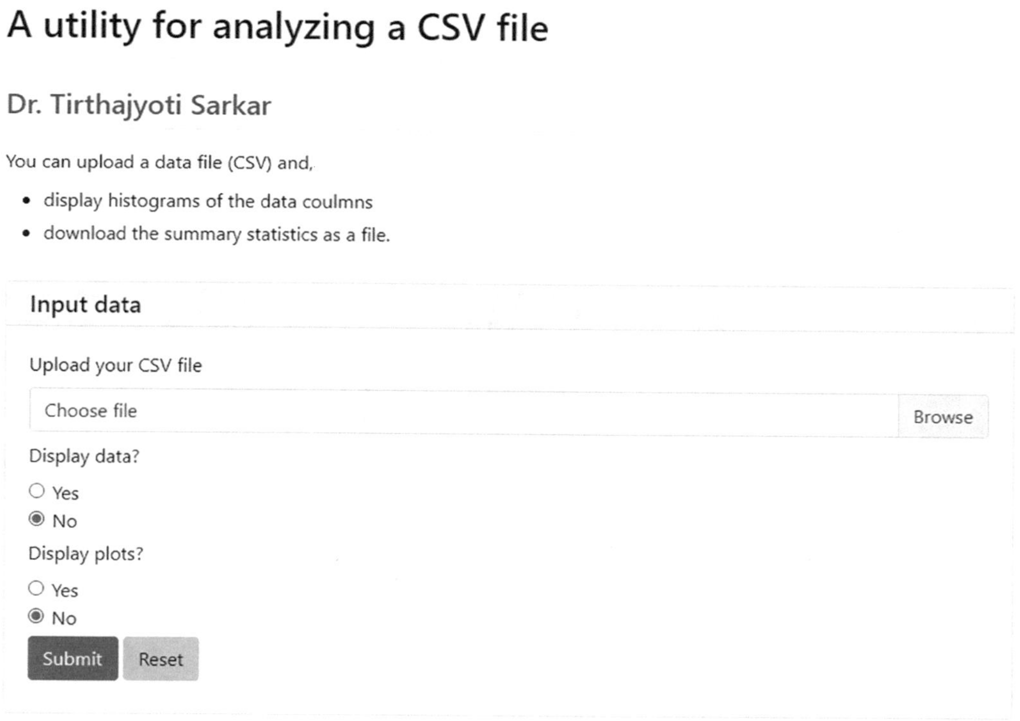

# A utility for analyzing a CSV file

## Dr. Tirthajyoti Sarkar

You can upload a data file (CSV) and,

- display histograms of the data coulmns
- download the summary statistics as a file.

**Input data**

Upload your CSV file

| Choose file | Browse |

Display data?

○ Yes
◉ No

Display plots?

○ Yes
◉ No

[Submit]  [Reset]

***Figure 12-7.*** *CSV analysis web app created by PyWebIO with just a single Python script*

Overall, this presents a HTML form (much like what you saw with the Flask example earlier) that accepts user input, does background Python processing, and presents the processed data back to the user. All the user needs to do is upload a file and press the Submit button.

The file upload functionality exposes the local filesystem for searching and choosing any file that the user wants to select. Figure 12-8 shows the state of the app after the user presses the Browse button on the file upload box.

**Figure 12-8.**  *The user chooses the file they want to analyze with the PyWebIo app*

After pressing the Submit button, the back-end processing happens and the page elements and states are updated to show the output in the bottom frame. Figure 12-9 shows the result. Note that here both the raw data table and plots section are truncated for intelligibility purposes.

# A utility for analyzing a CSV file

## Dr. Tirthajyoti Sarkar

You can upload a data file (CSV) and,

- display histograms of the data coulmns
- download the summary statistics as a file.

## The data

|   | X1 | X2 | X3 | X4 | X5 | X6 |
|---|-----|-----|-----|-----|-----|-----|
| 0 | 79545.5 | 5.68286 | 7.00919 | 4.09 | 23086.8 | 1.05903e+06 |
| 1 | 79248.6 | 6.0029 | 6.73082 | 3.09 | 40173.1 | 1.50589e+06 |
| 2 | 61287.1 | 5.86589 | 8.51273 | 5.13 | 36882.2 | 1.05899e+06 |
| 3 | 63345.2 | 7.18824 | 5.58673 | 3.26 | 34310.2 | 1.26062e+06 |
| 4 | 59982.2 | 5.04055 | 7.83939 | 4.23 | 26354.1 | 630944 |
| 5 | 80175.8 | 4.98841 | 6.10451 | 4.04 | 26748.4 | 1.06814e+06 |
| 6 | 64698.5 | 6.02534 | 8.14776 | 3.41 | 60828.2 | 1.50206e+06 |
| 7 | 78394.3 | 6.98978 | 6.62048 | 2.42 | 36516.4 | 1.57394e+06 |

Plots

Plots for X1

Plots for X2

Plots for X3

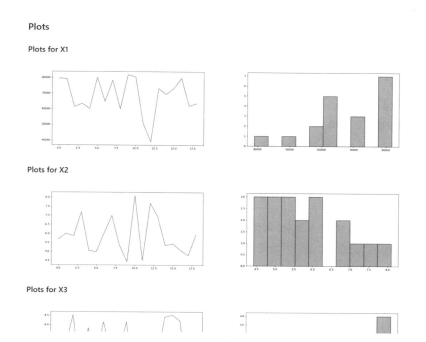

***Figure 12-9.*** *Typical output from the CSV analysis web app*

At the bottom of the page, the descriptive stats, calculated from the CSV file data, are also displayed and a download option is presented to the user (Figure 12-10).

## Descriptive stats

| | count | mean | std | min | 25% | 50% | 75% | max |
|---|---|---|---|---|---|---|---|---|
| X1 | 19 | 68391.4 | 11692.1 | 39033.8 | 61608.1 | 69391.4 | 79397.1 | 81885. |
| X2 | 19 | 5.86014 | 1.06293 | 4.42367 | 5.05422 | 5.68286 | 6.47244 | 8.0935 |
| X3 | 19 | 7.06813 | 1.14311 | 5.04275 | 6.24882 | 7.18777 | 8.15772 | 8.5175 |
| X4 | 19 | 3.83947 | 1.01868 | 2.27 | 3.11 | 4.04 | 4.335 | 6. |
| X5 | 19 | 35107.1 | 9041.33 | 23086.8 | 28067.9 | 35521.3 | 39469.1 | 60828. |
| X6 | 19 | 1.18541e+06 | 351690 | 528485 | 1.03112e+06 | 1.26062e+06 | 1.50397e+06 | 1.70705e+0 |

## Download stats here

Download stats file here

***Figure 12-10.*** *More output from the CSV analysis app including a download option*

Although you saw a very simple data analysis task, this example demonstrates the essential features and advantages of PyWebIO for this kind of workflow: user uploads of data files, background data transformations and visualizations, displaying the results, and a download option for the transformed data. You can create such an app just by coding a single Python script and abstracting away all the HTML/CSS/JavaScript front-end details using PyWebIO methods and utilities. This enhances your productivity and helps you **present the result of your data science exploration in a nicely organized visual manner to external stakeholders within a short span of time**.

# Other Options and GUI-Building Tools

Although I demonstrated the PyWebIO library in this section, there are quite a few options for a similar task: going from a Python script or Jupyter notebook to a full-fledged web app. Streamlit is one of the most prominent and widely used options. Interested readers can refer to this article that I wrote about working with Streamlit: `https://towardsdatascience.com/data-analytics-to-web-app-streamlit-made-easy-ed687266f0e8`.

There is a recently developed tool called mljar-mercury that lets you convert Jupyter notebooks into web apps with the minimal addition of some YAML config code. With this library, you define interactive widgets for the notebook with a YAML header, and the end users can change the widgets' values, execute the notebook, and save the results (as an HTML file). You can also hide the code to abstract the complexity from any non-technical collaborators. The library makes it easy to deploy the app to any server such as AWS or Heroku. For more information, please see the GitHub site (`https://github.com/mljar/mercury`) or the documentation (`https://mljar.com/mercury/`).

In many cases, building a stand-alone GUI app (not necessarily running on a web browser) may also be required to quickly demonstrate and disseminate some data science work or model. There are a host of options for doing that. Interested readers can check out this article that I wrote about a framework called PySimpleGUI and how to use it to build simple data science GUI apps: `https://towardsdatascience.com/building-data-science-gui-apps-with-pysimplegui-179db54a9a15`.

# Going from Local to the Cloud

Cloud technology, with any doubt, has ushered in the biggest revolution in both the personal and enterprise computing spaces in the modern era. It takes full advantage of the improved infrastructure of the global high-speed internet backbone that continues to reach an ever-expanding section of human society every day. And, with that advantage, it has democratized and commoditized the process of delivering goods and services of every kind imaginable, virtual and physical.

Data science is no exception in this regard. While a great many data scientists prefer to work and explore ideas on their local machines, for various reasons they may need to transport their workflow seamlessly on to cloud resources, or at least have the skills to do so at a moment's notice when the need arrives.

Some typical example scenarios include but are not limited to the following:

> Need to analyze a multi-terabyte-sized dataset that they cannot store properly on their local machine

> Large in-memory analytics requirements for which their local system memory is awfully inadequate

> Fast, distributed computing requirement with a cluster of CPU/GPU resources

Need to use highly specialized libraries, frameworks, and specially designed environments that come only with a prebuilt container/image that is difficult and time-consuming to set up on a local machine

In all these cases, the ability to quickly spin up a cloud resource and connect the existing data science codebase to that infrastructure determines the ultimate productivity and efficiency of the data science pipeline.

# Many Types of Cloud Services for Data Science

There is no denying the fact that a dizzying variety of cloud services exist that can be used to enhance the productivity and efficiency of regular data science work. Some of them fall under the category of **Infrastructure-as-a-Service (IaaS)**, where the end users rent the raw compute/storage power that exists in the cloud environment and just transport their local codebase to that layer. The typical usage scenarios in the previous section are applicable for this IaaS case. A specific example is to rent an EC2 compute node on AWS, connect it to some S3 storage bucket, and start doing large-scale data science work on this "rented" infrastructure that would not have been possible with limited local compute power.

## Platform-as-a-Service

A variety of new startups (and new service organizations of established corporations) are also working on services that can be classified as **Platform-as-a-Service (PaaS)**. Here a host of modules and submodules run on top of an IaaS layer (that is not chosen or entirely visible to the end user). These modules can perform all the necessary and expected tasks of a typical data science pipeline (data ingestion, transformation, machine learning, visualization, model deployment, long-term data and logs storage, etc.). Users may choose all or a mix of the modules/services that are part of a PaaS offering.

For example, AWS has many components (Amazon **QuickSight** (business analytics service), Amazon **RedShift** (data warehousing), AWS Data Pipeline, AWS **Data Exchange**, Amazon **Kinesis** (real-time data analysis), Amazon **EMR** (big data processing using map-reduce)) that can be used as per the requirements of the end user's data science workflow. Google Cloud also provides a host of similar services (**BigQuery** (data warehouse), Dataflow (streaming analytics), **Dataproc** (running Apache Hadoop, Apache Spark clusters), **Looker** (business intelligence and analytics), Google **Data**

**Studio** (visualization dashboards, data reporting), **Dataprep** (data preparation for analytics)) for the end user to pick and choose. At the other end of this spectrum, these services can be highly specialized, focusing on a single type of AI/ML job. AWS **Sagemaker** and Google **Vertex AI** are examples in this regard.

## Data-as-a-Service

**Data-as-a-Service (DaaS)** is also becoming a popular concept with the advent of cloud-based data services. DaaS is provided by a host of new and established cloud vendors that use cloud computing to provide data storage, data processing, multi-domain data sources integration, and advanced data analytics to clients using distributed network infrastructure. They have proper security and identity management layers integrated and their focus is on **AI/ML and data analytics without a limit on scaling**. This kind of service can be used by any organization to rapidly improve their business process and create long-term value using the power of data. Some prominent examples of service providers in this field include **Databricks** and **H2O.ai**.

There are also cloud services focusing on providing specialized data science coding and programming environments for end users. An example that you have already seen in this book is the **Saturn Cloud** service that you used in Chapter 11 to spin up a GPU-powered cloud instance with the RAPIDS framework preinstalled and configured. All you had to do was to click a few buttons and within minutes you could connect to a Jupyter notebook with access to all the RAPIDS libraries from your local browser.

**Paperspace Gradient** is another such successful hosted service provider for ML tasks. Without a doubt, these services enhance the productivity of data scientists by reducing the barrier of entry to environments that need special setup or a dedicated hardware configuration.

## Bringing Cloud Power to a Local Environment

There are a plenty of excellent resources to learn about cloud computing technologies and how they can help various data science tasks and projects. In fact, knowledge and basic experience of such technologies are becoming standard requirements for getting into the field of data science as a professional. This means, apart from studying programming languages, algorithms, machine learning theory and practices, and statistics concepts, a data scientist also needs to acquire skills and basic experience in cloud computing for prospective job interviews or career progression.

Therefore, a related question is, *how can you bring the power of cloud computing (mostly the infrastructure part, as mentioned in the previous section) to a local environment?*

This basically entails the following tasks:

- Spin up a EC2 instance on AWS.

- Set up a Python data science environment on that instance (basically a computer in the cloud).

- Start a Jupyter server.

- Securely connect to that server through a local browser.

If these tasks are completed successfully, **a data scientist will have a Jupyter notebook running on their local browser that is powered by the cloud computing instance**. Local files and existing code can be ported into an environment that is no longer restricted by the hardware limitations of a single system.

Fortunately, many excellent step-by-step tutorials on this topic are available on the Internet. Instead of repeating the steps from those articles, I will provide links so you can follow them directly. Many of these tutorials feature low-resource EC2 instances (e.g., t2-micro) to keep the cost of the AWS service minimal or even zero. However, **the concept is extendable to almost any kind of EC2 instance, and the data scientist can spin up as large and powerful cloud computing resource as needed by the data science workflow**. If it is a CPU-intensive data science task, a 32- or 64-core CPU instance can be chosen. It is a memory-intensive job, specialized high-memory instances can be used.

Additionally, the following links also include a guide for accomplishing the same goal with a Google Cloud Platform (GCP), which is a competitor and equivalent service to what AWS offers. GCP is powered by the vast distributed computing resource of Google and runs the familiar Jupyter notebook on a GCP computing node; it could be the first step towards extending your local data science pipeline to the amazing world of cloud computing. Furthermore, the similarity of the overall process in these two articles will prove that the **fundamentals of this local-to-cloud connection remain exactly same regardless of the cloud service adopted**.

Article/guide about AWS: "JupyterLab on AWS EC2" (`https://medium.com/ analytics-vidhya/jupyterlab-on-aws-ec2-d6b2cb945e54`)

Article/guide about GCP: ""Setting up Jupyter Lab Instance on Google Cloud Platform" (`https://medium.com/analytics-vidhya/setting-up-jupyter-lab-instance-on-google-cloud-platform-3a7acaa732b7`)

# Low-Code Libraries for Productive Data Science

Low-code libraries are becoming some of the most promising gateways for professionals who come from a diverse background such as web developers, business analysts, and even academic researchers in parallel fields and want to enter the world of data science and leverage its full power for their profession or daily work. In this section, I discuss the essential nature of low-code libraries and show a popular example.

## What Are These Low-Code Libraries?

At their core, these libraries are built atop the traditional data science ecosystem (e.g., programmatic frameworks with languages like Python, R, or Julia) with the goal of **abstracting away the coding portion of data science as much as possible while keeping the technical rigor largely intact**.

Naturally, these libraries act as thin wrapper layers on established coding-oriented libraries and frameworks. They provide easy and intuitive APIs and may even incorporate a lot of attractive visual elements and dashboard analytics tools to make the data science work ever more approachable and presentable.

In many cases, they incorporate some **Auto-ML bells and whistles** that help run a series of data science/machine learning experiments and tuning exercises with only a few lines of codes (or at the click of a button). When such a low-code library abstracts away all its direct programmatic APIs into a GUI-oriented, interactive front end, then it can also be called a **No-code** data science library.

## Example with PyCaret

As its website (`https://pycaret.org/`) says, "*PyCaret is an open-source, low-code machine learning library in Python that automates machine learning workflows*" (Figure 12-11). Although the emphasis on machine learning is heavy in this statement, it can support all the usual stuff in a typical data science pipeline, like

- Exploratory data analysis

- Data wrangling and preprocessing

- Model training and tuning

- Basic model explainability and model management (MLOps)

**Figure 12-11.** *PyCaret, a low-code, open source data science/ML library*

Here is a simple classification example with PyCaret to demonstrate the idea of low-code data science. First, install the library via `pip`:

```
pip install pycaret
```

PyCaret offers friendly data loading functions that can be used to import popular ML datasets, one of them being the diabetes dataset (`https://archive.ics.uci.edu/ml/datasets/diabetes`):

```
from pycaret.datasets import get_data
data = get_data('diabetes')
```

The next steps are almost magical! With a single function call (`setup`), the data is examined and set up (i.e., prepared for an ML experiment):

```
from pycaret.classification import *
s = setup(data, target = 'Class variable')
```

The inference algorithm embedded (and largely abstracted from the general user) inside PyCaret will automatically infer the data types for all features based on certain properties. If the inference is not 100% correct, PyCaret handles this by displaying a user prompt and asking for a confirmation of data types when the `setup` function is executed.

You can press Enter if the data types are correct, or type `quit` to exit the setup. Ensuring the correct data types is critically important in PyCaret as it automatically performs multiple type-specific preprocessing tasks that are imperative for accurate ML modeling.

The next step is equally magical in its simplicity and power. One function call of `compare_models()` trains and evaluates the performance of all the ML estimators available in the model library using cross-validation (CV). The output is a scoring grid with average cross-validated scores. CV metrics can be accessed with the `get_metrics` function and customized metrics can be added or removed using the `add_metric` and `remove_metric` functions, respectively.

```
Best = compare_models()
print(best)
```

Figure 12-12 shows the results.

| | Model | Accuracy | AUC | Recall | Prec. | F1 | Kappa | MCC | TT (Sec) |
|---|---|---|---|---|---|---|---|---|---|
| **catboost** | CatBoost Classifier | 0.7767 | 0.8309 | 0.6056 | 0.7114 | 0.6413 | 0.4823 | 0.4950 | 1.3870 |
| **lr** | Logistic Regression | 0.7564 | 0.8043 | 0.5056 | 0.6941 | 0.5786 | 0.4145 | 0.4285 | 1.1230 |
| **gbc** | Gradient Boosting Classifier | 0.7562 | 0.8239 | 0.5667 | 0.6731 | 0.6031 | 0.4314 | 0.4431 | 0.0900 |
| **ada** | Ada Boost Classifier | 0.7526 | 0.8016 | 0.5889 | 0.6524 | 0.6091 | 0.4310 | 0.4394 | 0.0800 |
| **lightgbm** | Light Gradient Boosting Machine | 0.7524 | 0.8028 | 0.5778 | 0.6614 | 0.6086 | 0.4299 | 0.4381 | 0.1430 |
| **rf** | Random Forest Classifier | 0.7488 | 0.8035 | 0.5111 | 0.6849 | 0.5740 | 0.4023 | 0.4182 | 0.2350 |
| **ridge** | Ridge Classifier | 0.7452 | 0.0000 | 0.4722 | 0.6844 | 0.5492 | 0.3816 | 0.3997 | 0.0150 |
| **lda** | Linear Discriminant Analysis | 0.7452 | 0.7912 | 0.4833 | 0.6783 | 0.5563 | 0.3859 | 0.4017 | 0.0130 |
| **xgboost** | Extreme Gradient Boosting | 0.7449 | 0.7896 | 0.5722 | 0.6442 | 0.5984 | 0.4140 | 0.4207 | 0.2640 |
| **knn** | K Neighbors Classifier | 0.7153 | 0.7261 | 0.5111 | 0.5962 | 0.5405 | 0.3379 | 0.3467 | 0.0220 |
| **et** | Extra Trees Classifier | 0.7134 | 0.7573 | 0.4333 | 0.6079 | 0.4968 | 0.3072 | 0.3204 | 0.1810 |
| **dt** | Decision Tree Classifier | 0.7075 | 0.6741 | 0.5722 | 0.5635 | 0.5630 | 0.3445 | 0.3481 | 0.0130 |
| **nb** | Naive Bayes | 0.6817 | 0.7064 | 0.2389 | 0.5527 | 0.3288 | 0.1657 | 0.1905 | 0.0110 |
| **svm** | SVM - Linear Kernel | 0.6015 | 0.0000 | 0.3611 | 0.3419 | 0.3251 | 0.0851 | 0.0924 | 0.0170 |
| **qda** | Quadratic Discriminant Analysis | 0.5759 | 0.5889 | 0.4833 | 0.4062 | 0.3705 | 0.1011 | 0.1281 | 0.0180 |

***Figure 12-12.***   *One function call trains a handful of ML estimators and displays the CV metrics of all kinds. Image from* `https://pycaret.gitbook.io/docs/ get-started/quickstart`*, used with permission from the PyCaret creator*

Next, you can analyze the performance of the trained model on the test set, again with a single function call. This actually gives you a choice of many types of plots, and you can select any one of them.

```
evaluate_model(best)
```

A typical result is shown in Figure 12-13 where the user has chosen to see a feature importance plot.

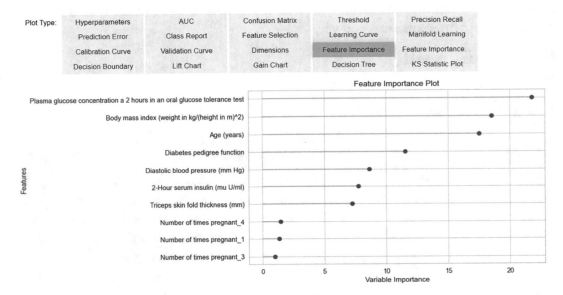

***Figure 12-13.*** *One function call analyzes the trained model against the test set and produces various plots. Image from* `https://pycaret.gitbook.io/docs/ get-started/quickstart`*, used with permission from the PyCaret creator*

Note that `evaluate_model` can only be used in a Jupyter notebook session since it uses `ipywidget` (to interactively show the user all the plot options). You can also use the following code to generate plots individually:

```
plot_model(best, plot = 'auc')
```

This produces the plot shown in Figure 12-14 showing the area-under-the-curve.

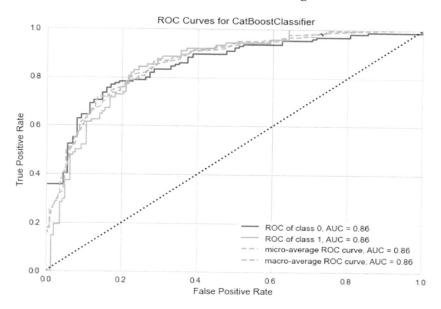

*Figure 12-14.* *Individual plot. Image from* `https://pycaret.gitbook.io/docs/` `get-started/quickstart,` *used with permission from the PyCaret creator*

Prediction is, as expected, one line of code. The evaluation metrics are calculated on the test set.

```
predict_model(best)
```

And finally, saving a model (the full pipeline, actually) and loading it back is simple, too (Figure 12-15).

```
save_model(best, 'my_best_pipeline')
loaded_model = load_model('my_best_pipeline')
```

```
Transformation Pipeline and Model Successfully Loaded
Pipeline(memory=None,
         steps=[('dtypes',
                 DataTypes_Auto_infer(categorical_features=[],
                                      display_types=True, features_todrop=[],
                                      id_columns=[],
                                      ml_usecase='classification',
                                      numerical_features=[],
                                      target='Class variable',
                                      time_features=[])),
                ('imputer',
                 Simple_Imputer(categorical_strategy='not_available',
                                fill_value_categorical=None,
                                fill_value_numerical=None,
                                numeri...
                ('cluster_all', 'passthrough'),
                ('dummy', Dummify(target='Class variable')),
                ('fix_perfect', Remove_100(target='Class variable')),
                ('clean_names', Clean_Colum_Names()),
                ('feature_select', 'passthrough'), ('fix_multi', 'passthrough'),
                ('dfs', 'passthrough'), ('pca', 'passthrough'),
                ['trained_model',
                 <catboost.core.CatBoostClassifier object at 0x0000020AF7A3ADF0>]],
         verbose=False)
```

*Figure 12-15.   Saved model. Image from* https://pycaret.gitbook.io/docs/ get-started/quickstart, *used with permission from the PyCaret creator*

It is clear from this hands-on demo that one of the primary goals of these libraries is to save time for the data science practitioner by simplifying the front API, reducing the lines of the raw coding needed, and even helping run multiple ML experiments in an autopilot mode. All these goals line up very well with that of the productive data science and therefore I strongly believe that **low-code libraries are going to be an important part of this initiative in the future ahead**.

# Summary

This chapter was not about a particular topic or a specific type of Python framework. It was an ensemble of topics and skills that often need to be studied and acquired by data scientists parallel to practicing a productive data science agenda. Although these skills do not feature directly in a data science pipeline as explicit components, they often provide additional value and foundation bedrock. Learning them can truly amplify the power and efficiency of a standard data science task flow.

In that spirit of learning, I started with a discussion on the importance of learning basic web technologies (HTML, CSS, and JavaScript). Next, I touched upon the utility of creating web apps for data science projects and made the point that the ultimate success of a data science task depends critically on communicating the insights that it generates and how this can be done best with an interactive web app. I showed how to build simple web apps with Python libraries of two distinct flavors, Flask and PyWebIO.

Almost invariably, web apps are supported by the cloud infrastructure that is the backbone of modern high-tech society. In the context of data science, I also talked about cloud technologies such as Amazon Web Service and Google Cloud Platform and data-focused platforms such as Databricks and Saturn Cloud. I also provided pointers to the simple process for bringing the power of cloud computing power to a local data science environment.

Finally, I switched gears and discussed how in many cases using a "low-code" framework can be useful and productive for a data science task. I demonstrated a ML classification task with PyCaret, a popular Python library in this genre, and showed how the low-code-focused abstraction made the whole affair of doing data science highly productive, faster, and intuitively simple.

# CHAPTER 13

# Wrapping It Up

You underwent a long and arduous journey over the course of the last 12 chapters. As you begin the last phase of this book, let's summarize the key takeaways and salient points of those chapters. This is important because one of the main things that I will focus on in this chapter is the topic of *what was not covered*. Naturally, you will appreciate the treatment of *what was not* by examining and recollecting *what was* covered.

## Chapter 1

Like any other computing (and non-computing) task in life, data science and machine learning can be practiced with various degrees of efficiency and productivity. Therefore, the goal of Chapter 1 was to introduce you to the benefits of performing data science tasks efficiently and productively. I also illustrated potential pitfalls in the everyday work of a regular data scientist to drive home the point of *efficient data science*.

## Chapter 2

The goal of Chapter 2 was to introduce you to the concepts of certain programming styles and habits that play an essential part in developing efficient data science systems and pipelines. I illustrated the concepts through brief examples and talked about how to measure or track inefficiency. Concepts of time and space complexities in programming and algorithms were introduced, as was the Big-O notation. Then I demonstrated practical examples of common, inefficient data science and ML coding practices to show you a glimpse of typically inefficient (but commonly used) coding patterns that do not scale well or make some aspects of the overall system design inefficient.

© Dr. Tirthajyoti Sarkar 2022
T. Sarkar, *Productive and Efficient Data Science with Python*, https://doi.org/10.1007/978-1-4842-8121-5_13

# Chapter 3

In Chapter 3, I came close to the root of this book in a sense. This is a book based on exploring productive data science with the Python programming language. The choice of this language is almost self-explanatory. Python is, without any doubt, the most used and fastest growing programming language of choice for data scientists (and other related professionals such as ML engineers or artificial intelligence researchers) all over the world. One of the primary reasons for this popularity is the availability of high-quality and powerful yet easy-to-learn libraries focused on data science.

However, just because these libraries provide easy APIs and smooth learning curves does not mean that everybody uses them in a highly productive and efficient manner. You must explore these libraries in depth and understand both their power and weaknesses to exploit them fully for productive data science work.

This was precisely the goal of this chapter: to show *how and why these libraries should be used in typical data science tasks for achieving high efficiency*. You started with the Numpy library as it is also the foundation of Pandas and Scipy. Then you explored the Pandas library, followed by a tour of the Matplotlib and Seaborn visualization packages.

# Chapter 4

This chapter built on the connection between data scientists and the Python language that was discussed in the previous chapter. Data scientists often come from a background that is quite far removed from traditional computer science/software engineering, one of physics, biology, statistics, economics, and electrical engineering, and they also use Python a lot for their work. While Python is the most widely used major language for modern data-driven analytics and AI apps, it is also used for simple scripting purposes, to automate stuff, and to build a web framework back end. It turns out that Python for data science work and Python for scripting and general software development can be quite different in style and temperament.

*Scripting is (mostly) the code you write for yourself. Software is the assemblage of code you (and other teammates) write for others*. It has been widely observed that when (a majority of) data scientists who do not come from a software engineering background write Python programs for AI/ML models and statistical analysis, they tend to write such code *mostly for themselves*. Writing high-quality, production level code is a skill to be learned and honed over a lifetime. It is the bread and butter of software engineers and developers. Not all data scientists will have the motivation and drive to acquire these skills. However, some good practices can be learned and applied in your everyday work. This chapter provided some pointers in the context of productive data science.

# Chapter 5

Functions, inheritance, methods, classes: they are at the heart of robust object-oriented programming. But a typical data scientist may not delve deeply into them if all they want to do is to create a Jupyter notebook with exploratory data analysis and plots. Therefore, they can avoid the initial pain of using OOP principles, but that almost always renders the Notebook code non-reusable and non-extensible. More precisely, that piece of code serves only the individual (until that individual forgets what exact logic was coded) and no one else.

But readability (and thereby reusability) is critically important for any good software product/service. Following a discussion about modular, readable, reusable coding practices in Chapter 4, this chapter focused on examples of such practices in the domain of deep learning. These days, powerful and flexible frameworks like TensorFlow or PyTorch make the actual coding of a complex neural network architecture relatively simple and brief. However, if the overall data science code is not modularized and well organized, then it can be plagued by the same issues of non-reproducibility and non-reusability.

Specifically, I discussed wrapping up the most essential tasks in a DL-based workflow, such as building and compiling a classification or regression model, creating targeted visual analytics, creating proper docstrings inside custom functions, and using them as the core building blocks of the main data science pipeline. Additionally, you can wrap up the task related to data formatting/transformation and prediction/inference in a similar fashion. Apart from simple functional wrappers, I also discussed a powerful construct called callback that caters to the dynamic nature of training a deep neural network. I showed how to extend this approach all the way to the full OOP paradigm, to build out classes and utility modules incorporating all these wrappers as special methods. I called this a DL utility module that can be called from any data science task.

# Chapter 6

In the previous two chapters, I showed that data scientists must learn how to write machine learning code (whether it is the final model or just some experimental prototype) efficiently. There must be proper organization and modularization in the code so that it can interface well with the standard software engineering tools and techniques. There must be some amount of automation in the code to reduce the time to explore, evaluate, and experiment with data and models. Data scientists must be comfortable with writing functional and module tests, incorporating object-oriented principles, and so on. And finally, data scientists must also develop the habit of producing good documentation for their code so that it can be reusable and readable by other developers.

This chapter took you through the journey of developing a lightweight but useful ML package of your own so that you can experience many aspects of producing a complete piece of software for data science. In my experience, this exercise of writing (and publishing) an ML package teaches several valuable lessons to any upcoming data scientist.

# Chapter 7

Python has an amazing ecosystem for data science work, starting from numerical analysis and going all the way to advanced deep learning or reinforcement learning, with statistical modeling and visualization thrown in the mix. A great open-source culture keeps new and exciting developments coming and thriving. Data scientists can learn, contribute code, share their experience, help debug, and support each other in this environment.

There are some predominant libraries and packages in this ecosystem that are used by almost all data scientists in their daily job: Pandas, NumPy, and Scikit-learn are three. However, there are also some little-known Python packages that can help you do some common data science jobs faster and more efficiently. These are not general-purpose large projects like Numpy or Pandas. Instead, they focus on niche aspects of similar data science tasks and do them really well.

In this chapter, I touched upon a few such nifty packages and showed hands-on examples of efficient data science. The goal was to induce the idea of exploration in your mind so that you can take full advantage of the great Python data science zoo.

# Chapter 8

Data science tasks come with a wide variety of computational costs of both space and time. Data wrangling jobs may need the support of large storage, while advanced ML algorithms need high intensity computing speed. Some ML algorithms work better with the support of large local memory (RAM) and cannot perform well with data situated far from the CPU on a hard disk, while others are optimized to perform well with distributed data storage.

Furthermore, the nature of the data may change slowly or frequently, depending on the application. Some models and data science code scale gracefully with increasing size and complexity of the input data, some do not. When their scaling is not properly planned or baked into the code, the performance can suffer, even leading to possible catastrophic failure in time.

To plan for such a situation or to design data science code robustly, you must start with the basic measurement of the efficiency of the code in terms of memory usage or profile. There are many tools and techniques for such measuring depending on the code and the underlying hardware. In this chapter, I introduced tools (with hands-on examples) that can be used to measure the memory usage profile of data science and ML code.

# Chapter 9

Data science tasks may cover a wide variety of dataset sizes, ranging from kilobytes to petabytes. Some datasets can have many rows and a small number of columns while others (e.g., genomic assay) may be extremely high-dimensional and consist of a few rows but millions of columns as feature dimensions. Even within the same organization or data science team, there can be multiple pipelines dealing with different types of input and they may face wide variation in the dataset size and complexity.

It is often a natural practice for data scientists to build a scaled prototype of a data science job (such as combining data wrangling, a ML algorithm, and some prediction functions). To support this quick analysis and prototyping, a data scientist must be able to quickly scale across a wide variety of dataset sizes and complexity as the need arises. They should not run into issues like out-of-memory while prototyping on their laptop.

This chapter talked about the common problems and limitations that arise while scaling out to larger datasets and what tools exist to address those issues. Specifically, you explored some of the limitations that arise while doing analysis with a large dataset using the most common data analysis library, Python Pandas, and discussed two alternative libraries or add-ons that can be used to overcome those limitations.

# Chapter 10

In almost all real-life scenarios, the success of a data science pipeline (and its value addition to the overall business of the organization) may depend on how smoothly and flawlessly it can be deployed *at scale*, such as how easily it can handle large datasets, faster streaming data, rapid changes in the sampling or dimensionality, and so on. This aspect of scalability is also closely related to the ability to do parallel processing of large data. Therefore, the theme of Chapter 9 was continued in this chapter where I discussed Python libraries that support parallel processing natively for data science tasks.

Much like the last chapter, I discussed limitations that arise while doing analysis with large and complex datasets using the most common data analysis and numerical computing libraries like Pandas or Numpy and I discussed some alternative libraries to help with those tasks. However, this chapter does not focus on an exhaustive discussion about the general parallel computing tricks and techniques with Python. It purposely avoids detailed treatment of the topics that often come up in a standard Python parallel computing tutorial or treatise such as working with built-in modules like `multiprocessing, threading,` or `asynco`. The focus, like any other chapter in this book, is squarely on data science, so I covered two libraries named `Dask` and `Ray` that truly add value to any data science pipeline where the user wants to bring in the power of parallel computing to their tasks.

# Chapter 11

Productivity in data science is often directly related to the speed of execution of various tasks including numerical processing, data wrangling, and feature engineering. When it goes to the advanced machine learning stage, depending on the modeling complexity, the matter of speed and performance assumes a critical role. It is now well established that the unprecedented success of modern ML systems has been critically dependent on their ability to process massive amounts of raw data in a parallel fashion using task-optimized hardware. The history of machine learning has clearly demonstrated that the use of specialized hardware like GPUs played a significant role in the early success of ML.

While the use of GPUs and distributed computing is widely discussed in academic and business circles for core AI/ML tasks, there is less coverage when it comes to their utility for regular data science and data engineering tasks. So, the important question is, *can we leverage the power of GPUs for regular data science jobs (e.g., data wrangling, descriptive statistics) too*? The answer is not trivial and needs some special consideration and knowledge sharing. In this chapter, I focused on a specialized suite of tools called RAPIDS that help any data scientist take advantage of GPU-based hardware for a wide variety of data science tasks (not necessarily deep learning or advanced ML). You explored how by utilizing the inherent parallel processing power of GPUs, you can enhance the productivity of such common data science tasks significantly.

# Chapter 12

I dedicated this complete chapter to the set of various disparate useful skills that a data scientist should strive to master to enhance their productivity. Unlike previous chapters where I examined and discussed similarly grouped skills (e.g., memory profilers or distributed computing tools), the tools and skills discussed in this chapter might have looked somewhat disjointed from each other. They do not fall under one unifying class, but taken as a whole, they can truly aid a data scientist in enhancing productivity.

I started with a discussion on the importance of learning basic web technologies such as HTML, CSS, and JavaScript. Building on the same concepts, next I discussed the utility of creating a simple web app for a data science project. You saw a hands-on example with two Python libraries, Flask and PyWebIO. Then I moved on to cloud technologies such as Amazon Web Services and showed (with lined resources) the simple process for bringing the power of the cloud to a local data science workflow. Finally, I switched gears and discussed how, in many cases, using a so-called "low-code" framework can be useful and productive for a data science task. I demonstrated PyCaret, a popular low-code Python library in this regard.

# What Was Not Discussed in This Book

Often, the most important thing that an author can (and should) discuss at the end of a book is not a running list of all the topics that were covered in the book, but *what was not covered*. In that spirit, in the following subsections, I identify some key topics that should be pointed out to you, the reader, for self-learning and exploring beyond this book. These topics should help you equip yourself with productive data science techniques.

## MLOps and DataOps

A typical (or traditional) software development lifecycle goes from requirement elicitation, to designing, to development, to testing, to deployment, and all the way down to maintenance. For many years, these practices were firmly in the realm of so-called DevOps.

As business and technological enterprises incorporate more and more data science and machine learning into their products and services, the new requirement of building ML systems modifies these time-tested principles of the SDLC to give rise to a new engineering discipline called MLOps (**a handshake between ML practices and traditional DevOps**). One of the most popular and widely used Python libraries for getting started with basic MLOps is MLFlow.

While MLOps deals primarily with ML models and artifacts, a similar and related concept is DataOps, which focuses data (and the various transformations, techniques, and systems associated with the processing and flow of data) as main artifacts. Like MLOps, this modern discipline tries to **blend the newer set of demands created by the unprecedented scale and complexity of data processing with traditional DevOps tool chain** and produce a homogenized pipeline that delivers value to any organization that wants to take advantage of the power of data science.

These are newly emerging disciplines with ever-changing standards and golden practices. To be productive and efficient, a data scientist must keep abreast of these developments. There are conferences exclusively dedicated to these spaces, and excellent books and blogs are being produced all the time. You are highly encouraged to start exploring these avenues to get a firm grasp of these concepts.

# Container Technologies

Containers have become an essential part of any modern software technology stack. Fundamentally, they enable packaging software code and services with all the necessary components like libraries, frameworks, and other dependencies so that they are "contained" and "isolated" in their own private space. This results in the ability of the software or application within the container to **move across and run consistently in any environment and on any infrastructure**, independent of that environment or infrastructure's operating system.

Although the core idea of such process isolation has been around for years, in 2013, **Docker** introduced Docker Engine, which set a standard for container use with easy-to-use tools and pioneered a universal approach for packaging. This accelerated the adoption of container technology with breakneck speed, leading to container orchestration tools like **Kubernetes** (developed and open sourced by Google). Today, developers can choose from a large selection of containerization platforms and tools that support the **Open Container Initiative** standards pioneered by Docker.

In fact, the adoption of containerization has pushed software development from being monolithic (where all services and components use the same language or a fixed set of technology) towards a much more diversified situation (each individual service is written in the best programming language for the task and then run as pods with a container orchestration tool like Kubernetes). Naturally, an increasing number of modern data science and ML services and platforms are also being built with containerization at their core. To take advantage of this mega-trend and to make it work for productive data science, you should familiarize yourself with the basic principles, workings, and features of container tools such as Docker and Kubernetes.

# Database Technologies

Database and related technologies have been around for much longer than modern data science and machine learning, going back to the early 1960s. For the longest time, they centered around relational database management systems or **RDMBS**. These systems mainly dealt with "structured data" such as business transactional records or tabular data coming from inventory, quality control, production, or other business processes of a similar nature. Structured Query Language or **SQL** (and the many variants it spawned) has been the mainstay of querying large databases with amazing speed and accuracy for more than five decades.

It is **imperative for any aspiring data scientist to acquire at least a rudimentary knowledge of databases and SQL** and to constantly practice and upgrade that knowledge. Almost every web app, platform, and enterprise software makes use of multiple databases in some form or another. In real-life scenarios, it is extremely likely that the raw data for a data science pipeline must come from a legacy database (or a combination of multiple such databases). Therefore, the data scientists in charge need to be proficient in SQL to perform those queries to extract raw data from the databases.

SQL, being a declarative language (`https://365datascience.com/tutorials/sql-tutorials/sql-declarative-language/`), does not necessarily have a steep learning curve. But a solid knowledge of database design and optimization can go a long way towards performing optimized queries for data extraction that enhances the efficiency of the entire data science pipeline. There are, in fact, many **database bindings or connector libraries in Python** that allow data scientists to build tight coupling with existing databases and extract data even from within a Python environment.

However, SQL and RDBMS are just the tip of the iceberg. With the growing importance of unstructured data such as images, videos, audio, natural language, handwritten notes, and streaming output from digital sensor networks, particularly in the field of data science and ML, there is a fresh revolution in database technologies leading to the development of **NoSQL technologies**. These tools and languages are generally designed and optimized for dealing with unstructured or semi-structured datasets.

You are duly encouraged to update your database knowledge, invest time in building solid fundamentals in SQL, and keep abreast of developments in the latest database trends and technologies. No matter what background you come from or what kind of business or scientific application you are working on, this knowledge will help you become highly productive and efficient with maximum impact.

# General Advice for Upcoming Data Scientists

It is not hard to imagine that the following question comes up often when a few data scientists gather for a drink, after work: *how can you distinguish yourself from hundreds of other data science practitioners/candidates at work or in a job interview?*

Why is this question important to ponder?

Because there is a tremendous amount of competition to get a job as a data scientist (`www.kdnuggets.com/2020/10/getting-data-science-job-harder.html`). Because there is a **mad rush**. Every kind of engineer, scientist, and working professional is **calling himself or herself a data scientist** (`www.linkedin.com/pulse/why-so-many-fake-data-scientist-bernard-marr/`). Because, as an aspiring data scientist, you may not be sure if you can cut your teeth in this field. The so-called ***imposter syndrome*** is alive and well in data science (`https://towardsdatascience.com/how-to-manage-impostor-syndrome-in-data-science-ad814809f068`).

I neither claim to have ready answers nor do I know whether you can truly distinguish yourself, but I will list a few pointers.

# Ask Questions and Learn Constantly

Ask yourself the following questions and count the number of YES answers. The more you have done, the more you can separate yourself from the masses.

## If You Are a Beginner

Have you **published** your own Python/R (whatever you code in) **package**?

If yes, have you written extensive **documentation** for it to be used easily by everyone else?

Have you taken your analysis from a Jupyter notebook to a fully published **web app**? Or have you investigated tools that help you do so easily?

Have you written at least a few **high-quality, detailed articles** describing your hobby project?

Do you try to practice the **Feynman method of learning**, which is to teach a concept you want to learn about to a student in the sixth grade?

## At a More Advanced Phase

If you consider yourself to be at a somewhat mature stage as a data scientist, answer these questions:

Do you consciously try to integrate good **software engineering practices** (e.g., object-oriented programming, modularization, unit testing) in your data science code at every chance you get?

Do you make it a point to not stop at the scope of the immediate data analysis required but imagine what would happen for 100X data volume or 10X cost of making the wrong prediction? In other words, do you think consciously about **data or problem scaling and its impact**?

Do you make it a point to not stop at the traditional ML metrics, but also think about the **cost of data acquisition** and **business value resulting from applying ML**?

## Learn a Diverse Set of Skills

I particularly would like to advise you to not spend all of your time and energy analyzing larger and larger datasets or experimenting with the latest deep learning model. As *well-rounded* data scientists, we should set aside at least a quarter of our time learning to do a couple of things that are valued everywhere, in every organization, in all situations.

Build a small but focused utility tool for your daily data analysis. Your creative juices will flow freely in this exercise. You are creating something that may not have thousands of immediate users, but it will be novel, and it will be your own creation.

Read and create high-quality documentation related to new tools or frameworks or the utility tool you just built (see above). This will force you to learn how to communicate the utility and mechanics of your creation in a manner that is intelligible to a wide audience.

As you can see, these habits are easy to develop and practice. They do not require backbreaking work, a years-long background in statistics, or advanced expertise in deep machine learning knowledge. But, surprisingly, not everybody embraces them. So, here's your chance to distinguish yourself from a set of large number of candidates either at a new job or at an interview (Figure 13-1).

***Figure 13-1.*** *Building data science tools (apps) and high-quality documentation could distinguish yourself from others. Image source: "How Can You Distinguish Yourself from Hundreds of Other Data Science Candidates?" by Tirthajyoti Sarkar* (https://towardsdatascience.com/how-to-distinguish-yourself-from-hundreds-of-data-science-candidates-62457dd8f385)

## Read About Broad Topics at Every Chance

Aspiring data scientists often spend a disproportionate amount of time reading about the latest deep learning trick or blog posts about the latest Python library. While these are positive attributes, in order to be productive and efficient, you should also allocate some time for reading broader topics in data science or artificial intelligence in general. I encourage you to read about broad and diverse topics in the industry's top forums and in good books. Figure 13-2 shows some of the books and forums that I enjoy.

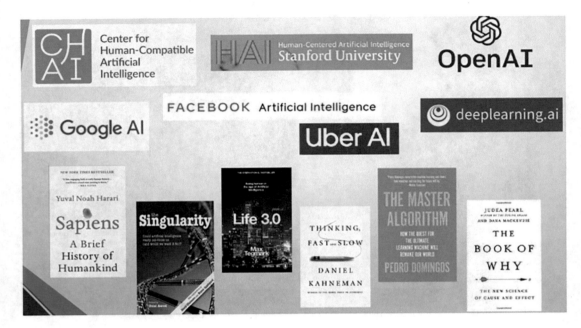

*Figure 13-2.* *Some high impact blogs, forums, and books on broad topics related to data science, machine learning, and artificial intelligence*

## Distinguish Yourself at a Job Interview

Following the goal of distinguishing yourself at a job interview, imagine yourself to be in such a situation. If you did have many YES answers to the questions above, you can mention something like the following to your interviewer:

- *"Hey, check out the cool Python package I built for generating synthetic time-series data at will."*

- *"I also wrote a detailed documentation which is hosted at MyApp. readthedocs.io website. It's built with Sphinx and Jekyll."*

- *"I write data science articles regularly for the largest online platform, Towards Data Science. Based on those articles, I even got a book publishing offer from a well-known publisher like Packt or Springer."*

- *"Everybody can fit an ML model in a Jupyter notebook. But I can hack out a basic web app demo of that Scikit-learn function where you can send data through a REST API and get back the prediction."*

- *"I can help in the cost-benefit analysis of a new machine learning program and tell you if the benefit outweighs the data collection effort and how to do it optimally."*

Imagine how different you will sound to the interview board from all the other candidates who do well on regular questions of statistics and gradient descent but do not offer demonstrable proof of all-around capabilities.

This shows that you are **inquisitive** about data science problems. This shows that **you read, you analyze, and you communicate**. This shows that You **create** and **document** for others to create. This shows that your thinking goes beyond notebooks and classification accuracy to the realm of **business value addition and customer empathy**. This is the secret sauce of being truly productive and efficient.

What company wouldn't love this kind of candidate?

# Some Useful Resources

There are so many great tools and resources for acquiring and practicing these skills. It is impossible to even list a good fraction of them in the space of a single chapter, but below I list some representative examples. The key idea is to instill the idea of exploring along these lines and discovering such learning aids for yourself.

## A Data Scientist's Amazing, Curated List of Useful Tricks and Tools

Khuyen Tran is a data science writer at NVIDIA and a data science intern at Ocelot Consulting. She has written over 200 data science articles and hundreds of daily data science tips at Data Science Simplified (`https://mathdatasimplified.com/`). Her current mission is to make open source more accessible to the data science community. She has curated a list of efficient Python tricks and tools that can act as a perfect supplement to this book. Check out the open-source book *Efficient Python Tricks and Tools for Data Scientists* (Figure 13-2) at `https://khuyentran1401.github.io/ Efficient_Python_tricks_and_tools_for_data_scientists/intro.html`.

# Build Installable Software Packages Using Only Jupyter Notebooks

This tool comes from the developers of FastAI, a popular deep learning framework and learning resource. They experimented with the idea that one can build an installable Python package right from the Jupyter notebook code and came up with this tool. Of course, the Jupyter notebook is where data scientists are mostly at ease and this kind of tool lets them publish packages right from their preferred coding and experimentation environment. Here are the details about this project: `www.fast.ai/2019/12/02/nbdev/`.

# Learn How to Integrate Unit Testing Principles

Testing software modules enhances robustness and trust in the final product/service. The importance of high-quality testing cannot be emphasized enough in any software development. The same argument goes for your data science pipeline. Even if you are developing a data science codebase mainly for prototyping and research, it's a good idea to know how to write basic testing modules to check if the functions and classes you are developing are working as expected.

It is often not about checking the input data type but about checking whether your data science pipeline can handle it. It is not only just randomly throwing out-of-range variables at the function but also about checking whether the response is as expected.

To get you started, here are references to a couple of useful articles in this regard. In these short articles, I looked at an example of a typical data science pipeline (consisting of small, dedicated functions) instead of a monolith, and showed how to write a Pytest module for it. I also looked at why writing test modules for data science can be slightly different from what software engineers or Quality Assurance folks do every day.

"PyTest for Machine Learning" (`https://towardsdatascience.com/pytest-for-machine-learning-a-simple-example-based-tutorial-a3df3c58cf8`)

"How to Write Test Code for a Data Science Pipeline" (`https://heartbeat.comet.ml/how-to-write-test-code-for-data-science-pipeline-4ee35956c513`)

# Write Whole Programming and Technology Books Right from Your Jupyter Notebook

This is an awesome open-source project to help develop code-oriented, quick-read books and booklets: "Books with Jupyter" (`https://jupyterbook.org/intro.html`).

# Get Started with MLOps

As discussed, MLOps was not covered in this book, and yet it deserves the full attention of aspiring data scientists to succeed professionally and be productive in today's business environment. Check out this high-quality introductory guide: "What is MLOps – Everything You Must Know to Get Started" (`https://towardsdatascience.com/what-is-mlops-everything-you-must-know-to-get-started-523f2d0b8bd8`).

# Understand the Multi-Faceted Complexity of a Real-Life Analytics Problem

Check out the following article to understand the multi-faceted complexities of a real-life analytics problem: "Why a Business Analytics Problems Demands all of your Data Science Skills" (`https://medium.com/analytics-vidhya/why-a-business-analytics-problem-demands-all-of-your-expertise-at-once-1290170808c4`). In this case study example, I describe in detail what could be a good analytics pipeline for a power company that wants to run a power shut-off campaign (for non-payment of electric bills), shown in Figure 13-3. Specifically, I analyzed

- What data needs to be collected and how it needs to be cleaned and prepared using wrangling techniques

- What the main components of the pipeline need to be

- What subcomponents or specific modeling technique may be used

- How to formulate the optimization problem

- What business and social factors to consider

- When to apply stochastic simulations and what kind of simulation runs need to be conducted

# Efficient Python Tricks and Tools for Data Scientists

Why efficient Python? Because using Python more efficiently will make your code more readable and run more efficiently.

Why for data scientist? Because Python has a wide application. The Python tools used in the data science field are not necessarily useful for other fields such as web development.

The goal of this book is to spread the awareness of efficient ways to do Python. They include:

- efficient built-in methods and libraries to work with iterator, dictionary, function, and class
- efficient methods to work with popular data science libraries such as pandas and NumPy
- efficient tools to incorporate in a data science project
- efficient tools to incorporate in any project
- efficient tools to work with Jupyter Notebook.

**Effective Python for Data Scientists**

Q Search this book...

Powered by Jupyter Book

***Figure 13-3.*** *Khuyen Tran's ebook on efficient Python tricks and tools for data science*

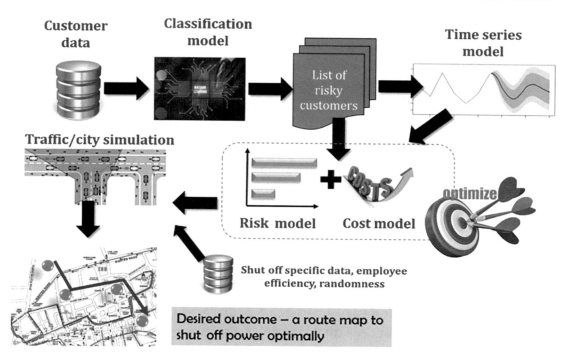

**Figure 13-4.** *An example of a real-life business analytics problem incorporating data science tools of all kinds, such as classification, simulation, time-series, risk and cost modeling, randomized (stochastic) analyses, optimization, etc. Image source: "Why a Business Analytics Problem Demands all of your Data Science Skills" by Tirthajyoti Sarkar (*`https://medium.com/analytics-vidhya/why-a-business-analytics-problem-demands-all-of-your-expertise-at-once-1290170808c4`*)*

You will appreciate, after reading this article, how the **modern practice of data-driven analytics, when applied to a real-life business problem, is always a complicated mixture of multiple techniques and frameworks** including data wrangling, machine learning, business logic, and even ethical choices.

# Begin a New Journey

Well, that's the end for this journey with this book. My goal was simple: to illustrate the concept of productive data science and introduce you to a few tools and techniques (all using the Python language and its rich ecosystem) that can help you achieve higher productivity (and efficiency) in your data science work. With that goal in mind, I covered a wide array of topics in the span of 13 chapters. Some of those topics dealt directly with the efficiency of the data science code and programming patterns, while others covered concepts that may play critically important roles in practical data science pipelines. There were discussions on as diverse topics as modularity, code packaging, memory and time profiling, GPU processing, parallel computing, web technologies, and everything in between.

I sincerely hope that this medley was useful and illuminating to you, and that you gained an insight or two about productive data science practices by making the journey through these chapters, either by following every example diligently or just browsing casually. As expected from a book on such a mixed topic, not everything that I know to be important for practicing productive data science could be covered within these chapters. Whenever possible, I encouraged you to explore those topics and concepts on their own.

Those explorations will surely lead to newer adventures, professional success, and pure joy for the practitioners of the wonderful enterprise (and transformative technology) that is data science. With this hope, I signal the start of that newer and future journey.

# Index

## A

Activation maps, 142
    activation, 144–146
    training, 143
    web-based UI, 147
AI/ML models, 9, 85, 358
Algorithmic complexity
    deep learning network, 25, 26
    image data, cubic-complexity, 22
    regression model, 23, 24
    relative growth comparison, 24, 25
Apache Arrow columnar memory
        format, 303
Artificial intelligence (AI), 9, 47, 85,
        300, 358, 370
Aspiring data, 369, 373
.at or .iloc methods, 61
AutoML tools, 10

## B

Back-end processing, 342
Base class, 119, 165, 166, 173, 175
Basic web technologies, 327, 355, 363
Best-matching distribution
    datasets, 206, 207
    plot, 204
    simple fitting, 203, 204
Binary search, 20
Boolean filters, 197
Business and technological
        enterprises, 364

## C

Cell magic, 44
Classification score, 322
Client-scheduler-worker, 264, 265
Cloud computing
        technologies, 347
Cloud instance, 233, 234, 261, 282,
        314, 347
Cloud technology, 345
Colab Pro, 236
ColDrop method, 189, 191
Computing, 212, 235, 254, 357
Containers technologies, 365
Convolutional neural
        network (CNN), 119, 138
cProfile library
    array operations, 225
    data science workflow, 227
    Profiler class, 226, 227
    usage, 223
cProfile.run function, 223, 224
Cross-validation (CV), 92, 95,
        148, 150, 351
CSV analysis app, 344
CSV analysis web app, 341, 343
CUDA programming, 303, 304
CUDA version, 309
CuDF DataFrame, 315, 317, 319
CuDF *vs.* pandas, 314
CuGraph, 304–305
CuML pipeline, 323
CuML version, 322

Printed in the United States
by Baker & Taylor Publisher Services